Free Will

Second edition

Sourcehood and its Alternatives

KEVIN TIMPE

B L O O M S B U R Y

LONDON • NEW DELHI • NEW YORK • SYDNEY

Bloomsbury Academic

An imprint of Bloomsbury Publishing Plc

50 Bedford Square   175 Fifth Avenue
London   New York
WC1B 3DP   NY 10010
UK   USA

www.bloomsbury.com

First published 2013

British Library Cataloguing-in-Publication Data
A catalogue record for this book is available from the British Library.

ISBN: HB: 978-1-4411-8993-6
PB: 978-1-4411-4642-7

Library of Congress Cataloging-in-Publication Data
Timpe, Kevin.
Free will : sourcehood and its alternatives / Kevin Timpe.– 2nd ed.
p. cm.
Includes bibliographical references and index.
ISBN 978-1-4411-8993-6 (alk. paper)– ISBN 978-1-4411-4642-7 (pbk. : alk. paper)–
ISBN 978-1-4411-7174-0 (ebook pdf : alk. paper)– ISBN 978-1-4411-9735-1 (ebook epub : alk. paper) 1. Free will and determinism. I. Title.
BJ1461.T48 2012
123'.5–dc23
2012015689

Typeset by Fakenham Prepress Solutions, Fakenham, Norfolk NR21 8NN
Printed and bound in India

Free Will

Second edition

For A, J, and E;
I will fight away the darkness. For you.

CONTENTS

10 Incompatibilism and luck 162

ACKNOWLEDGMENTS

This book is analogous to the Pokemon Charizard, in that it is the second major evolution of an earlier entity. The first stage of this project, the "Charmander" if you will, was my doctoral dissertation which I wrote at Saint Louis University over a decade ago. The first evolution occurred a few years later when Jim Fieser asked if I wanted to publish my dissertation in a series he edited for Continuum. I told him that I'd rather write a book which I, with a few more years of thought on free will, wished my dissertation had been. Jim allowed me to write what I think of as the Charmeleon stage—the first edition of *Free Will: Sourcehood and Its Alternatives*. The project evolved again in 2011 when Manuel Vargas suggested that if I added broader coverage, the book would be a better candidate for course adoption as a textbook. What you hold in your hands is the third, and probably last, stage in the project's evolution.

Of course, in the course of the previous decade, I have benefited greatly from many individuals. As will be clear from the text, I do not approach the issues I discuss in anything approaching an intellectual vacuum. During the past few years, I have received comments, suggestions, and criticisms on various parts of this manuscript from H. E. Baber, Chris Callaway, Joe Campbell, Alicia Finch, John Martin Fischer, Tom Flint, Chris Franklin, Carl Gillett, Bent Hart, Tyler Hower, Bob Kane, Neil Levy, Todd Long, Michael McKenna, Jason Miller, Mike Murray, Ryan Nichols, Tim Pawl, Derk Pereboom, Mike Rea, Seth Shabo, Dan Speak, Eleonore Stump, Matt Talbert, Neal Tognazzini, Manuel Vargas, Kip Werking, and Matt Zwolinski. A special note of gratitude is due to Zachary Bachman, who read the complete revised manuscript and gave me very useful guidance, both large and small, in shaping the second edition. Erin Diefenbach, my TA during the 2011–12 academic year, also helped with the preparation of the final manuscript. The editorial staff at Bloomsbury/Continuum—in particular Tom Crick, Sarah Campbell, and Rachel Eisenhauer—have once again been a model of support for their authors.

In addition to their comments, I have learned much about both free will and how to do philosophy from John Martin Fischer, Michael McKenna, Derk Pereboom, Eleonore Stump, Neal Tognazzini, and Manuel Vargas. Their work has shaped—in ways big and small, seen and unseen—my own work. While I have no doubt that they disagree with many of the claims I make in this book, I hope they can see their impact on the present volume.

I would also like to thank the universities which made this book possible. The first edition of the book was written while I was on the faculty of the University of San Diego. The second edition was written while I was at Northwest Nazarene University and during a Templeton Research Fellowship at Saint Peter's College at Oxford University. I am grateful for the support of these institutions without which the present book would not exist.

This volume makes considerable use of some of my previously published work. Parts of two entries I wrote for the *Internet Encyclopedia of Philosophy*, entitled "Free Will" and "Moral Character," can be found incorporated into Chapters 1, 2, and 5. Aspects of my "A Critique of Frankfurt-Libertarianism" (originally published in *Philosophia*) can be found in Chapter 2 and, more extensively, in Chapter 9. Chapter 9 also draws on my "Source Incompatibilism and its Alternatives" (originally published in *American Philosophical Quarterly*). Chapter 4 borrows heavily from a chapter I contributed to the *Continuum Companion to Metaphysics* (edited by Neil Manson and Bob Barnard), while Chapter 7 draws extensively from my "The Dialectic Role of the Flickers of Freedom" (originally published in *Philosophical Studies*). Much of my "Trumping Frankfurt: Why the Kane-Widerker Objection is Irrelevant" (originally published in *Philosophia Christi*) can be found in Chapter 6. Many of the ideas contained in Chapters 8 and 9 first saw the light of day in my "Free Will: Alternatives and Sources" (published in the collection *Sci-Phi: Philosophy Through Science Fiction*, edited by Ryan Nichols, Fred Miller and Nicholas Smith). Some of the dialectical issues discussed in Chapter 10 were first published in "Demotivating Semicompatibilism" (published in the Colombian journal *Ideas y Valores: Revista colombiana de filosofía*). The copyrights of these papers are held by the journal or book in which they were first published, and they are used here with permission. Complete bibliographic information on all these works may be found in the bibliography at the end of the volume.

PART ONE

Introducing the issues

CHAPTER ONE

The basics

Introduction

Imagine coming home one day to find your beloved yellow Labrador named Riley lying dead on the kitchen floor. How would you feel? At the very least, you are likely to feel quite heartbroken. ("Oh my blenker, I can't believe he's dead!") But beyond this grief, how you feel will depend largely on what else you find out about the cause of the dog's death. If, for instance, you discover that he died when your grandfather clock fell on him during an earthquake earlier that afternoon, you may regret having moved to southern California. If, on the other hand, you discover that someone—say Allison—is the cause of the dog's death, you will have a different reaction. Yet even here, the exact nature of your reaction will depend on answers to further questions: Did Allison kill the dog on purpose, or did she accidentally push the grandfather clock onto him when she tripped over your haphazardly strewn slippers? If the latter, is Allison a young child, or an adult? Among these questions, one question in particular that is likely to have a significant impact on your reaction is this: Was Allison acting freely when she killed Riley? If you learn that Allison was coerced or tricked or hypnotized into killing the dog, for example, you will respond to Allison differently than if you discover that she, as the phrase goes, "did it freely."

Although the phrase "did it freely" is quite commonplace, it is nevertheless a widely contested issue what it means to "do something freely." Presumably, to do something freely requires that you have free will and that you exercise it in the action in question. But what exactly is free will? As Manuel Vargas has recently noted, "'free will' is a term of both ordinary and technical discourse."[1] However, it is not clear if the ordinary use of the term always tracks the technical use. Minimally, both uses of the term involve a certain sort of control over one's behavior. But exactly what kind of control is involved is the subject of great dispute. According to David Hume, the question of the nature of free will is "the most contentious question of metaphysics."[2] More recently, Susan Wolf writes that "free will is arguably the most difficult problem in philosophy."[3] If Hume and Wolf are correct in this, then figuring out *what free will is* will be no small task indeed. It is for just this reason—the ambiguity of something that is so central to our thinking—that I think so many people have an intrinsic interest in free will. Besides this intrinsic interest, there is another important line of reasoning that has motivated much of the philosophical attention on free will, namely its connection with moral responsibility. Though, as we shall see below, there is some disagreement on this issue, it is both plausible and widely accepted that an agent must possess free will if she is to be morally responsible for her actions. Along these lines, Richard Taylor writes:

> It is this idea [i.e. responsibility], I believe, which is largely responsible for the philosophical concept of agency to begin with. Had people never conceived of themselves as responsible beings then it is doubtful whether they would ever have thought of themselves as agents either, in the philosophical sense of that term. The reason for this is that responsibility presupposes freedom. If anyone is responsible for what he has done, then he must have been free.[4]

The connection between free will and responsibility that Taylor is drawing our attention to is implicit in the above discussion of Allison and Riley—whether or not we blame Allison for the dog's death is likely to depend in part on whether or not she was acting freely when she killed him.

However, many think that the significance of free will is not limited to its being a necessary condition for moral responsibility. Various philosophers suggest that free will is also a requirement for agency, rationality, the autonomy and dignity of persons, creativity, ownership, cooperation, the value of friendship and love, and a proper understanding of the self.[5] Others suggest that a belief in free will is required for us to deliberate about what to do without contradicting ourselves.[6] John Martin Fischer also suggests that free will is crucial for self-expression, artistic creativity, and being able to make a certain kind of statement about one's self.[7] Fischer goes so far as to say that "when thinking and writing about free will ... the stakes are so high ... [that] the very meaning of life is at stake."[8] Even if one thinks that this last statement by Fischer is a bit of an exaggeration, we nevertheless see that free will is central to many philosophical issues. Though I won't be exploring many of these ideas in any detail in subsequent portions of this book, it should now be clear why free will has been a recurrent topic of philosophical inquiry.

The present volume aims to provide a fair and clear introduction to many of the central issues in contemporary debates about free will. I will not, of course, be able to address in any significant detail all of the issues, but I do hope to be able to provide the reader with some understanding of the breadth of the issues involved in philosophical discussions of the metaphysics of free will. In doing so, I also hope to give the reader a sense of how the debates surrounding free will have developed during the past few decades. Of course, the contemporary debates did not arise in a vacuum but were prompted by earlier discussions, which in turn were informed by prior dispute and debate.[9] One could easily trace this discussion of free will through the history of Western philosophy at least as far back as St. Augustine, who wrote extensively on the nature of free will and its implications for other issues in metaphysics.[10] In fact, nearly every major figure in the history of philosophy has had something or other to say about free will. But every discussion must have limits, even if those limits are in a certain sense arbitrary. Thus, though I will be focusing my discussion almost exclusively on the second half of the twentieth century and the first few years of the twenty-first century, I do not intend this to suggest that the historical issues are not worthy of consideration. I think they are, though their exploration will have to be the focus of another book. Furthermore, there is another reason to limit our coverage to contemporary issues, namely the significant amount of innovative work produced on these issues in the past few decades that has propelled and changed the philosophical discussion. In this regard, commenting on the contemporary treatment of free will, Saul Smilansky writes:

> In the last generation or two, the free will debate has been one of the most exciting areas of philosophical endeavour, where undeniable progress has been made both in clarifying older theories and understanding their strengths and weaknesses, and in discovering new pertinent questions and positions. The progress has been so great that it might be claimed that here (unlike with most philosophical problems) there is not much worth reading that was written before, say, 1960.[11]

While I'm not inclined to agree with Smilansky's claim that there isn't much worth to be found in reading historical work on free will, I think that he is correct in noting that contemporary discussions have made significant advances over previous works and that, as a result, limiting one's focus to contemporary works is neither unjustified nor without certain merits.

Moral responsibility

In light of the connection between free will and moral responsibility noted above, it will be helpful to consider briefly the nature of moral responsibility before turning toward free will *per se*. And here we encounter the question: What's at stake when we ascribe moral responsibility? According to Manuel Vargas, a key part of answering this question is figuring out what work moral responsibility does in justifying our moral practices:

The work of the concept of moral responsibility has to do with marking a set of inferences about differential moral praiseworthiness and blame-worthiness. People who knowingly and intentionally do the wrong thing deserve condemnation. People who do the right thing deserve approval. Keeping track of when people deserve praise and blame is the work of the concept of moral responsibility. It is, in some sense, why we rightly have a concept of moral responsibility.[12]

But beyond this, there is considerable disagreement about what the exact content of our concept of moral responsibility is. Though there exists a plethora of accounts of the exact content of our concept of moral responsibility, I will briefly discuss the three most influential ones.

The reactive attitudes

The first of these three accounts was developed initially by Peter Strawson.[13] According to Strawson, whose work on moral responsibility is quite influential, moral responsibility is to be understood in terms of certain social practices: to think that a person is a morally responsible agent is to think that it is proper to treat that person in certain ways and to adopt certain attitudes toward him. Strawson calls these attitudes the "reactive attitudes," because they are attitudes that arise in us in response to others. The reactive attitudes "are essentially natural human reactions to the good or ill will or indifference of others towards us, as displayed in *their* attitudes and actions. ... [The reactive attitudes are] non-detached attitudes and reactions of people directly involved in transactions with each other."[14] Strawson gives as examples of these attitudes "such things as gratitude, resentment, forgiveness, love, and hurt feelings."[15] The reactive attitudes can be either positive—as in cases of moral praise, gratitude, respect, love—or negative—as in cases of moral blame, resentment, and indignation. On Strawson's view, a person is morally responsible for performing some action X only if that person is the apt recipient of praise (or gratitude, etc.) or blame (or resentment, etc.) for her doing X. The reactive attitudes, according to Strawson, are foundational and essential aspects of interpersonal inter-action. As one commentator on Strawson's view puts the point, the reactive attitudes are "simply inescapable elements of the human condition."[16] It is also important to note that on such an account of moral responsibility, a person could be responsible for some action even if no other person, in fact, actually holds her responsible. A person could be deserving of resentment, for example, for performing some action even if no one does, in fact, resent her for performing that action. What is important on this view is whether or not the reactive attitudes are *justified*, not whether they are *present*.[17]

The ledger view

A second view of the nature of moral responsibility is often called "the ledger view". On this account, an agent's moral responsibility is thought of in terms of a metaphorical moral ledger. Michael Zimmerman describes one version of this view as follows:

> Praising someone may be said to constitute judging that there is a "credit" in his "ledger of life", a "positive mark" in his "report-card of life", or a "luster" on his "record as a person"; that his "record" has been "burnished"; that his "moral standing" has been enhanced. Blaming someone may be said to constitute judging that there is a "discredit" or "debit" in his "ledger", a "negative mark" in his "report card", or a "blemish" or "stain" on his "record"; that his "record" has been "tarnished"; that his "moral standing" has been "diminished". Someone is praiseworthy if he is deserving of such praise; that is, if it is correct, or true to the facts, to judge that there is a "credit" in his "ledger" (etc.). Someone is blameworthy if he is deserving of such blame; that is, if it is correct, or true to the facts, to judge that there is a "debit" in his "ledger" (etc.).[18]

Thus, on this view, marks are made in one's ledger when it is appropriate to ascribe to that individual certain ethical predicates such as "good," "bad," "right," "wrong," "ought," "ought not," etc. Zimmerman thinks that despite the metaphorical nature of this approach, it nevertheless captures the heart of moral responsibility. "Even if there is no such record, it remains a fact that certain events occur and that a person's moral worth is a function of these events."[19]

The accountability view

On a third view, which like Strawson's view is an inherently social approach, moral responsibility is a function of the appropriateness of expecting the agent to provide an explanation for his behavior. According to Marina Oshana, who develops a version of this sort of view, "when we say a person is morally responsible for something, we are essentially saying that the person did or caused some act (or exhibited some trait of character) for which it is fitting that she give an account."[20] For this reason, this understanding of moral responsibility is often called "the accountability view." To further understand the view, consider the following two descriptions of it:

> Suppose you are the chairman of my department, and the time has come to evaluate my teaching performance. As a junior member of the department,

I have been occupied by an array of academic duties. You suspect I might be less than stellar in the classroom, but you are inclined to be lenient in your assessment of my teaching. To your surprise, my teaching secures strong reviews. When you ask me to explain how I have managed to juggle the stresses of the year with apparent success, and I reply that hard work was the key, you might feel admiration (or envy) toward me; but then again, you might feel nothing. What expresses your belief that I am responsible for this situation is to be found in the fact that you believe I am in a position to explain the actions and motives that lead to my success.[21]

What is the popular notion of responsibility? ... We see ... at once the idea of a man's appearing to answer. He answers for what he has done, or (which we need not separately consider) has neglected and left undone. And the tribunal is a moral tribunal; it is the court of conscience, imagined as a judge, divine or human, external or internal. It is not necessarily implied that the man does answer for all or nay of his acts; but it is implied that he might have to answer, that he is liable to be called upon—in one word, ... it is *right* that he should be subject to the moral tribunal; or the moral tribunal has a *right* over him, to call him before it, with reference to all or any of his deeds.[22]

As seen in this example, the accountability view holds that the essence of moral responsibility is found in the expectation that the agent can provide a proper account or explanation for her behavior.

These three different approaches to the nature of moral responsibility, while conceptually distinct, need not be isolated from one another. Indeed, a significant amount of overlap is possible. John Fischer suggests, for instance, that a version of the ledger view follows from Oshana's accountability view.[23] Similarly, Oshana suggests that an agent is the apt recipient of the reactive attitudes precisely because it is fitting that she give an account of her action. Finally, it might also be thought that an agent is the proper recipient of the reactive attitudes if one has "added" to one's moral ledger in a particular way.

I am not wedded to any one of these accounts of moral responsibility. In addition, I think that nothing of what I say hinges on the truth of any particular account. For these reasons, and for simplicity's sake, in the remainder of this book I will use the language of just one of these views—the reactive attitudes view. The reader who favors one of the other accounts is welcome to translate what I say into her own preferred view.

Free will

None of these accounts of the nature of moral responsibility proves that it exists; that is, an account of what moral responsibility is doesn't, by itself, mean that anyone has it. And while most of us probably think that there is such a thing as moral responsibility, there are a number of philosophers who think that none of us are morally responsible for anything. I discuss a number of such views in Chapter 4. In fact, some philosophers think that the reason we lack moral responsibility is because it is impossible for anyone to be morally responsible for anything. But let us assume that moral responsibility is possible. That is, assume that it is possible that at least some agents are at least some times morally responsible for their actions. (I put it this way because affirming the existence of free will doesn't mean that everyone has free will, or that those who have it always have it.) If it is possible that an agent is morally responsible, what conditions would have to be the case in order for the agent to *actually* be morally responsible? At least two different kinds of conditions must be met: an epistemic condition and a control condition.[24] The idea behind the epistemic condition is that moral responsibility requires a certain kind of knowledge or perhaps just a belief about the nature of one's actions or choices and what could result from them. Peter van Inwagen captures the basic idea here as follows: "[N]o one, I suppose, would seriously maintain that we can be blamed for *all* of the consequences of *any* of our acts. ... Obviously, I can be blamed only for those consequences of my acts that are in some sense 'foreseeable'."[25] One might initially think that an agent can only be morally responsible for a decision if she was aware of the morally salient feature of her action. But this can't be right either. To begin with, it doesn't take into account cases of culpable ignorance—that is, cases where an agent is herself morally blameworthy for failing to have the required knowledge. The epistemic requirement should thus require that, in order for an agent to be morally responsible, she must not be ignorant of the relevant facts or else that there be something she should have done at some earlier time such that, had she done it, she would not now be ignorant of the relevant facts. But even this is only a first approximation of a satisfactory presentation of the epistemic condition. While further specification and unpacking of the epistemic condition is an important issue, it is not one that I will be able to pursue here.[26]

The second requirement for moral responsibility is often called the "control condition" or the "freedom-relevant condition" for moral responsibility. As Susan Wolf puts it, "An agent that has a will can be responsible only for things that are related to her in such a way that they fall, so to speak, within the sphere of influence of her will."[27] And free will is often taken to be simply the capacity or set of capacities needed to fulfill the control condition for moral responsibility. In other words, an agent acts freely when he controls his actions in the way needed for him to be morally praiseworthy or blameworthy for that action. If there is no free will, then no agent has the kind of control needed for moral responsibility: "Without free will there is no moral responsibility: if moral responsibility exists, then someone is morally responsible for something he has done or for something he has left undone. ... Therefore, if moral responsibility exists, someone has free will. Therefore, if no one has free will, moral responsibility doesn't exist."[28]

That being said, the contemporary free will literature contains two dominant general conceptions of the nature of free will, as we shall see more fully in subsequent chapters. According to the first of these, which has received the majority of the attention in the literature, free will is primarily a function of being able to do otherwise than one in fact does. For example, I have free will to order a salad for lunch if I could have ordered a sandwich or a pizza instead, or even refrained from eating anything for lunch at all. According to the second approach, free will is primarily a function of an agent being the source of her actions in a particular way. On this approach, I order the salad of my own free will if nothing outside of me is the ultimate explanation of my action or choice. Both of these notions can be seen in the following passage taken from Robert Kane:

> We believe we have free will when we view ourselves as agents capable of influencing the world in various ways. Open alternatives, or alternative possibilities, seem to lie before us. We reason and deliberate among them and choose. We feel (1) it is "up to us" what we choose and how we act; and this means we could have chosen or acted otherwise. As Aristotle noted: when acting is "up to us," so is not acting. This "up-to-us-ness" also suggests (2) the ultimate control of our actions lies in us and not outside us in factors beyond our control.[29]

The vast majority of the contemporary free will literature focuses on the first of these two approaches, so much so that John Martin Fischer sometimes speaks of this as being the traditional view: "Traditionally the most influential view about the sort of freedom necessary and sufficient for moral responsibility posits that this sort of freedom involves the availability of genuinely open alternative possibilities at certain key points in one's life."[30] In contrast, a smaller percentage of the extant literature focuses primarily on the issues of "source," "ultimacy," and "origination" that are at the heart of the second approach to free will. In what follows, I will call the first of these conceptions—the conception that free will is primarily a matter of having alternative possibilities—the "alternative-possibilities condition." Similarly, I will call the second of these conceptions—that free will is primarily a matter of our being the source of our choices in a particular way—the "sourcehood condition." As Kane suggests, I think that most of us think about free will along the lines of one or the other, or both, of these conditions. In subsequent chapters, I demarcate these two different conceptions of the concept of free will (i.e. *free will as having the ability to do otherwise* and *free will as being the source of one's actions*) and explore the relationship between them.

Some philosophers simply define free will as one of these two conditions. Peter van Inwagen, for instance, writes that "to be able to have acted otherwise is to have free will"[31] thereby identifying free will with the alternative-possibilities condition. Similarly, Randolph Clarke writes: "I shall say that when an agent acts freely (or with free will), she is able to do other than what she does."[32] I think, however, that there is reason to resist this practice, particularly in the context of the issues to be addressed in this book. For, as will be discussed at greater length in the second part of this volume, it is a contentious issue whether the satisfaction of the alternative-possibilities condition is required for moral responsibility. I could, of course, reserve the use of "free will" to mean the alternative-possibilities condition, and use the phrase "the control condition" to refer to the kind of control required for moral responsibility. But I find this way of speaking to be clumsy and awkward. Consider also John Fischer's "semi-compatibilist" position. On the semi-compatibilist's view, satisfaction of the alternative-possibilities condition—which he often refers to as "regulative control"—*is not* required for moral responsibility, but another kind of control—"guidance control"—*is* required for moral responsibility.[33] Fischer writes: "moral responsibility does not require the sort of control that involves genuine metaphysical access to alternative possibilities ('regulative control'). Rather, 'guidance control' is the freedom-relevant condition necessary and sufficient for moral responsibility."[34] The substantial influence of Fischer's view on the contemporary free will literature gives us another reason to resist equating free will with the alternative-possibilities condition at the very beginning. For these reasons, in what follows I will use the term "free will" to refer to the kind of control required for moral responsibility rather than equating it with one or other of these two free will conceptions.

In later chapters, I will explore whether or not free will is best understood as involving the alternative-possibilities condition, the sourcehood condition, or both. I will argue that the sourcehood condition is more important for free will than the mere having of alternatives, though I think the relationship between the sourcehood condition and the alternative-possibilities condition is complex. To anticipate what is developed in greater detail later, at the heart of my preferred view is the claim that what is most important for an agent's free will is the agent being the source of her actions in a certain way and that being this sort of source for one's actions requires features of the world at large to be certain ways. To return to the above example involving Allison, a first approximation is that Allison freely killed Riley only if the dog's death was the result of her rational or volitional faculties and there is nothing outside of her cognitive and volitional faculties that was sufficient for her action. This is obviously an overly simplistic characterization, but I will elaborate and clarify this basic idea throughout the rest of the book. While I think that it would be overly ambitious to think that this book will fully defend the view I develop from all its competitors and against all possible objections, I do hope to go a considerable distance toward showing that this view is worthy of significant attention, if not acceptance.

Choice and actions

Before progressing, however, it will be helpful to address the relationship between the exercise of free will and our actions. This book is about free will. But one of the reasons we care about whether or not we have free will is because of its relationship to our actions. As indicated earlier, we hold people morally responsible not only for their choices or willings—I shall take these terms to be synonymous—but for their actions as well. And while there is, or at least can be, a connection between doing an action freely and freely willing that action, the two are not coextensive.

In the eighteenth century, Thomas Hobbes famously defined freedom of action as the lack of external obstacles or constraints to doing what you want to do.[35] On this understanding, Emmaline is free to go outside and play so long as there are no external impediments to her doing so—that is, the front door is not locked, or she's not shut in the closet, or tied to a chair, etc. But it seems to be the case that Emmaline could have freedom of action and lack freedom of the will. Suppose, for instance, that while the door is unlocked and she's not tied to the chair (and that there are no other similar impediments to her going outside if that's what she chooses to do) she's incapable of willing to go outside. Perhaps, for instance, she thinks the Boogey Man is outside waiting for her, and she's so petrified with fear that she is incapable of forming the volition to go outside. In this case, it looks as though she has freedom of action (since there is nothing preventing her from going outside) but lacks freedom of the will. And if that is the case, then obviously freedom of action and free will cannot be the same thing.

Conversely, an agent may have the free will to form a particular volition, but lack the freedom to carry out that volition. Rogers Albritton gives the following example of such a mismatch:

> Suppose I am chained up so that I can't walk, but don't yet know it. I deliberate about what to do next and decide on a little tour of my cell. Then I discover that I can't walk. They've chained me up, the swine! ... Do I have reason to think not only, "They've chained me up!" but, "Good God, they've been tampering with my free will!"? No, I don't. ... It's nothing against my freedom of will if I "can't walk" because [I'm chained up or] the floor will collapse, or because it has been arranged for me to explode if I shift my weight. These difficulties in the way of my actually getting any walking accomplished are on the side of the world, not the will; and they don't in themselves interfere with the will's part in walking (that is, in these cases, its part in deciding and trying to walk). They don't affect its freedom, therefore. Where there's a will, there just isn't always a way.[36]

As Albritton points out in this quotation, it is possible to freely will to do some action and not be free to perform that action. This distinction is sometimes described as the difference between formal freedom and material freedom, a distinction which traces back to the medieval period. Formal freedom is an agent's freedom to will what she wants to will, apart from whether or not she is able to realize the object of her choice. In contrast, material freedom involves "whether we are also able to effectuate the volition, i.e. whether we also have the freedom to realise the object of choice."[37] An agent has formal freedom when she has free will, but she has material freedom when she has the further ability to actually perform what she has chosen to do formally. In cases where an agent has formal freedom but lacks material freedom, she has free will but lacks freedom of action.

If free will and freedom of action can come apart in both of these ways, what then is the relationship between the two? As already indicated, the relationship will likely be complex. But, for present purposes, we can take as a starting point the connection with moral responsibility. Earlier, I defined free will as the control condition on moral responsibility. Given this understanding, if an agent is to be held morally responsible for some free action of hers, then it must be the case that she freely willed to do that action. In other words, free and responsible action presupposes an exercise of free will, just as material freedom presupposes formal freedom. To return to the example involving Allison at the beginning of the chapter, Allison clearly acted freely in Hobbes's sense in knocking over the clock in the sense that there were no external impediments preventing her action. But if we are justified in holding her responsible for her action, then we must know that the action was the result of her choice of volition; that is, we must know that she freely willed to do it if we are justified in blaming her. Though at times throughout this study I'll use examples involving material freedom, my main interest is with formal freedom. The examples involving external actions are intended for ease of description, and the reader should keep in mind that the key issue is the exercise of free choice that underlies those free and responsible actions.

The thesis of causal determinism

Much of the contemporary scholarship on free will focuses on whether or not it is compatible with causal determinism. Robert Kane has labeled this "the Compatibility Question."[38] In addressing the Compatibility Question, it is important to keep causal determinism distinct from other sorts of determinism, such as logical determinism or theological determinism. Causal determinism—hereafter, simply "determinism" for short—is the thesis that the course of the future is entirely determined by the conjunction of the non-relational past and the laws of nature. An event is causally determined when the event's happening just as it did was necessitated by causes and the laws of nature. So, to take a mundane example, consider that you're playing billiards. Imagine that you could somehow "pause" a particular shot right after you struck the cue ball with your pool cue, and before the cue ball has hit another ball. Let us call this time *t1*. Where the balls will end up on the table once the shot has been completed and all the balls have eventually come to rest—let's call this time *t2*—is entirely a function of the location of the balls on the table when you struck the cue ball, the force and spin you hit the cue ball with, the various properties of the balls (their weight, etc.) and the laws of nature, here, the laws of physics (e.g. the law of conservation of energy, the law of angular momentum, the laws governing friction, etc.). So where the balls end up on the table at *t2* is causally determined by how things are at *t1* and the relevant laws of nature. Now, the thesis of causal determinism says that everything is like the balls on the billiard table in this sense—everything that happens is causally necessitated by the past and the relevant laws of nature. As Bertrand Russell once put it, according to the thesis of causal determinism, "there are such invariable relations between different events at the same or different times that, given the state of the whole universe throughout any finite time, however short, every previous and subsequent event can theoretically be determined as a function of the given events during that time."[39] So, if the thesis of causal determinism is true, your reading this very book at this very moment was necessitated by the past and the laws of nature.

Consider a proposition that completely describes the way that the entire world was at some point in the distant past.[40] Let us call this proposition "*P*." Consider also another proposition that expresses the conjunction of all the laws of nature; call this proposition "*L*." Determinism is the thesis that the conjunction of *P* and *L* entails a further proposition describing a unique future. Given *P* and *L*, there is only one possible future, one possible way for things to end up. So, to use an example, the way the universe was in 1,847 BCE, together with the laws of nature, necessitate that you are reading this very book at this very instant. The only way for you to not read this book at this instant, on the assumption of determinism, is if either the past had been different or the laws of nature had been different. To make the same point using possible-world semantics, the thesis of causal determinism is the claim that all the states of affairs that obtain at some time in the past, when conjoined with the laws of nature, entail which possible world is the actual world. Since a possible world includes those states of affairs that will obtain, the truth of determinism amounts to the thesis that the past and the laws of nature entail what states of affairs will obtain in the future, and that only those states of affairs entailed by the past and the laws will in fact obtain. Similarly, David Lewis defines the thesis of causal determinism in such a way that, if true, "the prevailing laws of nature are such that there do not exist any two possible worlds that are exactly alike up to some time, which differ thereafter, and in which those laws are never violated."[41]

Being determined differs from being predictable. It is possible for determinism to be true and for no one to be able to predict the future. The fact that there are some future truths that no human agent knows (or even if there are some future truths that no human agent is able to know) has no bearing on whether there are future truths entailed by the conjunction of the past and the laws. However, there is a weaker connection between the thesis of determinism and the predictability of the future. If determinism were true, then a being with a complete knowledge of P and L and with sufficient intellectual capacities should be able to predict infallibly the way that the future will turn out. However, given that we humans lack both the relevant knowledge and the required intellectual capacities, the fact that we are not able to predict the future is not evidence for the falsity of determinism.

Most philosophers agree that whether or not determinism is true is a contingent matter; that is, determinism is neither necessarily true nor necessarily false. If this is so, whether or not determinism is true becomes an empirical matter, to be discovered by investigating the way the world is, not through philosophical argumentation. This is not to deny that the truth of determinism would have metaphysical implications. For one, the truth of determinism would entail that the laws of nature are not merely probabilistic—for if they were, then the conjunction of the past and the laws would not entail a unique future. Furthermore, as we shall see shortly, philosophers care very much about what implications the truth of determinism would have for free will. But the point to note here is that if the truth of determinism is a contingent truth about the way the world actually is, then scientific investigation should give us insight into this matter.[42] Let us say that a possible world is deterministic if causal determinism is true in that world. There are two ways that a world could fail to be deterministic. First, as already noted, if the laws of nature in that world were probabilistic, then such a world would not be deterministic. Second, if there are entities within a world that are not fully governed by the laws of nature, then even if those laws are themselves deterministic, that world would not be deterministic. Is the actual world deterministic? I do not know. During the eighteenth, nineteenth, and early twentieth century, most philosophers and scientists thought that it was.[43] But the contemporary scientific consensus seems to go the other way. At a recent conference, I had the opportunity to ask a Nobel-Prize-winning physicist if the world's leading physicists think determinism is likely to be true, and he indicated otherwise. Of course, it is possible that all of the current leading physicists are wrong in thinking the world is indeterministic. However, following Randolph Clarke, I would say "perhaps the best that can be said … is that … there is no good evidence that determinism is true."[44]

Numerous scientists suggest a stronger claim, and that is that certain parts of physics give us reason to doubt the truth of determinism.[45] For example, the standard interpretation of Quantum Theory, the Copenhagen Interpretation, holds that some of the basic laws of physics are indeterministic and probabilistic. According to this interpretation, whether or not a subatomic particle such as a quark swerves in a particular direction at a particular time is described properly only by probabilistic equations. Although the equations may predict the likelihood that a quark swerves to the left at a certain time, on this view whether or not it actually swerves is indeterministic or random.

There are also deterministic interpretations of Quantum Theory. Fortunately, the outcome of the debate regarding whether Quantum Theory is most properly interpreted deterministically or indeterministically can be largely avoided for our present purposes. Even if (systems of) micro-particles such as quarks are indeterministic, it might be that (systems involving) larger physical objects such as cars, dogs, and people are deterministic. It is possible that the only indeterminism is on the scale of micro-particles and that macro-objects themselves obey deterministic laws. If this is the case, then causal determinism as defined above is, strictly speaking, false, but it is "nearly" true. That is, we could replace determinism with what Ted Honderich calls "near determinism," or "determinism-where-it-matters". This view

> allows that there is or may be some indeterminism but only at what is called the micro-level of our existence, the level of the small particles of our bodies, particles of the kind studied by physics. At the ordinary level of choices and actions, and even ordinary electrochemical activity in our brains, [deterministic] causal laws govern what happens. It's all cause and effect in what you might call real life.[46]

In what follows, I shall only explicitly speak of determinism, and drop further reference to near-determinism. But this is done only for purposes of ease of discussion, and many of the points made about determinism should also be taken to hold about near-determinism.

A central issue in the present volume, as in the philosophical debates about free will in general, is what the implications would be for questions involving free will if determinism were true. One way to think about the implications would be by asking the following question: Could we still be free even if scientists were to discover that causal determinism is true? This question shall be the focus of the next chapter.

CHAPTER TWO

The compatibility question

Compatibilism and incompatibilism

The Compatibility Question, introduced at the end of the preceding chapter, is also a helpful way to differentiate two of the main positions in the contemporary free will debate. Recall that the Compatibility Question asks if the existence of free will is compatible with the truth of the thesis of causal determinism. Compatibilists answer the Compatibility Question in the affirmative, believing that agents could have free will even if causal determinism is true. In other words, the existence of free will in a possible world is compatible with that world being deterministic. It is for this reason that the position is known as "compatibilism" and its proponents are called "compatibilists." According to the compatibilist, it is possible for an agent to be determined in all her choices and actions and still make at least some of her choices freely. "Incompatibilists," on the other hand, answer the Compatibility Question in the negative. According to incompatibilists, the existence of free will is logically incompatible with the truth of determinism. If a given possible world is deterministic, then no agent in that world has free will for that very reason. Furthermore, if one assumes that having free will is a necessary condition for being morally responsible for one's actions, then the incompatibility of free will and determinism would entail the incompatibility of moral responsibility and determinism.

Clearing away confusions

It is important to keep in mind that both compatibilism and incompatibilism are claims about possibility. According to the compatibilist, it is possible that an agent is both fully determined and yet free. The incompatibilist, on the other hand, maintains that such a state of affairs is impossible and that free will is possible only if determinism is false. But neither position by itself is making a claim about whether or not agents actually do possess free will. Assume for the moment that incompatibilism is true. If, as suggested above, the truth of determinism is a contingent matter, then whether or not agents have free will depends on whether or not the actual world is deterministic. Furthermore, even if the actual world is indeterministic, it doesn't immediately follow that the indeterminism present is of the sort required for free will. But the view according to which incompatibilism is true and that free will does exist is a view which goes by the name "libertarianism."[1]

It is also important to keep in mind that compatibilism makes no claim about whether or not determinism is true. In the 1930s, a then influential compatibilist named R. E. Hobart published a paper entitled "Free Will as Involving Determination and Inconceivable Without It."[2] Though the title includes "determination" rather than "determinism," the article begins with the claim that "the doctrine of free will and determinism, that it is based upon a misapprehension, that the two assertions are entirely consistent, that one of them strictly implies the other." In this article, Hobart suggests that any amount of indeterminism, at least as related to choice and action, is detrimental to moral agency. For Hobart, an action which is not determined is actually not an action of the agent at all, since it is something that *happens to* the agent rather than something the agent *does*. He writes: "such absence of determination, if and so far as it exists, is no gain to freedom, but sheer loss of it; no advantage to the moral life, but blank subtraction from it. ... Freedom is something that we can attribute only to a continuing being, and he can have it only so far as the particular transient volitions within him are determined."[3]

To be fair to Hobart, it is doubtful that he intended his title to be taken as literally true.[4] He is willing to grant, for instance, that the presence of indeterminism wouldn't necessarily undermine freedom and responsibility if that indeterminism was causally irrelevant to the action (or volition) in question.[5] But most contemporary compatibilists want their view of free will to be compatible not only with the truth of determinism, but also its falsity. That is, they want their view to be one according to which the truth or falsity of determinism is irrelevant to whether or not we are free.[6] John Martin Fischer, one of the most influential contemporary compatibilists, thinks that it is a major advantage of his particular brand of compatibilism that we can be free whether determinism ends up being true or false. Here is one of Fischer's presentations of how compatibilism is resilient to the discoveries of physicists in a way that libertarianism is not:

> I could certainly imagine waking up some morning to the newspaper headline, "Causal Determinism Is True!" (Most likely this would not be in the *National Enquirer* or even *People*—but perhaps the *New York Times*...) I could imagine reading the article and subsequently (presumably over some time) becoming convinced that causal determinism is true—that the generalizations that describe the relationships

between complexes of past events and laws of nature, on the one hand, and subsequent events, on the other, are universal generalizations with 100 percent probabilities associated with them. And I feel confident that this would not, nor should it, change my view of myself and others as (sometimes) free and robustly morally responsible agents.... The assumption that we human beings—most of us, at least—are morally responsible agents (at least sometimes) is extremely important and pervasive. In fact, it is hard to imagine human life without it.... A compatibilist need not give up this assumption [that we are at least sometimes free and morally responsible], even if he were to wake up to the headline, "Causal Determinism is True!" (and if he were convinced of its truth).... A compatibilist need not "flipflop" in this weird and unappealing way.[7]

In contrast, if the libertarian were to become convinced that determinism were true, she would have to give up at least one of her beliefs under threat of inconsistency. That is, she would either have to abandon her belief that we are morally responsible beings, or she would have to abandon her incompatibilism. "One of my main motivations for being a compatibilist," writes Fischer, "is that I don't want our personhood and our moral responsibility, as it were, to hang on a thread, or to be held hostage to the possible scientific discovery that determinism is in fact true."[8]

However, surely some readers will think that compatibilism is false by definition, for free will and determinism are by definition in conflict. There are a number of ways this concern can be fleshed out. One is the view that determinism threatens free will because, if true, then an agent's volitional structure (that is, the totality of his volitions and the other agential features like desires, beliefs, values, goals, etc. that they depend on) is causally irrelevant to what the agent does. Susan Wolf describes this worry as follows:

A naïve reaction to the idea that everything we do is completely determined by a causal chain that extends backward beyond the times of our births involves thinking that in that case we would have no control over our behavior whatsoever. If everything is determined, it is thought, then what happens happens, whether we want it to or not.[9]

As Wolf goes on to show, however, this initial worry is misplaced for it confuses determinism with fatalism, the view that future events—including an agent's actions—are inevitable and will happen no matter what the agent does. The truth of determinism would not mean that our volitions, desires, beliefs, values, etc. play no causal role in explaining our actions. The thesis of causal determinism itself puts no limits on the *relata* of causation; rather, it is simply a view about the relationship that holds between the *relata*. The truth of determinism is completely compatible with our actions being in part determined by our choices such that if we had not made a particular choice, we would not have done a particular action. Of course, if determinism is true, then our choices are themselves causally necessitated by earlier factors in a way that one might think threatens free will. But the worry that determinism rules out the causal efficiency of our volitions is misguided.

Another typical initial confusion regarding compatibilism is to think that if determinism is true, then the causal processes which bring about our volitions are constrained or coerced in a way that undermines our freedom. But determinism does not imply that the causal processes which result in our volitions act contrary to our wills; instead it says that they are a necessary causal contributor to the volition in question. As Philippa Foot put it:

> To say that a man acted freely is, it is often suggested, to say that he was not constrained, or that he could have done otherwise if he had chosen, or something else of that kind; and since these things could be true even if his action was determined it seems that there could be room for free will even within a universe completely subject to [deterministic] causal laws.[10]

Once the central compatibilist claim is understood to imply neither fatalism nor constraint, at least some of the initial resistance to compatibilism should be avoided.

The previous paragraphs are intended to clearly explain what exactly compatibilism is, not to argue for its truth. In a similar manner, the failure of these initial confusions about compatibilism doesn't mean that it's not false for some other reason. What then should we think about the dispute between compatibilists and incompatibilists regarding the relationship between free will and the truth of determinism? Is compatibilism correct? Or is incompatibilism?

Where should we start?

In the past, some philosophers have suggested that incompatibilism is the "common" or "folk" view about the relationship between causal determinism and free will, thereby making incompatibilism the default position. Laura Ekstrom, for instance, writes that "we come to the table, nearly all of us, as pre-theoretic incompatibilists"[11] and thus the compatibilist "needs a positive argument in favor of the compatibility thesis."[12] A similar endorsement can also be found in Robert Kane's work:

> In my experience, most ordinary persons start out as natural incompatibilists. They believe there is some kind of conflict between freedom and determinism; and the idea that freedom and responsibility might be

compatible with determinism looks to them at first like a "quagmire of evasion" (William James) or "a wretched subterfuge" (Immanuel Kant). Ordinary persons have to be talked out of this natural incompatibilism by the clever arguments of philosophers—who, in the manner of their mentor Socrates, are only too happy to oblige.[13]

And an even stronger claim can be found in a recent book by J. P. Moreland:

It is widely acknowledged that worldwide, the commonsense, spontaneously formed understanding of human free will is what philosophers call libertarian freedom: one acts freely only if one's action was not determined—directly or indirectly—by forces outside one's control, and one must be free to act or refrain from acting; one's choice is "spontaneous", it originates with and only with the actor. Unless one has an ideological axe to grind, one will be a libertarian.[14]

These comments, and others like them, might be taken to suggest that the onus is on the compatibilist to show that causal determinism is in fact compatible with free will: short of an argument to the contrary, incompatibilism carries the day.

There are at least two reasons why I think that this suggestion should be resisted. First, a number of recent philosophers—called "experimental philosophers"[15]—have called into question the claim that incompatibilism is more intuitive than compatibilism. In arguing for various positions, contemporary philosophers often appeal to intuitions, and, as the following chapters will illustrate, this tendency is also true of those philosophers working on issues related to free will. Rather than relying on their own intuitions, some experimental philosophers want to figure out the intuitions of the general population—or "the folk," as they are often called. Though the exact percentage of compatibilist responses varies from study to study, experimental philosophers have been able to secure as high as 83 percent compatibilist intuitions from the folk. While many of the studies involved here are tentative, these initial findings call into doubt the claims given by Ekstrom and Kane above.[16]

The second reason for not taking incompatibilism to be the default position regarding the Compatibility Question comes from William Lycan. Lycan argues that in general, one ought to assume the compatibility of any two theses unless one has an argument for their incompatibility. He elaborates this point as follows:

Compatibilism, not just about free will but generally, on any topic, is the default. For any modal claim to the effect that some statement is a necessary truth, I would say that the burden of proof is on the claim's proponent. A theorist who maintains of something that is not obviously impossible that nonetheless that thing *is* impossible owes us an argument.

And since entailment claims are claims of necessity and impossibility, the same applies to them. Anyone who insists that a sentence S1 entails another sentence S2 must defend that thesis if it is controversial. If I tell you that "Pigs have wings" entails "It snows every night in Chapel Hill," you need not scramble to show how there might be a world in which the first was true but the second false; rather, you would rightly demand that I display the alleged modal connection. And of course the same goes for claims of impossibility. The point is underscored, I think, if we understand necessity as truth in all possible worlds. The proponent of a necessity, impossibility, entailment or incompatibility claim is saying that *in no possible world whatever* does it occur that so-and-so. That is a universal quantification. Given the richness and incredible variety of the pluriverse, such a statement cannot be accepted without argument save for the case of basic logical intuitions that virtually everyone shares.[17]

While philosophical issues surrounding burdens of proof are quite contentious,[18] I think that Lycan is right in thinking that logical possibility should generally be assumed until an argument can be given to show logical impossibility.[19] Relatedly, Kadri Vihvelin argues that if free will is possible, then incompatibilism has a higher burden of proof insofar as incompatibilism requires determinism to be false in those worlds where free will exists but, unlike Hobart's view mentioned earlier, most contemporary compatibilist accounts can accommodate either determinism or indeterminism.[20] And if Lycan and Vihvelin are correct, then incompatibilists have an obligation to provide arguments for the incompatibility of free will and determinism.

Kinds of incompatibilism and compatibilism

Before turning to a leading argument for incompatibilism at the end of the present chapter, it will be helpful to look at some sub-categories of incompatibilism and compatibilism. There are myriad ways that one could categorize the various incompatibilist and compatibilist positions. The matter is further complicated by the fact that many of the ways of categorizing these views are orthogonal to one another. This results in more possible permutations than can be dealt with in any significant degree of detail. One might, for example, begin by differentiating those views which think we do have free will from those views which deny that we have free will.[21] There are forms of both compatibilism and incompatibilism which affirm the existence of free will. As indicated in the previous chapter, the conjunction of incompatibilism with the claim that some of us, at least some times, have free will is a position known as libertarianism. There is no catchy title for compatibilist views which affirm the existence of free will, perhaps in part because nearly every contemporary compatibilist thinks that free will does exist.[22] But it is not a part of compatibilism *per se* that we have free will.

It is also open to both compatibilists and incompatibilists to deny that there is such a thing as free will. I will refer to those views which deny the existence of free will as "free will skepticism." While not all free will skeptics are incompatibilists, most are. One reason that an incompatibilist might be a free will skeptic is if she thought that the thesis of causal determinism were in fact true; for, as an incompatibilist, she thinks that it is not possible for agents to be both free and determined. This position is known as "hard determinism". (Another incompatibilist view which denies the existence of free will, but not because determinism is true, is called "hard incompatibilism." For more on hard incompatibilism and other skeptical views, see Chapter 4.) So one way to sub-categorize both incompatibilist and compatibilist views is between those views which think we do have free will and those which deny its existence.

Event-causation and agent-causation

Another way of classifying both compatibilist and incompatibilist views is between event-causal and agent-causal views. Here, the fundamental disagreement concerns *how* an agent causes her free choices. Causation is a central issue in many areas of metaphysics, but there is considerable disagreement on exactly how the causal relation should be understood. One set of questions focuses on the nature of the relation itself. Is the causal relation constant conjunction, production, a kind of counterfactual dependence, a probability raiser, or something else? Or is it instead a primitive notion that cannot be further analyzed? Fortunately, for present purposes, the dispute over the nature of the causal relation need not concern us.[23] Rather, the relevant issue at present is regarding the *relata* of the causal relation—that is, what kinds of things are being related by the causal relation. More specifically, when an agent freely wills to do a particular action, to what ontological category do the *relata* belong? There is little debate about the nature of the effect insofar as it is going to be an event, such as a volition (in the case of formal freedom) or an action (in the case of material freedom). But there is considerable disagreement about the nature of the cause of a free choice. Most typically, the cause is also taken to be an event, such as the agent's considering a particular reason for making the choice in question. While the details vary from view to view, event-causal approaches to free will take both the cause and the effect to be events. To oversimplify, if Noah chooses to jump in a lake, the idea is that some event or other (or even some set of events) in Noah's volitional structure was the cause of his choosing to jump in the lake; perhaps he thought that he had a good reason for jumping in the lake insofar as his sister promised to pay him $20 if he would.

Most incompatibilists and compatibilists alike adopt such a view. Where they differ is whether or not all the causation involved is deterministic. Insofar as they think that free will and causal determinism are compatible, compatibilists will hold that the relationship between the cause (here, Noah's consideration of his reasons) and the effect (here, Noah's choice to jump in the lake) can be deterministic; that is, that the occurrence of the cause can be sufficient, given the laws of nature, for the occurrence of the effect. And this could be true, the compatibilist will also hold, even if the occurrence of the cause was itself the determined effect of a previous causal chain. In contrast, the incompatibilist will insist on the falsity of determinism at some point in the story if Noah's choice is to be a free choice. Exactly where the determinism occurs will vary among incompatibilist theories. Most hold that the causal relationship between the cause and the effect is not deterministic but merely probabilistic. On these views, Noah's having the reasons in question does not necessitate his making the choice to jump in the lake. Instead, the reasons only make possible the occurrence of the choice. Other incompatibilists accept that the relationship between the agent's reasons and his choices is deterministic, so long as his having the reasons that he does is not itself the effect of a deterministic causal chain.[24]

But other philosophers think that event-causation is not the right way to understand the causation involved in free will. According to these philosophers, there is another kind of causation at work in which the first causal *relatum* is not an effect, but an agent.[25] For this reason, this approach to free will is called "agent-causation." Ned Markosian describes agent-causal views as follows:

> The Theory of Agent Causation is based on a very important—and controversial—assumption, namely, that events are not the only entities that can cause events. According to the Theory of Agent Causation, agents—things like you and me—can also sometimes cause events. ... The idea is that ... the [choice] is not caused by any previous event, but it is caused by something else, namely, the agent. The agent just somehow causes the [choice] to occur. ... The further idea is that it is precisely in cases like this that our actions are morally free. For in such cases, we are the causes of our actions, and nothing else causes those actions.[26]

Agent-causal theories have typically been associated with incompatibilism, insofar as the leading proponents of such views are incompatibilists. But recently Markosian has argued that there can be compatibilist agent-causal views as well. Via a consideration of six thought-experiments (the details of which need not concern us for present purposes), Markosian argues that the most plausible agent-causal requirement for free and responsible agency is as follows:

> An action *A* is performed freely *iff* that action is caused by *A*'s agent.[27]

He then notes that this account of agent-causation is compatible with the truth of determinism insofar as determinism is irrelevant to whether the second half of the biconditional is true. "[This] Theory of Agent Causation is not in fact based on a genuinely incompatibilistic intuition. Rather, it is based on an intuition—that you cannot be morally responsible for an action that is caused by something outside of you, but not caused by you—that might appear at first glance to be incompatibilistic, but that, upon examination, turns out to be a compatibilistic intuition that supports the main idea behind [this understanding of agent-causation]."[28] The result is a compatibilist view of agent-causation. If Markosian is right about this, what then explains why agent-causation has historically been linked only with incompatibilism? According to Markosian, this connection is only the result of contingent biographical reasons:

> My guess is that something like the following happened. Before they became proponents of the Theory of Agent Causation, these people first became persuaded, by familiar kinds of arguments, that incompatibilism is true. Then they worried about the problem of reconciling moral responsibility with indeterminism. If we want to say that an agent is morally responsible for an action, and we are worried about incompatibilistic considerations, it doesn't seem to help much just to say that the action is uncaused (or not physically necessary, or whatever). How can the agent be responsible for her action if nothing—not she or anything else—causes that action? Finally, the relevant people decided that in order for an agent to be morally responsible for an action, the agent would have to be the cause of her own action.[29]

The coherence of agent-causation has been severely criticized by parties on both sides of the Compatibility Question. Others, such as Peter van Inwagen, question whether the addition of agent-causation actually succeeds in providing an account of how an agent can control her actions in the way needed for moral responsibility. (I shall return to this issue later in Chapter 10 when discussing the relationship between indeterminism and control.) It is not my intention, however, to decide between event-causal and agent-causal views. The present point is just to show that the distinction between event-causal and agent-causal views is one way to differentiate various compatibilist and incompatibilist views.[30]

Leeway vs sourcehood

Yet a third way of differentiating both compatibilist and incompatibilist views harkens back to the two general approaches to the nature of free will introduced in the previous chapter. According to the first of these approaches, free will is primarily a function of being able to do otherwise than one in fact does. To use the example introduced in that chapter involving Allison and Riley, the now-dead labrador, Allison freely killed the dog only if she could have avoided killing him. According to the second general approach, free will is primarily a function of an agent being the source of her actions in a particular way. On this approach, Allison freely killed the dog only if she was the appropriate source of her action. According to the terminology introduced earlier, I will refer to the first of these conceptions as the "alternative-possibilities condition." Those incompatibilists who think about free will along the lines of the alternative-possibilities condition are Leeway Incompatibilists, and those compatibilists who think about the nature of free will along the lines of the alternative-possibilities condition could be called Leeway Compatibilists. However, for reasons that are introduced below in Chapter 5, Leeway Compatibilism is more commonly referred to as "Classical Compatibilism," and I shall follow this terminology.

I will call the second of these two conceptions of the nature of free will the "sourcehood condition." Those incompatibilists that focus on this condition are Source Incompatibilists, and those compatibilists who endorse such a view are Source Compatibilists. In subsequent chapters, I will focus primarily on this way of classifying the various positions with regard to the nature of free will. However, I shall treat skeptical views in Chapter 4 and return to the difference between event-causal and agent-causal incompatibilist views in Chapter 10 when I deal with the issue of luck, and explore the claim that agent-causal views are less lucky than are event-causal views. It seems to me, however, that the most important distinction regarding the nature of free will is between leeway and source-based approaches, and this is the distinction that shall guide the subsequent discussion.

The consequence argument

One of the most well-known and influential arguments for incompatibilism in the past 40 years is called the "Consequence Argument," and was first formulated by Peter van Inwagen.[31] The Consequence Argument is based on a fundamental distinction between the past and the future. Given the direction of the flow of time and the normal direction of causation, it seems as if the future is open in a way that the past is not. For example, it looks as though there is nothing that Emmaline can now do about the fact that Booth killed Lincoln, given that Lincoln was assassinated by Booth in 1865. And this point holds even if we admit the possibility of time travel. For if time travel is possible, Emmaline can influence what the past became, but she cannot literally change the past. Consider the following argument:

(1) The proposition "Lincoln was assassinated in 1865" is true.

(2) Propositions cannot change their truth-value; that is, a true proposition cannot become false, and a false proposition cannot become true.

(3) If Emmaline travels to the past, she could prevent Lincoln from being assassinated in 1865 (temporarily assumed for *reductio*).

(4) If Emmaline were to travel to the past and prevent Lincoln from being assassinated in 1865, the proposition "Lincoln was assassinated in 1865" would be false.

(5) A proposition cannot both be true and false.

(6) Therefore, 3 is false.

So, at most, the possibility of time travel allows for agents to have causal impact on the past, not for agents to change what has already become the past. The past thus appears to be fixed and unalterable. However, it seems that the same is not true of the future, for it seems as if Emmaline can have an influence on the future through her volitions and subsequent actions. For example, if she were to invent a time machine, then she could, at some point in the future, get in her time machine and travel to the past and try to prevent Lincoln from being assassinated. However, given that he was assassinated, we can infer that her attempts would all fail. On the other hand, she could refrain from using her time machine in this way. This asymmetry between past and future is also illustrated by the fact that we don't deliberate about the past in the same way that we deliberate about the future. While Emmaline might deliberate about whether a past action was really the best action that she could have done, she deliberates about the future in a different way. Emmaline can question whether her past actions were in fact the best, but she can both question what future acts would be best as well as which future acts she should perform. Thus, it looks like the future is open to Emmaline, or up to her, in a way that the past is not.

But the Consequence Argument calls into question this difference between the past and the future. First, consider an informal presentation of the argument from van Inwagen's influential *An Essay on Free Will*:

> If determinism is true, then our acts are the consequences of the laws of nature and events in the remote past. But it is not up to us what went on before we were born, and neither is it up to us what the laws of nature are. Therefore, the consequences of these things (including our present acts) are not up to us.[32]

As even this informal presentation shows, the Consequence Argument builds upon this view of the fixed nature of the past to argue that if determinism is true, the future is not open in the way that the above reflections suggest. For if determinism is true, the not-up-to-us-ness of the past and the laws of nature transfers to the future, rendering it also not-up-to-us.[33] Van Inwagen also gives three formal versions of the Consequence Argument in the same book, though he says that "the principle of individuation is far from clear."[34] Whether he gives three different but related arguments or one argument put three different ways is irrelevant, for "these three arguments, or versions of one argument, or whatever they are, are intended to support one another."[35] Van Inwagen writes that each version uses a different structure and vocabulary, but all aim at making the same point. So, for purposes of simplicity, I'm going to focus on only one version of the Consequence Argument.[36]

The version that I'm going to focus on here is the third version, which makes explicit use of modal operators.[37] According to van Inwagen, a modal operator is "an operator that attaches to sentences that have (or that express propositions that have) truth-values, to form sentences that have truth-values; and the truth-value of a sentence formed in this way is not in every case a function of the truth-value of the sentence to which the operator attaches."[38] Consider, for example, the following sentence:

Washington DC is the capital of the United States.

The proposition expressed by this sentence is (at least presently) true. But if you attach a modal operator to it, the newly formed sentence (and the proposition it expresses) need not also be true. Take, for instance, a modal operator that will figure into the third version of the consequence argument: □. When attached to a proposition, p, the newly formed proposition, $\Box p$, is "It is logically necessary that p." So the proposition

□(Washington DC is the capital of the United States.)

means

It is logically necessary that Washington DC is the capital of the United States.

But of course this new proposition formed by adding the necessity operator to the original sentence is false, for it is only a contingent matter that there is such a thing as the United States, and had there not been then it would be false that Washington DC is its capital. The third version of the Consequence Argument also makes use of another modal operator, N. Attaching N to a proposition, p, results in the following proposition:

p is true and no one has, or ever had, any choice about whether p was true.

So, for example,

N(All men are mortal)

means

All men are mortal and no one has, or ever had, any choice about whether all men are mortal.

This version of the Consequence Argument also makes use of two inference rules, which van Inwagen labels α and β.

α: $\Box p$ implies Np
β: $[Np + N(p \rightarrow q)]$ implies Nq

According to α, if a certain proposition is logically necessary, then that proposition is true and no one has, or ever had, a choice about its being true. According to β, if no one has, or ever had, a choice about a proposition p being true, and no one has, or ever had, a choice about the truth of q following from the truth of p, then no one now has, or ever had, a choice about q's being true. That is, the lack of control over p and the relationship between p and q transfers to q. To see the plausibility of β, consider the following application. Let p be the proposition "The earth was struck by a meteor weighing 100 metric tons one billion years ago," and let q be the proposition "If the earth was struck by a meteor weighing 100 metric tons one billion years ago, then thousands of species went extinct." Since no one had a choice about such a meteor hitting in the past, and had no choice that if such a meteor hit, it would cause thousands of species to go extinct, it follows that no one had a choice that thousands of species went extinct. β thus looks extremely plausible.

The Consequence Argument holds that these two inference rules, if valid, when joined with some reasonable assumptions about the past and laws of nature show that the truth of determinism is incompatible with free will. Recall the definition of causal determinism from Chapter 1: causal determinism is the thesis that the past and the laws of nature entail a unique future. Let "P" refer to a true proposition that expresses the complete state of the world at some point in the past. Similarly, let "L" denote the conjunction of all the laws of nature into a single proposition. Finally, let "F" refer to a true proposition about the future. The argument takes as its first premise the definition of determinism given above:

(1) $\Box[(P + L) \rightarrow F]$

Using a valid logical rule of inference (exportation), we can transform (1) into (2):

(2) $\Box[P \rightarrow (L \rightarrow F)]$

Applying α, we can derive (3):

(3) $N[P \rightarrow (L \rightarrow F)]$

The second premise in the Consequence Argument is called the "fixity of the past." No one has, or ever had, a choice about the true description P of the universe at some point in the distant past:

(4) NP

From 3, 4, and β, we can deduce 5:

(5) N(L $\rightarrow$ F)

The final premise in the argument is the fixity of the laws of nature. No one has, or ever had, a choice about what the laws of nature are:

(6) NL

And from 5 and 6, again using β, we can infer that no one has, or ever had, a choice about F:

(7) NF

Given that F could be any true proposition about the future, the Consequence Argument concludes that if determinism is true, then no one has or ever had a choice about any aspect of the future, including what we would normally take to be our free actions. Thus, according to the Consequence Argument, if determinism is true, we do not have free will—for if we have no choice about any of our actions, it is hard to see how we control them in the way required for moral responsibility.

Is the Consequence Argument decisive for incompatibilism? No. In later chapters, I will return to a number of compatibilist responses to the argument.[39] But in the closing part of the present chapter, I want to focus on two issues regarding the logical form of the Consequence Argument. The first of these is the inference rule β.[40] Van Inwagen thinks that all sound arguments for incompatibilism must either explicitly or implicitly appeal to β.[41] Despite β's initial plausibility, it has been shown to be formally invalid by Thomas McKay and David Johnson (though the details of their proof need not concern us here).[42] Various incompatibilists have sought to salvage the Consequence Argument by replacing β with another inference rule which will do the same work in the Consequence Argument but which avoids McKay's and Johnson's counterexample to β. Alicia Finch and Ted Warfield, for example, replace β with β^*:

β^*: $[Np + \Box \, (p \rightarrow q)]$ implies Nq[43]

β^* is a stronger principle than β, and according to even one compatibilist, "there are no known counterexamples to principle β^*."[44] So in this respect, it seems as if the Consequence Argument can be bolstered.

Another thing to note regarding the Consequence Argument is its assumptions. For example, premise (4) makes the assumption that there is a past that no one now or ever had a choice about. The most obvious way of supporting this assumption is to make the moment of time that P is about be a time before there were any human agents. But this assumption introduces a contingency into the argument that is problematic, as pointed out by Joseph Campbell:

> Incompatibilism holds that determinism is incompatible with the free will thesis. Incompatibilism is a noncontingent thesis: if it is true, it is necessarily true. The [third formulation of the Consequence Argument] depend[s] on contingent assumptions about the actual world, for example, that every person has a remote past, a time where the world existed but he did not. Necessary truths do not follow from contingent assumptions. Thus, the [third formulation of the Consequence Argument] cannot prove incompatibilism.[45]

Unless a version of the Consequence Argument can be given which does not assume a contingent truth, then it will not be able to prove that incompatibilism is necessarily true. Recently, Alicia Finch has argued (persuasively, in my mind) that one can formulate a version of the Consequence Argument which does not assume the existence of a distant past, and that Campbell's objection can thereby be avoided.[46] While I think that Finch is right that this objection to the Consequence Argument can be rebutted, even if she's wrong, the failure of the Consequence Argument to establish the truth of incompatibilism doesn't mean that incompatibilism isn't true, and thus that compatibilism is true. In section II, I shall return to another influential argument for incompatibilism. But first, in the following chapter I discuss a set of views which claim to be neither compatibilist nor incompatibilist.

CHAPTER THREE

Revisionist accounts

Moving beyond compatibilism and incompatibilism

In the previous chapter, I differentiated between compatibilist and incompatibilist views about free will. Compatibilist views hold that the existence of free will is compatible with the truth of the thesis of causal determinism, while incompatibilists think that we can be free only if determinism is false. (Keep in mind that neither compatibilism nor incompatibilism *per se* makes a claim on whether or not free will exists, or if determinism is true. Both are simply positions regarding the relationship between freedom and determinism.) Much of the contemporary literature begins with this distinction. And if we take the amount of literature written on the Compatibility Question into account, it can easily seem as though this is the most important issue in the free will debate. However, a number of philosophers have suggested that the distinction between compatibilism and incompatibilism is unhelpful, and perhaps even misguided. In this chapter, I consider two views which purport to be neither compatibilist nor incompatibilist. The first of these is advanced by Ted Honderich. The second view, that articulated and defended by Manuel Vargas, is called "revisionism," a term which can also be used to describe Honderich's view. The present chapter focuses on revisionism, a view which according to Robert Kane is "comparatively new and has come into prominence only in the past decade."[1] At the heart of revisionist accounts is the belief that we need to revise our view of free will.

Ted Honderich

Honderich is one philosopher who thinks that the contemporary focus on the Compatibility Question is misguided. The reason why is not just that he thinks the Compatibility Question is not the most important question regarding the nature of free will. He also thinks that the Compatibility Question falsely suggests that one must be either a compatibilist or an incompatibilist, as can be seen from the title of one of his articles: "Determinism as True, Both Compatibilism and Incompatibilism as False, and the Real Problem."[2] This is, no doubt, a provocative title, and one that also calls for explanation. It is to this task that I first turn.

Neither compatibilism nor incompatibilism

As indicated in Chapter 1, Honderich distinguishes the thesis of causal determinism, as it traditionally figures in the debates about free will and moral responsibility, from the thesis of near determinism. Causal determinism is the thesis that the course of the future is entirely determined by the conjunction of the non-relational past and the laws of nature, whereas near determinism "allows that there is or may be some indeterminism but only at what is called the micro-level of our existence, … [while] at the ordinary level of choices and actions, and even ordinary electrochemical activity in our brains, [deterministic] causal laws govern what happens."[3] In the present context, what Honderich means by determinism is as follows:

> Let us understand by determinism the family of doctrines that human choices and actions are effects of certain causal sequences or chains— sequences such as to raise the further and separate question, as traditionally expressed, of whether the choices and actions are free. … Determinism so conceived is a matter only of macro events. … This macro determinism, determinism as defined, raises exactly the traditional problem of freedom despite being married to micro indeterminism. It leaves exactly where it was the question about determinism most attended to by philosophers, that of its consequences for our lives—our freedom in choosing and acting.[4]

In other words, in claiming that "determinism is true," Honderich is not embracing the thesis of causal determinism defined earlier in Chapter 1; he is instead making a weaker claim that all macroscopic events, including all human actions and choices, are effects of causal chains that necessitate their occurrence. Later in the same book, he writes that "neuroscience gives … clear and strong support to our theory of determinism."[5] Honderich seems willing to grant that "if determinism is true then my action today, perhaps of complying or going along again with my unjust society, is the effect of a causal circumstance in the remote past."[6] But this, by itself, doesn't settle the question of whether those choices and actions are free or not.

Here, it is important to note that Honderich makes a distinction between free will and Free Will. When Honderich uses the term "Free Will" (that is, the capitalized form of the term), he means an incompatibilist conception of free will in which our choices are not causally determined:

> According to this idea [of Free Will], each of us has a kind of personal power to *originate* choices and decisions and thus actions. Their coming-about or initiation definitely wasn't just a matter of [deterministic] cause and effect. Thus on a given occasion, with the past just as it was and the present and ourselves just as they are, we can choose or decide the opposite of what we actually do choose or decide.[7]

The last part of this quotation makes clear that Honderich understands Free Will as incompatible with the truth of causal determinism and involving both the ability to do otherwise and origination (or sourcehood). But he does not think free will—what he calls "free will in the ordinary sense"[8]—is undermined by the truth of determinism; this kind of free will is compatibilist.

It is here that we begin to see Honderich's view, for he thinks that there isn't just one kind of freedom. And he thinks that the presumption that there is has led astray both compatibilists and incompatibilists:

> Might it not be that both sides are wrong? ... Might they be wrong in believing that one side or the other in their battle has got to be right? Might they be wrong in believing that one side or the other must have hold of the truth about the bearing of determinism on other things, however few or many of those things there are? It's easy to be inclined to agree with that belief of theirs. You will want to say either that determinism is consistent with freedom or that it isn't. One of those *has* to be true. Just as it *has* to be true that either you're over six feet tall or you're not.[9]

But Honderich himself doesn't believe that either compatibilism is true or incompatibilism is true; keep in mind part of his title mentioned above: "Both Compatibilism and Incompatibilism as False." How can this be? What goes wrong in the "easy to agree with" belief in the passage above?

To show where he thinks it goes wrong, Honderich begins by describing two kinds of reactions we could have to the truth of determinism: dismay and intransigence. Dismay is "the sad response to determinism ... of thinking that something ... [is] destroyed or must be entirely given up because determinism is true, or that this is the likely prospect because determinism is likely to be true."[10] In contrast, intransigence is "the tough response to determinism" in which we realize that things "are untouched by it."[11] For Honderich, the real problem of determinism is not whether or not it is incompatible with the one idea of freedom (and the one idea of moral responsibility) that we have; that is to say, the problem isn't one of logical compatibility or the lack thereof. Instead, the real problem is how it would be appropriate to respond to being convinced of the truth of determinism as found in these two different reactions:

> What all this leads to is the real problem of the consequences of determinism—which is not the problem of proving something to be our one idea of freedom, or our only self-respecting one, or what you will along these lines. The real problem of the consequences of determinism is that of dealing with the situation in which we have both the idea of voluntariness and also the idea of voluntariness plus origination, and these two ideas run, shape, or at least color our lives, and the second conflicts with determinism. We may attempt to bluff and carry on intransigently in the pretence that what matters is only the first idea and what it enters into, our family of attitudes. This is the response of intransigence. On the other hand we may respond with dismay to the prospect of giving up the second idea and what it enters into, the other family of attitudes.[12]

Honderich then claims that various aspects of human attitudes—he discusses life-hopes, personal feelings, attitudes about knowledge, and various moral feelings—are not uniform. Given my interest in the connection between free will and moral responsibility, I'll focus primarily on what he says about moral feelings; but what he says there parallels what he says about the other kinds of attitudes. Honderich agrees with compatibilists and incompatibilists that free will and responsibility are inseparable: "any ascription of responsibility that there is ... contains a conception of freedom. ... So if you ascribe responsibility, you have an idea of freedom that goes with this, and vice versa."[13] But insofar as we really have two conceptions of free will, he thinks that we also have two sets of the related attitudes, like moral responsibility, mentioned above. Here Honderich writes:

> Consider moral responsibility. The subject-matter is sometimes left or made obscure, but it comes to holding people (including ourselves) morally responsible for something bad, and crediting people (including ourselves) with moral responsibility for something good.... These attitudes fall into two kinds, and each of us has both. ... If a man injures my daughter in the street, or defrauds her in a financial transaction, or concocts evidence against her in a court, I can focus on his action as voluntary but also originated. I hold him responsible where that involves my seeing his action in a certain way. It came out of his desires and the person he is, *and* it was such that he could have stopped himself from doing it given things as they were.[14]

These feelings, Honderich grants, would be unjustified if determinism were true—for if determinism were true, then there is neither Free Will nor origination which undergirds this set of feelings. "What these reflections show is that holding someone responsible can be something that is inconsistent with determinism. To think of this way of holding people responsible, and to contemplate that determinism is true, is to face dismay."[15]

But this isn't the whole of the story according to Honderich, for there is another set of feelings which are also involved:

> There is no doubt that I can in another way hold the injurer of my daughter responsible. I can focus just on the fact that the injury he did to her was voluntary. It was really owed to him and to his own desires. I can enlarge on this fact to myself in various ways. I can without doubt have strong feelings about him, and speak of his voluntariness as the reason. They will include feelings of repugnance for this person who was able to do the thing in question, and desires for the prevention of such injuries. There is the same possibility in the different case where I morally approve of someone.[16]

Honderich doesn't give us a good idea of just how he understands moral responsibility, as it seems to involve aspects of both the reactive attitude view and the accountability view discussed in Chapter 1. However, it is clear from the above comments that he thinks we can be intransigent about one set of attitudes involved in moral responsibility even if we became convinced, as he is, of the truth of determinism. As for the other set of attitudes, we'd have to give these up, leading to dismay for it is true that "determinism *does* threaten something important to us."[17] Honderich calls this view—that we have these two kinds of attitudes—"Attitudinism."

Attitudinism

Where Honderich's Attitudinism differs from both compatibilism and incompatibilism is in taking seriously the idea that we do not have a single settled idea of what it means to say that a choice is free, just as we do not have a single settled idea of what it means to be morally responsible.

> They [both compatibilists and incompatibilists] share some single settled idea of what has to be true of a choice if it counts as free, and hence of what has to be true of an action if it counts as free. ... Both sides agree in assigning to all of us a certain belief, which they take to be a plain truth. It is the factual belief that something is necessary for something else. A free choice is necessary for holding the person responsible. The sides differ, as just remarked, about what we are supposed to take a free choice to be. ... They are both mistaken.[18]

The mistake is the presupposition that there is a single idea of freedom which undergirds the plethora of our emotions and practices. "We don't have *any* definition of a free choice if a definition is supposed to be the one and only correct description of a thing."[19] As a result, we need not be led to feel simply intransigence (as compatibilists think) or simply dismay (as incompatibilists think) if determinism is true. Both of these responses are unsatisfactory. "The short version of the hopelessness of both traditions is simply that there is reference-failure or reference-ambiguity with respect to asserting or denying that freedom is compatible or incompatible with determinism."[20] Fortunately, Honderich thinks we need not pick between these two failed options for there is a third response based on the idea that "there are two notions of freedom at issue, one compatible, one incompatible, with determinism."[21] Honderich calls this realization "affirmation":

> What we have to do is try to give up whatever depends on thoughts inconsistent with [the truth of determinism]. Above all we have to try to accept the defeat of certain desires. ... What we need to see first is that our attitudes involving voluntariness cannot really allow us to be intransigent, to go on as if determinism changes nothing. We can't successfully barricade ourselves in them. And secondly, our attitudes involving both voluntariness and origination need not give rise to dismay, taking everything as wrecked. That is to forget that in part or in a way these attitudes can persist. They can persist in so far as they involve voluntariness.[22]

We should thus try to accommodate ourselves and our beliefs to what we can possess if determinism is true—to *affirm* them—while also realizing that there are other beliefs and attitudes we are no longer justified in holding. Such affirmation, Honderich thinks, will require us to believe determinism is true if we are to succeed.

I shall return to evaluating Honderich's view later in this chapter. But first it will be helpful to consider another recent view regarding free will which shares a number of important parallels with Honderich's view. This view, called revisionism, is most thoroughly developed and defended by Manuel Vargas.

Manuel Vargas

In a series of recent papers, Manuel Vargas has elaborated and defended a revisionist approach to free will and moral responsibility which he says is distinct from both compatibilism and incompatibilism. In fact, according to Vargas, one of the virtues of revisionism is its ability to help avoid some of the traditional stalemates between these two groups:

> Every dialectical stalemate between incompatibilists and compatibilists seems to be superseded by a similar though often more subtle stalemate.

The stalemate has two sources. On the one hand, incompatibilists again and again find intuitive support from our folk concept. On the other hand, compatibilists seem right to insist that even if determinism were true, this would not mitigate our need for a concept of responsibility. ... I attempt to show how principled and systematic pursuit of an approach I call *revisionism* might push us through this stalemate.[23]

In the remainder of this chapter, I explore revisionism, paying special attention to the particular form Vargas advocates. I then develop two inter-related arguments for the claim that Vargas' revisionism is a particular species of compatibilism, and thereby ought to be labeled as such. Nevertheless, Vargas' reasons for resisting this label make salient some important methodological issues that the contemporary debates could benefit from, as he's right that the compatibility issue may not track all important aspects of the free will and moral responsibility literatures.

Kinds of revisionism

Most fundamentally, revisionism is motivated by two questions, and the apparent difference between the answers to those questions:

What *do* we think about free will and moral responsibility?
What *should* we think about free will and moral responsibility?

For the revisionist, both of these are important questions, in part because they have different answers:

Revisionism emerges out of a difference between the projects invited by the last two questions. One project is *diagnostic*, for it attempts to give a diagnosis for our commonsense reflections regarding responsibility. A diagnostic account of responsibility would be concerned to reflect the facts that our concept of moral responsibility and its conditions of application. The second project is something we might call *prescriptive*, for it aims at generating a theory that can guide our thinking about (and practice of) responsibility. In other words, it tells us what we should think and do.[24]

As support for the incompatibilist diagnosis, Vargas offers three sets of considerations. The first of these consists of the traditional arguments for incompatibilism, such as the Consequence Argument (discussed in Chapter 2) and the Core Argument for Incompatibilism (to be discussed in Chapter 5). While Vargas doesn't consider these arguments sound, he thinks they do show us an important aspect of the allure of incompatibilist thought. "What makes these arguments powerful is not so much that they rule out the possibility of compatibilism but rather that they show how easily incompatibilism seems to capture ordinary ways of thinking about our own agency."[25] The allure of these arguments is related to, and perhaps in part grounded in, the second consideration in favor of an incompatibilist diagnosis—namely, the prevalence of incompatibilism in pre-philosophical thought. Here, Vargas draws upon recent work in experimental philosophy which provides evidence for incompatibilist folk-thinking (even if, as indicated in Chapter 2, one can also elicit compatibilist intuitions in different contexts). The data from these studies are complex and varied, but with respect to revisionism Vargas

> take[s] all of this to be good news. Even if it turns out that we have mixed commitments—compatibilist commitments sometimes, incompatibilist commitments other times—as long as there are consistently conditions under which a not insignificant number of us have genuinely incompatibilist commitments, then it seems correct to say that some important aspect of our ordinary commitments is genuinely incompatibilist.[26]

Vargas also writes that "a third possible source of the incompatibilist intuitions we tend to have may be rooted in the cultural history of the West."[27] He mentions both the influence of dualism and Christianity as two aspects of the cultural history of the West which could partly explain why many of the folk have incompatibilist intuitions. "There is considerable complexity to the theological tradition in the West, but there is also a clear and influential strand of religious thinking that treats free will, understood in an incompatibilist sense, as the only thing adequate for getting God off the hook for the world's evils. These convictions are often intertwined with an implicit commitment to a dualist metaphysics."[28]

What differentiates revisionism from incompatibilism, however, is the former's commitment to the claim that the folk incompatibilist account of freedom and responsibility is wrong. For reasons that we'll see shortly, Vargas thinks that we *ought* to hold that both free will and moral responsibility are compatible with the truth of determinism. (To prefigure, what he says about what we ought to think will form the basis of my argument that revisionism is a species of compatibilism.) It is this disconnect between the diagnostic and prescriptive elements that is the hallmark of his account of revisionism. While he thinks that there are other ways that one could characterize revisionism, "this possibility, the one that allows for a difference in diagnostic and prescriptive projects, captures the idea of revisionism that is central" to his view.[29] Vargas elaborates:

> A theory is for our purposes *paradigmatically revisionist* if it prescribes something other than what it diagnoses. In contrast, the central case of a conventional, *non*-revisionist theory is one where the diagnostic and prescriptive aspects of the theory do not bifurcate, treating diagnostic

and prescriptive aspects of the theory in a unified way. Thus, to determine whether a theory is revisionist or not in the paradigmatic sense, we need only determine whether its diagnosis and prescription are the same or different.[30]

In what follows, when I speak of revisionism, I shall be speaking of specifically paradigmatic revisionism of this sort.

Vargas is aware that a certain amount of revisionism, even paradigmatic revision of the sort described in the previous paragraph, goes on within some incompatibilist accounts as well as some compatibilist accounts.[31] In order to demarcate his preferred revisionism from these other competing accounts, he differentiates three different forms that paradigmatic revisionist accounts may take: weak revisionism, moderate revisionism, and strong revisionism. Vargas describes weak revisionist theories as follows:

> A *weak revisionist* theory revises beliefs about the various elements of concern for a theory of responsibility. According to weak revisionism, the concept of responsibility and the associated practices and attitudes do not themselves require revision, but our understanding of one or more of them does. As weak revisionists see it, we have come to misunderstand our own concept, practices, or attitudes, as they actually exist. Usually, our misunderstanding is a result of some confusion introduced by philosophical speculation, or some other correctable defect of cognition that keeps us from seeing what we *really* believe, mean, feel, or do.[32]

Vargas gives as examples of weak revisionists classical compatibilists who give conditional accounts of the ability to do otherwise and semi-compatibilists such as John Fischer (discussed at greater length in Chapter 8). Strong revisionists, in contrast, engage in a more thoroughgoing revisionist project:

> In contrast to weak revisionism, *strong revisionism* maintains that our concepts, practices, or attitudes themselves are in need of elimination. Where weak revisionism merely maintains that we need to modify our understanding of responsibility, strong revisionism argues that we must dispose of some or all of the main elements addressed by a theory of responsibility.[33]

Examples of strong revisionist accounts are Derk Pereboom's hard incompatibilism and Galen Strawson's Impossibilism, both of which are discussed in the next chapter.[34] Vargas objects to strong revisionist accounts because they "too readily reject what can be repaired."[35]

In between weak and strong revisionism is moderate revisionism, which is the form of paradigmatic revisionism that Vargas himself endorses:

> Moderate revisionism is the idea that the folk concept of responsibility is inadequate until it has been modified in some way. Unlike strong

revisionism, moderate revisionism's revision does not involve straight-forward elimination of the concept, practices, or attitudes characteristic of responsibility. Rather, it amounts to a "pruning" of that element. This pruning may itself involve eliminating some aspect of the considered element but it does not require elimination of the entire element.[36]

Unlike weak revisionism, moderate revisionism involves the modification of our extant concepts and practices; yet unlike strong revisionism, it does not revise these concepts and practices to the point of wholesale elimination. According to Vargas, moderate revisionism is a particularly promising species of revisionism because it appears

> to be immune to many of the worries that seem to fuel hesitancy and resistance to [other] revisionist approaches. By combining the folk conceptual analysis of incompatibilism with the metaphysical minimalism of compatibilism, these sub-species avoid many of the strongest objections leveled at both [revisionist forms of] incompatibilism and compatibilism while picking up many of their chief advantages.[37]

More recently, however, Vargas has given a new characterization of revisionist accounts.[38] For our present purposes, most of the differences between Vargas' original presentation of revisionism and his more recent treatment will not be relevant. He still marks the key distinction between revisionist accounts and their conventional counterparts as "the contention that we should abandon some of our commitments that constitute our ordinary way of thinking about free will."[39] But he now describes the difference between the diagnosis and the prescription in a slightly stronger way than he did before:

> Notice that if we maintain that any difference between diagnosis and prescription is sufficient for revision, then revisionism threatens to become an uninteresting category. After all, many conventional accounts of X invoke commitments that are not a part of the ordinary beliefs about X. ... This suggests revisionist accounts are best construed as those on which the prescription includes commitments that are not merely absent from common sense, but that are in conflict with it.[40]

Instead of differentiating between weak, moderate, and strong revisionism, Vargas now differentiates diagnostic correction, connotational revisionism, denotational revisionism, and eliminativism. A person engaged in diagnostic recognizes that the initial diagnostic process she'd engaged in was in error, and corrects the diagnostic element of her view. According to Vargas, this is an epicycle on a conventional view rather than an indication of revisionism since there is no conflict between the proper, corrected diagnosis and the proper prescription. According to connotational revisionism, we need to not just change our diagnosis, but actually expunge aspects of our folk-thinking about free will. But this will not involve changing the referent of the term "free will," for on this view "we have been talking ... about free will all along, even if we had erroneous beliefs about it." While denotional revisionism also involves expunging aspects of folk thinking about free will, it is stronger insofar as it involves the need to "reanchor the referent of 'free will' ... on some [similar] property whose existence is in most or even all of the places we used to refer to free will"[41] and whose presence warrants the appropriateness of our responsibility practices. Finally, according to Vargas, eliminativism regarding free will involves the outright rejection of its existence. (To use the language of the next chapter, eliminativist accounts of free will are skeptical accounts.) Vargas now thinks that this classification system is an improvement on his earlier account of revisionist views:

> In prior work, I have distinguished between weak, moderate, and strong revisionism. Weak revisionism is what I am here calling diagnostic correction. Strong revisionism is eliminativism. Moderate revisionism was ambiguous between connotational and denotational revision. I am now unhappy about the weak/moderate/strong distinction for several reasons. First, moderate revisionism's ambiguity between connotational and denotational revisionisms invited confusion. Second, weak and strong revisionism are not ordinarily revisionism at all. Weak revisionism (i.e. diagnostic correction) is a conventionalist's admission that he or she mischaracterized our commonsense views about free will. Strong revisionism (i.e. eliminativism) is a view that holds that we should reject the existence of free will, irrespective of whether our best account of free will's nature is at odds with our folk conception of it. So, I now propose that we regiment terminology in the way I have suggested here, reserving "revisionist" for those theories that are committed to either denotational or connotational revision.[42]

Revisionism, both in general and in the more reserved use that Vargas now favors, is a family of views rather than a particular view. In "Responsibility and the Aims of Theory," Vargas gives the following guidelines for developing an acceptable revisionist theory:

1 Take your favorite compatibilist theory of responsibility and invoke standard revisionist tropes (e.g. a folk conceptual error theory, the naturalist and normative standards, etc.) to justify the theory's partial departure from common sense.

2 Revise the theory's account of morally responsible agency so that it reflects our best picture of moral psychology.

3 Strip the account of morally responsible agency of any features that do not meet the naturalist and normative standards.

4 Show how the resultant specification of conditions for holding
people responsible meets schema M [where M holds that agent
S is morally responsible for some action x if it would be *morally
appropriate* to hold S morally responsible for x].

There we have it—a method to build revisionist theories.[43]

Vargas elaborates what he means by the two standards mentioned in step
3 above. According to the standard of naturalistic plausibility, an adequate
moderate revisionism should not

> require things that are implausible under some broad-minded conception
> of substantive naturalism. As I use it here, "naturalism" need not be
> understood in an especially contentious way (e.g. as committed to strict
> reductionism). Rather, we should think of it as helping to adjudicate a
> proposal's plausibility, based on what we know about science and the
> kinds of demands the considered theory makes on future sciences.[44]

This requirement will prevent a wide swath of otherwise revisionist
theories from being viable accounts. For example, Vargas intends for
various revisionist forms of libertarianism to be excluded by the standard
of naturalistic plausibility. By requiring indeterminism, and often indeterminism at specific points in the causal history of purportedly free actions
(the details of exactly *where* the indeterminism is required will depend on
the particular form of libertarianism at issue), libertarian views are less
plausible than are compatibilist accounts. "In the absence of any evidence
for the theory, these [libertarian] accounts will be less likely to be vindicated
by further discoveries about the nature of human beings, all other things
being equal."[45] In other words, in order to ensure that a revised concept of
free and responsible agency can be satisfied, revisionism ought to place few
specific demands that are open to scientific falsification.

Turning then to the second—and "more profound"[46]—standard that an
adequate revisionism needs to satisfy, Vargas writes:

> The standard of normative adequacy holds that however the revision
> goes, the result must include a concept that is justified and well integrated
> with our network of mutually supporting norms and practices. A revised
> concept of responsibility that made responsibility-characteristic practices
> immune to consideration of (for example) fairness, proportional praise
> or punishment, and differences of moral agency (from moral patients
> to fully moral agents) would hardly count as being well integrated. A
> revised concept of responsibility that played no justified normative role
> in our moral thinking, that systematically conflicted with other pieces of
> justified moral thinking, or that lacked normative force altogether would
> also fail to meet the standard of normative adequacy.[47]

While these guidelines don't specify a fully worked out revisionist theory, they do provide parameters for developing an acceptable variety of revisionist theory that is worth wanting. But Vargas realizes that revisionist accounts of free will may in fact require some revision to our responsibility practices and attitudes, perhaps along the lines discussed with respect to Honderich above.[48]

Moderate revisionism as compatibilism

The previous section provided an overview of the sort of revisionist account of free will and moral responsibility Vargas advocates. Such a theory is desirable, he thinks, because it does not require elimination of our responsibility practices (as skeptical and other strong-revisionist accounts do), it does not require that its picture of moral agency satisfies all of our pre-theoretical intuitions (as weak-revisionist compatibilist accounts do), nor does it require implausible accounts of agency (as libertarian accounts do). In this section, I want to advance two interrelated arguments for the conclusion that despite presenting moderate revisionism as an alternative to existing positions in the free will debates, revisionism is best understood as a species of compatibilism. While moderate revisionism differs in important ways from other compatibilist accounts, it is not clear that it does so to such a degree that it deserves to be treated as a standalone position in these debates.

I call the first of the two arguments of this section "the Logical Argument" insofar as it is based on the logical notion of bivalence. Consider the central compatibilist claim about free will and causal determinism:

CCC: Free will is compatible with the truth of determinism.

What makes an account of free will a compatibilist account is simply its endorsement of CCC. According to incompatibilists, CCC is false and the truth of determinism is sufficient to show that there is no free will. Applying bivalence to CCC, we get as a matter of logical necessity either compatibilism or incompatibilism is true.[49]

Here then is the Logical Argument that Vargas' moderate revisionism is really a form of compatibilism:

(1) A theory is compatibilist by definition *iff* according to that theory CCC is true.

(2) According to Vargas' revisionism, CCC is true.

(3) Therefore, Vargas' revisionism is a species of compatibilism.

The key premise in this argument is obviously (2). Why think that Vargas' revisionism holds that free will is compatible with the truth of determinism? As seen above, the prescriptive element of revisionism is compatibilist, holding that we ought to accept the truth of CCC. A number of further quotations provide further support for (2). First, consider also the following passage from a discussion of a specifically Strawsonian moderate revisionism:

> What we are giving up is the idea that an adequate theory of responsibility is one that fully captures folk beliefs about responsibility. In short, revisionist Strawsonians will admit that the best theory of responsibility might well be *revisionist* in the sense that it will depart (to some extent) from our commonsense understanding of responsibility, and ultimately, require some revision of commonsense. But, nothing in such a concession requires that revisionist Strawsonians give up a commitment to the property of responsibility being compatible with the truth of determinism.[50]

As with before, we see here that Vargas thinks that the prescriptive elements are thoroughly compatibilistic in nature. Furthermore, consider what Vargas holds to be the two principal requirements for free will:

> Responsible agency [according to the moderate revisionist] has two principal requirements for responsibility-supporting freedom: a detection or sensitivity requirement and a self-governance condition. Where free will is to be located, then, is in the satisfaction of these conditions. An agent can be said to have free will or to be acting from or with free will when that agent, in the context of deliberation or action, has the capacity to detect moral considerations and can govern him or herself [in an] appropriate way in light of those moral considerations.[51]

Insofar as both of these requirements could be satisfied if determinism were true, his theory again accepts the truth of CCC.

As final support here for the crucial second premise of the Logical Argument, consider Vargas' response to John Fischer's thought experiment of waking up and finding out that physicists had discovered that determinism is true:[52]

> Recall the morning of the fabled declaration of universal determinism. On this morning, moderate revisionists of many stripes will smile, perhaps stretch, and begin propagating a theory of responsibility that respects the psychology we have, the world in which we live, and the norms that make our attitudes and practices justifiable. What more should we expect from a theory of responsibility?[53]

As with Fischer's semi-compatibilism, Vargas' moderate revisionism would not need to "flip-flop" with respect to its prescriptive account of free will and moral responsibility in light of such a discovery—and the reason in both cases is that the theories are compatibilist in nature.

I will call the second argument that Vargas' moderate revisionism is properly understood as a species of compatibilism "the Resemblance Argument." The Resemblance Argument and the Logical Argument are intended to mutually reinforce each other, rather than be taken as independent arguments, and points of connection between them will be evident. The Resemblance Argument begins by pointing out that the amount of revision a theory of morally responsible agency calls for does not affect whether or not the core prescriptive element of that theory is compatibilist or not. Consider, for example, John Martin Fischer, who, as seen earlier, Vargas classifies as a weak revisionist.[54] The mere fact that Fischer's semi-compatibilism involves weak revisionism doesn't mean that he is no longer a compatibilist. One could also imagine a compatibilist account which is strongly revisionist in the sense described above. Suppose, for example, that someone thought that not only was free will compatible with the truth of determinism, but that free will *required* the truth of determinism.[55] Suppose further that this individual became convinced of the falsity of determinism, and thus came to believe that free will didn't exist. Such a person would be, according to Vargas, a strong revisionist since strong revisionism "holds that the correct prescriptive account is one that jettisons talk of responsibility and free will, at least in the senses that are central to free will debates."[56] But jettisoning responsibility and free will because one of the necessary conditions for their applications wasn't met would not affect the modal claim that their proper application is compatible with the truth of determinism. So, whether a view is a compatibilist account of free will is independent of the amount of revision of our folk understanding of free will that the view in question commits one to. (The same is true of incompatibilist accounts.) While Vargas' moderate revisionism involves an incompatibilist descriptive element, the next step in the Resemblance Argument is to point out that this does not change the fact that the core prescriptive element of his view is compatibilist insofar as it affirms *CCC*. Thus, insofar as the amount of revision of folk concepts required by a view does not affect whether or not that view is compatibilist or incompatibilist in nature, one again sees that Vargas' account is fundamentally a form of compatibilism.[57]

The moral of the story

I take the Logical Argument and the Resemblance Argument to together show that Vargas' moderate revisionism is a form of compatibilism. Returning to Honderich, similar considerations also show that his view is a form of compatibilism as well—insofar as he thinks that there is a kind of free will and responsibility which could exist even if it turns out that determinism is true, he too affirms CCC. In fact, I take these conclusions to be so obvious that one might reject it on the grounds that it is not worth stating. To this charge I reply as follows: no, clarity and consistency of terminology is important. Insofar as Vargas' revisionism satisfies the defining criterion for compatibilism, we ought to call it what it is.[58] Honderich anticipates an objection to Attitudinism along the lines of the Logical Argument:

> You may want to reply quickly that logically or necessarily it either has to be true that our ordinary conception of freedom is compatible with determinism or that it is not. Just as it either has to be true that you're over six feet tall or that you're not. One or the other has to be true. You may say there is a law of logic about that. But the either-or statement states, or anyway presupposes, something else—that *there is one thing in question with respect to what is called our ordinary idea of freedom.* If there isn't one thing, then saying that our ordinary idea of freedom either is or is not compatible with determinism may be perfectly pointless and in fact as good as false.[59]

Insofar as there are numerous different concepts that are picked out by the term "free will," and if more than one of these concepts falls under "the ordinary idea of freedom," then there is a sense in which Honderich is right. But, as indicated in Chapter 1, the concept of free will at issue in the present volume is that which is the control condition on moral responsibility. And there is a kind of moral responsibility which Honderich thinks is compatible with the truth of causal determinism. Of course, as we've already seen, he thinks that the truth of determinism would not leave moral responsibility untouched, insofar as he thinks there are two aspects to moral responsibility, only one of which is compatible with determinism:

> Compatibilists say determinism leaves it where it is, Incompatibilists say that determinism wrecks it. Both are wrong. Compatibilists are wrong because we know from our reflections that we have one way of holding people responsible, involving an image of origination, that is out of place if determinism is true. Incompatibilists are wrong because we know that we have one way of holding people responsible, involving only an idea of voluntariness, that goes perfectly well with determinism.[60]

Unlike other compatibilists, Honderich thinks that some aspect of moral responsibility would have to be abandoned if we were to come to discover that determinism were true. But he is quite clear that another aspect of responsibility would remain untouched. Thus, on his view there is a kind of moral responsibility (and thus a kind of free will) which is possible even if determinism were true, and his comments above do not prevent Attitudinism from properly being labeled compatibilism.[61]

However, at this point a more pressing objection surfaces. Writing about the compatibilist and incompatibilist labels, Vargas says

> Reflecting on the way traditional categories obscure widely shared projects in the theory of moral responsibility can help us to acknowledge an important point—we have paid entirely too much attention to the labels of traditional philosophical categories.[62]

And this is a sentiment which Honderich would endorse as well. Following Vargas' lead, one may go on to state any of the following claims: (i) too many positions fall under the label of compatibilism to carve the terrain in a helpful way, (ii) there is a web of important issues about free will and moral responsibility that the categories of compatibilism and incompatibilism don't neatly track, and (iii) that calling moderate revisionism a form of compatibilism obscures important differences between traditional compatibilist accounts and moderate revisionism. Insofar as such an obscurity can and should be avoided, one might think that it would be better to treat Honderich's and Vargas' views as distinct from compatibilism.

There is something correct in this line of response, though I do not think it is sufficient to diffuse the Logical and Resemblance arguments. I grant that there is perhaps a danger of such obscurity insofar as there are important differences between moderate revisionism and other extant compatibilist theories. But the term "compatibilism" (as with the term "incompatibilism") isn't meant to capture *every* important (or even *the most important*) feature of free will. It may well be that a cluster of theories sharing certain key features cuts across the compatibilism/incompatibilism divide; for example, in some ways Ned Markosian's agent-causal compatibilist view, discussed in the previous chapter, shares more in common with Timothy O'Connor's libertarian agent-causalism than it does with Harry Frankfurt's hierarchical compatibilism.[63] Nevertheless, moderate revisionism does share a key feature with other compatibilist theories: it holds that agents could be free and morally responsible even if causal determinism were true.

Consider the following ways that Vargas differentiates moderate revisionism from compatibilist theories at various places in the literature. First, "Moderate revisionist theories start with the advantage of not having to deny the plausibility of arguments for incompatibilism when they are construed as arguments about our folk concept of responsibility."[64] For present purposes, I'm willing to grant Vargas his claim about the relationship between the folk concept of free will. But note that what Vargas says here about moderate revisionism is *also* true of Fischer's semi-compatibilism. According to Fischer, there is an intuitive kind of freedom (regulative control) that can be plausibly shown to be incompatible with determinism via the Consequence Argument. But Fischer is still a compatibilist insofar as he thinks that there is another kind of freedom (guidance control) that is compatible with the truth of determinism.[65] Vargas himself grants this:

As an aside: thinking about free will in this way does raise a puzzle about semicompatibilism: how is it different than more traditional forms of compatibilism? What does the "semi" add, given that it holds that responsibility is compatible with determinism and given that it contains an account of the freedom-relevant condition on moral responsibility, i.e. free will?[66]

If the "semi" of semi-compatibilism is insufficient to differentiate it from compatibilism *simpliciter* even though semi-compatibilism differs in various ways from other compatibilist accounts, the same would also seem to be true of Vargas' view. There is nothing to differentiate it from compatibilism since moderate revisionism's concession about the folk concept is insufficient to deny the truth of CCC.

Elsewhere, Vargas makes a similar point in the context of addressing terminological issues more directly:

> There is significant overlap between compatibilism and the kind of revisionism I recommend. On one way of looking at the issue, my revisionism can be considered a species of compatibilism. Philosophical labels tend towards plasticity, and the important thing is not the label but the commitments of the theory. Thus, it is important to recognize substantial differences between revisionism and traditional conceptions of compatibilism. An obvious point of disagreement concerns the diagnosis of commonsense. … Revisionists are not bound by intuitions in the same way as compatibilists; revisionists are prepared to acknowledge a difference between what we believe and what we should believe and traditional compatibilists are not.[67]

I grant that there is an important lesson here. But even if extant compatibilist theories have been beholden to intuitions in a way that moderate revisionism or Honderich's Attitudinism are not, nothing in compatibilism *per se* requires such a commitment. There are certainly important differences between these views and other forms of compatibilism, but this doesn't mean that they do not share a common commitment to CCC. Similarly, even if moderate revisionism and other forms of compatibilism differ with respect to various aspects of their account of free will, insofar as they both assert the truth of CCC, they all share a commitment to compatibilism.

Conclusion

I've argued that Vargas' revisionism and Honderich's Attitudinism ought properly to be considered as species of compatibilism, and that as a result they ought to be called as such.[68] Vargas instead wants to foreground the issue of revisionism rather than simply focusing in the debate over the compatibility of free will and responsibility with the truth of determinism; he also doesn't want to force his view to deal with all the aspects of compatibilism as it has historically been understood. In a slightly different way, Honderich also wants us to be aware of ways in which not all of our actual attitudes and practices are justified given that he thinks we lack libertarian free will. While I commend them for these sensitivities, I think that they are insufficient for the terminological distancing of their views from compatibilism. If people were instead to pay careful attention to what compatibilism *per se* is and is not committed to, I believe the same result could be achieved. But on this way of moving forward, it would still have to be recognized that these leading forms of revisionism are themselves still forms of compatibilism.

CHAPTER FOUR

Free will skepticism

Introduction

Belief in free will is a cultural heritage for those of us who live in the West. According to a recent unpublished study, Eddy Nahmias found that 86 percent of undergraduates surveyed believe that all humans have free will.[1] And in another study, David Rose and James Petrik found that 92 per cent of participants indicated a belief that some choices made while awake are free.[2] Another recent survey found that the majority of philosophers, like the folk, believe in free will. As part of their PhilPapers online repository of philosophy scholarship, David Bourget and David Chalmers recently conducted a "survey as an information-gathering exercise concerning the distribution of philosophical views within the philosophical profession."[3] Of those who either are philosophy faculty or hold a PhD in philosophy, over 87 per cent of participants indicate a belief in free will.[4] And though the survey didn't ask explicitly about the existence of moral responsibility, it is plausible to believe that most philosophers have similar views about it. Though they may not speak for the rest of the discipline, or for the folk for that matter, a number of philosophers think that there is something wrong with denying moral responsibility. Peter van Inwagen, for instance, writes that "surely we cannot doubt the reality of moral responsibility"[5] and that denying the existence of moral responsibility is "absurd."[6]

This tendency to assume that we are free and responsible agents is not new, and can be traced at least as far back as Augustine, who has been described as having discovered the faculty of the will.[7] While Augustine addressed the importance of free will in many of his works, including the *Confessions*, *City of God* and the aptly named *On Free Choice of the Will*, he never seems to have questioned whether or not humans have free will. That is, the following question is one that Augustine never seems to raise because he thought the answer was an obvious yes:

The Existence Question: Do any agents have free will?

But in recent years, a number of philosophers have begun to not only raise the Existence Question, but proceed to answer it in the negative. The position which claims that free will doesn't exist is known as free will skepticism.[8] (Some make the skeptical claim in terms of free will, and some make the claim in terms of moral responsibility. Given the way in which I see the relationship between free will and moral responsibility in Chapter 1, I shall move back and forth between these two ways of putting the skeptical view in the present chapter.) This chapter focuses on skeptical views. But I begin with a pair of recent argumentative strategies for establishing the claim that free will does exist. These strategies will parallel the two general strategies that skeptics use. The majority of the chapter focuses on looking at these strategies for the skeptic, as well as a closer look at an exemplar of each strategy.

Free will affirmation

I begin with ways one could attempt to justify a positive answer to the Existence Question. There are at least two general ways one could attempt to argue for the existence of free will, which I will call "indirect" and "direct." The difference between these two approaches is whether one has to move "through" some other contentious existant before arriving at the conclusion that free will does exist.

Indirect proofs

What makes an argument for the existence of free will "indirect" is that it proceeds by showing that free will is a necessary condition on something else that is itself actual; they are indirect in the sense that they go "through" this other existant.[9] Peter van Inwagen provides an exemplar of this argumentative strategy as follows:

> There are, moreover, seemingly unanswerable arguments that, if they are correct, demonstrate that the existence of moral responsibility entails the existence of free will, and, therefore, if free will does not exist, moral responsibility does not exist either. It is, however, evident that moral responsibility does exist: if there were no such thing as moral responsibility nothing would be anyone's fault, and it is evident that there are states of affairs to which one can point and say, correctly, to certain people: That's *your* fault.[10]

Other indirect proofs could be offered that free will is necessary for basic desert, justified deliberation, agency, rationality, the autonomy and dignity of persons, creativity, cooperation, self-expression, artistic creativity, or the value of friendship and love.[11] Whatever form an indirect proof takes, two steps will be needed for such a proof to be successful:

(i) the proof will have to succeed in showing that free will is necessary for this further object, x; and

(ii) it will have to be the case that the actuality of x is evident or established by a further argument.

So by their very nature, indirect proofs for the existence of free will involve two steps, both of which will be open to dispute. Consider van Inwagen's indirect proof for the existence of free will based around moral responsibility described above. As indicated at the start of this chapter, van Inwagen thinks that it is "evident" that there is moral responsibility; but a number of philosophers—moral responsibility skeptics, a few of which we'll consider below—deny the existence of free will, thereby taking issue with step (ii) of van Inwagen's indirect proof. Or consider, for example, another indirect proof offered by van Inwagen, this one based on justified deliberation. According to van Inwagen, deliberating about performing a particular activity presupposes that one believes that it is possible to perform it:

> If someone deliberates about whether to do A or to do B, it follows that his behavior manifests a belief that it is *possible* for him to do A—that he *can* do A, that he has it within his power to do A—and a belief that it is possible for him to do B. Someone's trying to decide which of two books to buy manifests a belief with respect to each of these books that it is possible for him to buy *it* just as surely as would his holding it aloft and crying, "I can buy this book".[12]

Van Inwagen considers Baron Holbach, who denied the existence of free will. Van Inwagen thinks it obvious that Holbach deliberated: "Does he deliberate? Well, of course he did."[13] Van Inwagen concludes not only that free will exists, but that either Holbach really believed in it as well or had inconsistent beliefs:

> There is at least some reason to suspect that he [Holbach] did not believe that *he* lacked free will. I have given arguments above for the conclusion that no one could deliberate about whether to perform an act that he does not believe it is possible for him to perform. Even if these arguments are wrong, their *conclusion* has been accepted by everyone I know of who has thought about deliberation.[14]

And lest the reader think that only van Inwagen, or libertarians in general, give indirect arguments of this sort, similar arguments are advanced by a number of leading compatibilists.[15]

Given their structure, there are two ways to resist indirect arguments for the existence of free will, each taking aim at one of the steps in the general form that indirect arguments take above. One could, for instance, deny the existence of the "further thing" that the indirect argument claims requires free will, be that moral responsibility, basic desert, or deliberation. This is exactly what Saul Smilansky does, for example, with respect to van Inwagen's indirect argument based on moral responsibility:

> Van Inwagen seems to think that the reality of libertarian moral responsibility *can* be proved in a way that he himself admits fails in the case of libertarian free will: the existence of libertarian moral responsibility is, in some unclarified way, immediately obvious, while this is not so with libertarian free will. As he puts it, "surely we cannot doubt the reality of moral responsibility?" (p. 206) ... We all just know, it is claimed, that we are sometimes morally responsible in the libertarian sense. This of course would seem to contradict what many philosophers have claimed. ... The existence of libertarian moral responsibility is far from being obvious: many people have doubted this and still doubt it. Since libertarian moral responsibility depends on the at best problematic notion of libertarian free will, it is highly implausible to see the existence of libertarian moral responsibility as obvious; and this is even more implausible if the existence of libertarian moral responsibility is thought to be obvious independently of the case for libertarian free will.[16]

As Smilansky here shows, in order for an indirect argument for the existence of free will to be successful, it must proceed via something which both requires free will and which itself has been successfully established to exist.

A second way to resist indirect arguments for an affirmative answer to the Existence Question would be to attack the other step in the general schema of indirect arguments. On this tack, one calls into question free will's purported necessity for the further thing which is taken to exist. Derk Pereboom, for instance, argues that van Inwagen's indirect argument on the basis of rational deliberation fails insofar as it is false that one must believe (and thus false that one must *truly* believe) that one has the metaphysical ability to pursue either of two courses of action (which is what van Inwagen thinks free will is) in order to rationally deliberate.[17]

Direct proofs

I turn then to direct proofs for an affirmative answer to the Existence Question. Unlike indirect proofs, direct proofs don't try to establish that free will exists by showing how it is a necessary condition for some further thing (like moral responsibility or rational deliberation). Direct proofs work as follows. First, one specifies an account of what exactly free will is (e.g.

free will is *xyz*) and then one attempts to show that that thing exists (e.g. "Hey look, there's *xyz* in the world").[18] One can take the direct approach to show the existence of compatibilist free will, or to show the existence of libertarian free will. (As we'll see below, one can also take a direct approach to show that free will does not exist.)

Consider first a direct proof for the existence of free will by a compatibilist. John Martin Fischer's particular version of compatibilism is the most influential compatibilist view in the contemporary free will and moral responsibility literature, and it is one to which we shall return in considerable more detail in a later chapter.[19] According to Fischer's specific brand of compatibilism, which he calls "semi-compatibilism", the truth of causal determinism is *compatible* with moral responsibility even if causal determinism ends up being *incompatible* with a certain kind of freedom. Fischer differentiates between two kinds of control (or what he sometimes calls two kinds of free will): guidance control and regulative control. Regulative control involves having control over which of a number of genuinely open possibilities becomes actual; regulative control is thus a leeway notion of freedom as introduced in Chapter 1. While semi-compatibilism is officially agnostic about whether regulative control is compatible with the truth of causal determinism, Fischer himself finds it "highly plausible" that regulative control is incompatible with causal determinism.[20] However, Fischer thinks that regulative control is not required for moral responsibility. Instead, the freedom-relevant condition necessary for moral responsibility is guidance control, which is a source-based rather than leeway-based kind of control; such control, he thinks, is compatible with determinism. Fischer's discussion of guidance control is extensive and need not concern us here, though we shall return to his view later in Chapter 8. For present purposes, it is enough to note that his discussions of guidance control makes it clear that he thinks that at least some individuals are morally responsible. And if we take free will to be the control condition on moral responsibility, his answer to the Existence Question is an affirmative.[21]

Robert Kane is the libertarian who has done the most to prove via a direct route the existence of free will. Kane writes of the "two pronged modern attack on free will":

> The first prong of the modern attack on libertarian free will comes from *compatibilists*, who argue that, despite appearances to the contrary, determinism does not really conflict with free will at all. ... The second prong of the modern attack on libertarian free will goes a step further, ... arguing that libertarian free will itself is *impossible* or *unintelligible* and has no place in the modern scientific picture of the world. Such an ultimate freedom is not something we could have anyway, says its critics.[22]

In response to the first prong, Kane endorses a number of arguments which aim to show that free will is incompatible with the truth of causal determinism. Kane also endorses a version of the Consequence Argument,[23] but as we'll see below, his account of what free will is entails another argument for incompatibilism.

For present purposes, I'll focus on Kane's response to the second prong of the attack, insofar as it is more related to Kane's attempt to prove the existence of free will. He writes:

> I think libertarians must accept the empirical challenge of determinism (that it might turn out to be true), if libertarians are going to be serious about finding a place for free will *in the natural order* where we exist and exercise our freedom. This is the "Existence Question" for free will, and ... it cannot be finally settled by armchair speculation, but only by future empirical inquiry.[24]

Kane wants to avoid appeal to "extra-factor strategies" such as immaterial souls, noumenal selves, agent-causation, etc. if at all possible. He thinks it is possible to avoid extra factors because the conditions required for free will are (i) indeterminism, (ii) alternative possibilities (or "the ability to do otherwise") and (iii) ultimate responsibility. Since Kane is an incompatibilist, it is easy to see why he thinks free will requires indeterminism. Furthermore, not all indeterminism is relevant for free will; the indeterminism must be related to what the agent is able to do. Shortly, we'll see below that the need for alternative possibilities is also entailed by the third condition, which Kane thinks is more fundamental for the existence of free will. The basic idea behind ultimate responsibility is as follows: "to be ultimately responsible for an action, an agent must be responsible for anything that is a sufficient reason, cause, or motive for the action's occurring. ... [This] tells us that free will is only possible if *some* voluntary choices or actions in our life histories did *not* have sufficient causes or motives that would have required us to have formed them by still earlier choices."[25] Kane doesn't think that every free and voluntary choice needs to lack sufficient causes or motives; he allows for the fact that some of an agent's actions can be necessitated by her character—that is, by her will, motives, purposes, etc. In these cases, the necessitated action will be free only if the agent freely formed her character which necessitated the later action.

> If agents are to be ultimately responsible for their own wills, then if their wills are already set one way when they act, *they* must be responsible for their wills having been set that way—not God ... or fate or society or behavioral engineers or nature or upbringing. And this means that some of their past voluntary choices or actions must have played an indispensable role in the formation of their present purposes and motives.[26]

On these will-setting occasions, the agent will satisfy what Kane calls the plurality condition, for on these occasions the agent is choosing between two competing options that are each such that she could have done them voluntarily, intentionally and rationally.[27] Kane's classic example of a will-setting occasion is the story of a business woman, Anne:[28]

> Consider a business-woman who faces a conflict of this kind [as described in will-setting actions]. She is on the way to a meeting important to her career when she observes an assault taking place in an alley. An inner struggle ensues between her moral conscience, to stop and call for help, and her career ambitions that tell her she cannot miss the meeting. She has to make an effort of will to overcome the temptation to go on to her meeting. If she overcomes this temptation, it will be the result of her effort, but if she fails, it will be because she did not *allow* her effort to succeed. And this is due to the fact that, while she wanted to overcome temptation, she also wanted to fail, for quite different reasons.[29]

When properly elaborated, Kane contends that this case shows the various conditions that must be met in order for an agent, such as Anne, to have free will.

So far, this establishes what Kane thinks is *required for* free will. But it does not establish that we *have* free will. In order to do the latter step, Kane appeals to recent work in the philosophy of mind which can help explain how human agents can have free will:

> Imagine in cases of conflict characteristic of self-forming actions ..., like the businesswoman's, that the indeterministic noise which is providing an obstacle to her overcoming temptation is not coming from an external source, but has its source in her own will, since she also deeply desires to do the opposite. To understand how this could be, imagine that two crossing recurrent neural networks are involved in the brain, each influencing the other, and representing her conflicting motivations. ... The input of one of these neural networks consists in the woman's reasons for acting morally and stopping to help the victim; the input of the other network comprises her ambitious motives for going on to her meeting.
>
>   The two networks are connected so that the indeterminism that is an obstacle to her making one of the choices is present because of her simultaneous conflicting desire to make the other choice—the indeterminism thus arising from a tension-creating conflict in the will, as we said. This conflict ... would be reflected in appropriate regions of the brain by movement away from thermodynamic equilibrium. The result would be a stirring up of chaos in the neural networks involved.[30]

According to Kane, whichever of these two networks wins out, it will be the case that the agent has willed the outcome in the sense required for free will. Kane then cites the work of neurobiologists Gordon Globus, Francis Crick and Christof Kock, and philosopher of mind Owen Flanagan as providing some empirical support for this account of competing neural networks.[31]

While Kane doesn't think that this empirical support is conclusive, he does think that it gives "tentative"[32] support to the existence of libertarian free will.

Free will skepticism

I turn then to negative answers to the Existence Question. Why might one think that free will doesn't exist? Here, as with a positive answer to the same question, there are a number of different argumentative routes; but they are not the same routes as for arguments in favor of the existence of free will. There are no arguments for a negative answer to the Existence Question that are clearly indirect.[33] Even if one showed (i) that free will was necessary for some further thing, x, and (ii) that x does not exist, that would be insufficient to prove that there was no free will. For while on this approach the existence of free will is necessary for the existence of the further thing, the existence of the further thing is not necessary for the existence of free will. So arguments for the non-existence of free will will be direct arguments. But here, as we'll see, there are two different ways direct arguments are developed. I shall refer to these two strategies as contingent denials and categorical denials. A contingent denial will be a view which holds that while it is possible for free will to exist, it is a contingent fact that free will does not exist. Categorical denials will be stronger: free will does not exist because it is impossible for it to exist. Views which engage in categorical denials are thus sometimes referred to as impossibilism.[34]

Contingent denials

Derk Pereboom's "hard incompatibilism" is an excellent example of the contingent denial strategy. Pereboom's case for hard incompatibilism has a number of steps. First, he argues against compatibilist accounts of free will. He offers a manipulation-based argument against compatibilism, which aims to show that "an action's being produced by a deterministic process that traces back to factors beyond the agent's control, even when she satisfies all the conditions on moral responsibility specified by the prominent compatibilist theories, presents in principle no less of a threat to moral responsibility than does deterministic manipulation."[35] (We shall return to this argument in a later chapter, so I set discussion of it aside for now.)

The second step in Pereboom's argument is to argue that any satisfactory incompatibilist view which affirms the existence of free will must be of a certain sort. One way of classifying varieties of incompatibilism is in terms of what kind of indeterminism is required for free will. Some forms of incompatibilism hold that the indeterminism is (or needs to be) found in ordinary causation between events, while others postulate an additional kind of causation—agent-causation—to account for the indeterminism.[36] According to agent-causal views, the indeterminism involved in event-causation provides the opportunity for free will, but doesn't by itself provide for the kind of control needed. As Pereboom says in an early paper,

> According to one libertarian view, what makes actions free is just their being constituted (partially) of indeterministic natural events. ... But natural indeterminacies of these types cannot, by themselves, account for freedom of the sort required for moral responsibility. As has often been pointed out, such random physical events are no more within our control than are causally determined physical events, and thus, we can no more be morally responsible for them than, in the indeterminist opinion, we can be for events that are causally determined.[37]

Insofar as he thinks that event-causal libertarian views are unable to secure any more control than are compatibilist accounts, if there is to be libertarian free will, we would have to be agent-causes.

However, Pereboom thinks it unlikely that we are agent-causes. "Although our being undetermined agent-causes has not been ruled out as a coherent possibility, it is not credible given our best physical theories. Thus we need to take seriously the prospect that we are not free in the sense required for moral responsibility."[38] Why think that we are not agent-causes, given our best physical theories?

> If agent-causes are to be capable of such free decisions, they would require the power to produce deviations from the physical laws—deviations from what these laws would predict and from what we would expect given these laws. But such agent-causes would be embodied in a world that, by the evidence that supports our current theories in physics, is nevertheless wholly governed by the laws of physics.[39]

Therefore, according to Pereboom's hard incompatibilism, unless future investigation warrants a substantive rethinking of our view of the world in which we live, we ought to conclude that we lack the kind of free will required for moral responsibility. Given that we *could* have such freedom if the world were different (e.g. if we were agent-causes), his view is only a contingent denial of free will. Whether or not it's a *successful* denial will depend largely on two issues. First, is the question of whether event-causal libertarian views are less able to respond to the worries about luck and control than are agent-causal libertarian views. (I shall return to this issue below in Chapter 10.) According to Pereboom, the only successful libertarian views with regard to the worries about luck are agent-causal views. This leads to the second issue, namely Pereboom's claim that our best physical theories are ones according to which we are not agent-causes in the requisite way. An investigation into the relevant empirical issues here cannot be done in the present work; but the ways in which Pereboom's denial depend upon contingent features of the actual world should be clear by now.[40]

Categorical denials

In contrast, Saul Smilansky and Galen Strawson both advocate versions of categorical denial. Unlike a number of other philosophers who deny the existence of libertarian free will, Smilansky sees the attraction it presents:

> The various things that free will could make possible, if it did exist, such as deep sense of desert, worth, and justification *are* worth wanting. They remain worth wanting even if something that would be necessary in order to have them is not worth wanting because it cannot be coherently conceived. It is just this, the impossibility of the conditions for things that are so deeply worth wanting, which makes the realization of the absence of free will so significant.[41]

But the existence of free will is impossible, Smilansky thinks, because "the conditions required by an ethically satisfying sense of libertarian free will, which would give us anything beyond sophisticated formulations of compatibilism, are self-contradictory and hence cannot be met."[42] Insofar as Smilansky thinks these conditions *cannot* be met while Pereboom thinks they merely *are not* met, Smilansky's denial is a logically stronger claim. Every categorical denial will be stronger than every contingent denial for the same reason.

In rejecting the possibility of free will at this step, Smilansky draws on the influential work of Galen Strawson. (Galen Strawson is the son of P. F. Strawson, who was discussed in Chapter 1.) Galen Strawson is probably the most influential categorical denier of the existence of free will. Strawson's categorical denial is the conclusion of his Basic Argument, which comes in a variety of expressions. Let us begin with the simplest of them:

(1) Nothing can be *causa sui*—nothing can be the cause of itself.

(2) In order to be truly morally responsible for one's actions, one would have to be *causa sui*, at least in certain crucial mental aspects.

(3) Therefore nothing can be truly morally responsible.[43]

The idea behind this argument can be elaborated as follows. In order for an agent, such as Allison, to be responsible for some action of hers, that action must be a result of the kind of person that Allison is. We might say, for instance, that Allison is blameworthy for eating too many cupcakes at time t because she is a gluttonous individual. But in order for Allison to be responsible for being a gluttonous individual at t, she would have to be responsible at some earlier time t_1 for being the kind of person that would later become a gluttonous person. But in order for Allison to be responsible for being the kind of person who would later become a gluttonous person, she would have to be responsible at some earlier time t_2 for being the kind of person who would later become the kind of person who would later become a gluttonous person. According to Strawson, this line of thinking begins an infinite regress. A more elaborate version of the Basic Argument is as follows:

> (1) It is undeniable that one is the way one is, initially, as a result of heredity and early experience, and it is undeniable that these are things for which one cannot be in any [way] responsible (morally or otherwise). (2) One cannot at any later state of life hope to accede to true moral responsibility for the way one is by trying to change the way one already is as a result of heredity and previous experience. For (3) both the particular way in which one is moved to try to change oneself, and the degree of one's success in one's attempt to change, will be determined by how one already is as a result of heredity and previous experience. And (4) any further changes that one can bring about only after one has brought about certain initial changes will in turn be determined, via the initial changes, by heredity and previous experience. (5) This may not be the whole story, for it may be that some changes in the way one is are traceable not to heredity and experience but to the influence of indeterministic or random factors. But it is absurd to suppose that indeterministic or random factors, for which one is *ex hypothesi* in no way responsible, can in themselves contribute in any way to one's being truly morally responsible for how one is.[44]

Although both versions of the Basic Argument given here are expressed in terms of moral responsibility, it should be clear from the context that at issue here is the kind of control required for moral responsibility—that is, free will as defined in Chapter 1.[45] And if it is true, as Strawson claims, that such free will requires control over things that it is impossible for us to control, then it will be the case that free will is not only non-existent, but necessarily so. The existence of free will (and, in turn, moral responsibility) is categorically denied.

A similar argument has also recently been advocated by Bruce Waller. According to Waller, no one is "morally responsible for her character or deliberative powers, or for the results that flow from them. ... Given the fact that she was shaped to have such characteristics by environmental (or evolutionary) forces far beyond her control, she deserves no blame [nor praise]."[46] And Carlos Moya has recently devoted an entire book to developing, though not ultimately endorsing, an argument similar to both Waller's and Strawson's.[47]

Evaluating free will skepticism

What should one make of these arguments? John Martin Fischer writes that Strawson's arguments against the possibility of free will are based on an "'inflated' notion of self-creation or autonomy."[48] According to Fischer, there is no reason that a person must have control over all the features that go into her moral agency in order for the agent to be responsible for what she does with her agency:

> Suppose my parents had beaten me mercilessly when I was very young, so that I had significant physical (neurological) and emotional damage. If the damage had been sufficiently bad, I would never have developed into an agent at all. And yet it is quite clear that I never had any control over whether my parents beat me in this way. Similarly for an infinitely large number of factors. ... I had no control over the fact that I was not dropped on my head (accidentally or deliberately) by my parents when I was very young. But had I been dropped on my head in a certain way, I would not have developed into an agent at all, or might have developed into a very different sort of agent. When one begins to think about this sort of thing, one quickly realizes that we are incredibly lucky to be as we are. I had no control over the fact that I was not hit by a bolt of lightning when I was young (or, for that matter, yesterday), or that I was not hit by a meteorite, and so forth. But had any of these things occurred, I would not be the way I am today. ... Intuitively speaking, I am not "ultimately responsible" for my particular psychological traits or even for my very agency. We are not "ultimately responsible" for "the way we are," and yet it just seems crazy to suppose that we are thereby relieved of moral responsibility for our behavior. Does it not seem highly counter-intuitive to suppose that I am not a morally responsible agent in virtue of the fact that I had no control over whether the earth was hit by a meteorite or the sun flickered out when I was young (or yesterday, for that matter)? How could my moral responsibility hinge on whether or not I can prevent the sun from rising or flickering out? We do not have "ultimate responsibility," but it would seem much more plausible to suppose ... that such responsibility is not required for genuine, legitimate moral responsibility than to conclude that we are thereby rendered incapable of being held morally responsible.[49]

According to Fischer, Strawson's account of what is required for freedom and responsibility are too demanding and based on "a wild extrapolation from the quite legitimate desire to be the initiator or source of one's behavior, in some genuine and reasonable sense."[50] Such extravagant requirements are indicative of "metaphysical megalomania."[51] It is much more sensible to believe that we are sometimes free and responsible than to think that freedom requires this kind of control. While Fischer agrees with Strawson that the relevant kind of control should be thought of along the lines of sourcehood rather than alternative possibilities, he doesn't think that the proper understanding of sourcehood requires nearly as much as Strawson does. (Fischer's account of sourcehood is dealt with extensively in Chapter 8 below.)

A different sort of response to Strawson's argument for the impossibility of free will is given by Joseph Campbell. Campbell points out that in order for Strawson's argument to establish its intended conclusion—namely, that free will and responsibility are impossible—the argument must make use of an assumption that is only contingently true: namely that the interaction between the way one is and what one does is not an infinite series extended without limit into the past.

> Add the possibility of eternal existence and you can't show that creatures lack free will, even if having free will requires their being *causa sui* [in the way claimed by Strawson's Basic Argument]. The argument hinges on the fact that there is a time at which we were not free and then uses a kind of transfer principle to argue that there is no point of time at which we can become free. But if you extend the individual's life into the eternal past and deny a first moment of existence, Strawson's skeptical conclusion does not follow.[52]

Campbell's criticism on this point is correct, but it will likely come as little succor to those who believe in free will, as it merely changes Strawson's denial from categorical to contingent. Given that the best scientific evidence currently available suggests that our universe (and our lives) are not eternally old, a different response is needed if one is to defend the notion that there is free will and moral responsibility in our world.

Randolph Clarke offers yet another response to Strawson's Basic Argument. (This version of this objection targets the first way of putting the argument above, but the reader should be able to see how it applies to the more developed version of the argument as well.) Clarke asks us to look at premise (2) of the argument:

(2) In order to be truly morally responsible for one's actions, one would have to be *causa sui*, at least in certain crucial mental aspects.

Why should one accept this premise? Strawson gives two reasons in support of it, the second of which is supposed to follow from the first:

(i) You do what you do, in any situation in which you find yourself, because of the way you are.

(ii) To be truly morally responsible for what you do you must be truly morally responsible for the way you are—at least in certain mental respects.[53]

But according to Clarke, the inference from (i) to (ii) requires the following rules:

(O) When you do what you do because of the way you are, to be truly morally responsible for what you do, either (a) you must be truly [morally] responsible for the way you are, at least in certain crucial mental respects, or (b) it must be up to you whether if you are that way, in certain mental respects, then you perform that action.

(P) When you do what you do because of the way you are, it is not possible for it to be up to you whether if you are that way, in certain crucial mental respects, then you perform that action.[54]

But Clarke thinks that many philosophers who believe in the existence of free will and moral responsibility will reject (O); as will be discussed later in Chapter 8, both John Martin Fischer and Harry Frankfurt think that (O) requires too much of the control condition for moral responsibility. But even those that do accept (O), Clarke claims, have been given no reason to assent to (P). And without such an argument, Strawson's attempt to show that moral responsibility (and free will) are impossible is incomplete at best: "If (P) is false, then moral responsibility is possible (or, at least, not shown to be impossible by any issue raised in Strawson's argument). Everyone should accept, then, that Strawson's argument for the impossibility of moral responsibility requires a defense of (P)."[55]

There are thus reasons to not be convinced by Strawson's Basic Argument. (However, I return to reasons for being skeptical about the existence of free will in Chapter 10 below.) Before leaving categorical denials, it will be helpful to consider, even if briefly, their relationship to the debate between compatibilism and incompatibilism. Kadri Vihvelin argues that impossibilism is a position which differs from both compatibilism and incompatibilism. She writes: "Neither the compatibilist nor the incompatibilist is an impossibilist. ... The compatibilist and the incompatibilist disagree with the impossibilist and agree with one another that there are worlds where human-like creatures have free will."[56] But this is to build more into incompatibilism than should be. Michael McKenna responds to Vihvelin's taxonomy as follows: "As I understand it, incompatibilism is simply the thesis that, at any world at which determinism is true (and there exist non-godlike creatures like ourselves), owing to determinism, there is no free will. It is a different matter whether, in any worlds in which determinism is not true, there is free will."[57] Insofar as categorical denials hold that free will is metaphysically impossible, this particular kind of free will skepticism should be understood as a species of incompatibilism. After all, if free will is impossible, then it is not compatible with anything, including the truth of determinism.[58] Contingent denials, on the other hand, can be species of either compatibilism or incompatibilism, depending on the details of the denial involved.

PART TWO

Alternative possibilities

CHAPTER FIVE

The debate over the ability to do otherwise

Introduction

In Chapter 2, I introduced one very influential argument for incompatibilism, the Consequence Argument. The primary goal of this chapter is to explore another of the most influential arguments for the incompatibility of free will and determinism. More specifically, this chapter will focus on one particular premise in this influential argument that has attracted a considerable amount of attention in the past 40 years. Focusing on this one argument, and the one particular premise in that argument, will provide an overview of much of the recent free will literature. The other two chapters in Part II will examine the larger dialectical context of this argument.

The core argument and alternative possibilities

The particular argument for incompatibilism that we shall consider here is as follows:

(1) Free will requires the ability to do otherwise.

(2) If causal determinism is true, then no agent has the ability to do otherwise.

(3) Therefore, free will requires the falsity of causal determinism.[1]

I will refer to this argument as the "Core Argument for Incompatibilism," or simply the Core Argument.[2] The conclusion of this argument is that compatibilism is false. Compatibilists, of course, will reject the argument.

According to Gerald Harrison, the Core Argument has "historically ... been one of the main reasons why many have argued that determinism and moral responsibility are incompatible."[3] Insofar as it is a formally valid argument, the only way to reject the conclusion of the Core Argument is to deny the truth of one or both of its premises. At one point in relatively recent history, the literature suggests that incompatibilists and compatibilists alike accepted the truth of premise (1). If (1) is true, then in order for an agent to be morally responsible for an action, she must be able to do otherwise; that is, the agent must have alternative possibilities. Premise (1) of the Core Argument is intimately related with what is often called the "Principle of Alternative Possibilities" or simply *PAP*. In an important article discussed at greater length below, Harry Frankfurt defined *PAP* as follows:

> *PAP*: a person is morally responsible for what he has done only if he could have done otherwise.[4]

As stated, Frankfurt's presentation of *PAP* is expressed in terms of what is required for moral responsibility. But my interest is primarily with free will rather than moral responsibility. So the analogue principle that I'm interested in is as follows (called "*AP*" for alternative possibilities condition, which we already encountered earlier in Chapter 1):

> *AP*: a person has free will only if he could have done otherwise.[5]

As Robert Kane notes, "the two principles (*PAP* and *AP*) would be equivalent, if the moral responsibility at issue (in *PAP*) were precisely the kind that free will (in *AP*) is supposed to confer; and this assumption has been commonly made in free will debates."[6] As I indicated in Chapter 1, by "free will" I mean the kind of control an agent must have over his decisions (choices, actions, etc.) in order for him to be morally responsible for those decisions (choices, actions, etc.), and thus think that the alternative possibilities condition for free will and *PAP* as defined by Frankfurt stand and fall together.

As mentioned above, there was a time in the debates about free will when the alternative possibilities condition, and thus premise (1) of the Core Argument, was accepted by virtually all participants. This fact also helps explain why, as discussed in Chapter 1, some philosophers, like Peter van Inwagen, simply define free will as the alternative possibilities condition. However, in 1969 Harry Frankfurt published a seminal article that would change how the Core Argument was approached. There, Frankfurt observed that

> [a] dominant role in nearly all recent inquiries into the free will problem has been played by a principle which I shall call "the principle of alternate possibilities." ... Its exact meaning is a subject of controversy.

... Practically no one, however, seems inclined to deny or even to question that the principle of alternate possibilities (construed in some way or other) is true. It has generally seemed so overwhelmingly plausible that some philosophers have even characterized it as an *a priori* truth. People whose accounts of free will or moral responsibility are radically at odds evidently find in it a firm and convenient common ground upon which they can profitably take their opposing grounds.[7]

Frankfurt's article is famous (or perhaps infamous) for challenging the principle and thereby changing the debate over the Core Argument. Michael McKenna has recently written that "the implications of Frankfurt's argument cannot easily be overestimated,"[8] and the degree to which the contemporary free will debate has been shaped by Frankfurt bears this out. In the remaining sections of this chapter, I discuss the monumental impact of Frankfurt's argument on the debate. I shall proceed as follows in the remainder of this chapter: in the next section, I discuss how compatibilists before Frankfurt's argument—as well as a number of compatibilists since— have responded to the Core Argument. (In the next chapter, I will discuss how a number of compatibilists writing after Frankfurt have attempted to revive this line of response to the Core Argument.) I then discuss Frankfurt's article and how it afforded compatibilists a new way of responding to the Core Argument. The final section outlines the major strategies that incompatibilists have developed to respond to Frankfurt's argument. These strategies will then be examined in greater detail in subsequent chapters.

Compatibilism and alternative possibilities

Recall from the previous section that the conclusion of the Core Argument is that free will requires the falsity of determinism; in other words, it is an argument that incompatibilism is true and that compatibilism is false. Compatibilists, thus, will want to reject this argument. Insofar as it is formally valid, the only way to reject the conclusion of the Core Argument is to deny the truth of one or both of its premises. There are two general compatibilist responses to the Core Argument, and these track the two kinds of compatibilism introduced in Chapter 2: leeway compatibilists and source-based compatibilists.

Classical compatibilism

Given its widespread acceptance among compatibilists prior to Frankfurt's influential article, I will refer to forms of compatibilism which accept premise (1) of the Core Argument as "classical compatibilism." Elsewhere,

Joseph Keim Campbell refers to this kind of compatibilism as "strong compatibilism."[9] For reasons related to its acceptance of premise (1) of the Core Argument, classical compatibilism adopts a leeway-based approach to free will. (I discuss another kind of compatibilism which rejects the other premise of the Core Argument below in the next section.) There are a number of routes along which classical compatibilism can be developed. Peter Forrest, for example, argues that we have the ability to do otherwise even if determinism is true because we have the ability to causally affect the past:

> When a person acts he or she affects the *whole causal chain*, stretching back into the past, as well as forwards into the future. … And, to the extent that the person's reasons for acting *explain* the act, they explain why there is *that* causal chain … rather than *some other* causal chain— the one which would have occurred if the person had acted otherwise. My proposal, then, is that in acting … I affect the past.[10]

Similarly, Torbjörn Tännsjö writes that if determinism is true, then "sometimes we can perform actions such that, if we did perform them, then the past would have been different (while the laws of nature were the same)."[11] So Tännsjö rejects the fixity of the past premise in the Consequence Argument, discussed in Chapter 2. Tännsjö then goes on to argue that this view, coupled with what he considers some plausible moral principles, means that "we are morally responsible, not only for future consequences of our actions, but also for events in the (remote) past."[12] This version of classical compatibilism, however, faces considerable obstacles in terms of its plausibility, and for this reason few classical compatibilists defend such a view.[13]

There are other versions of classical compatibilism that do not involve affecting or being morally responsible for the past. Consider, for instance, the position advocated by David Lewis in "Are We Free to Break the Laws?"[14] In this article, Lewis is primarily concerned with "soft determinism," the view that "sometimes one freely does what one is [causally] predetermined to do; and that in such a case one is able to act otherwise though past history and the laws of nature determine that one will not act otherwise."[15] Though he himself thinks that causal determinism is false, Lewis thinks that soft compatibilism is possibly true (i.e., in at least one possible world where determinism is true, agents in that world would still have the ability to do otherwise) and thus that strong compatibilism is also true. Slightly modifying Lewis's own example, imagine a deterministic world in which an agent, Holli, fails to raise her hand at t_3. Since we are here assuming the truth of determinism, Holli's action at t_3 is the result of the conjunction of the way the world was at a previous time t_1 (where t_1 is in the distant past of t_3) and the set of all the laws of nature $L1$, $L2$, $L3$, etc. Let us refer to the proposition expressing all the individual laws of nature as

L. According to Lewis, if Holli's not raising her hand at t_3 is a free action, then she could have raised her hand at t_3 since free will requires the ability to do otherwise. However, given that the past at t_1 and L together entail that she not raise her hand at t_3, if Holli were to raise her hand at t_3, then one of the following would be true:

(a) contradictions could be true,

(b) the past would not have been as it actually was at t_1, or

(c) L would not have been true.

Lewis dismisses the first two options and embraces the third. Thus, he is "committed to that consequence that if [Holli] had done what [she] was able to do—raise [her] hand—then some law would have been broken."[16] As counterintuitive as this may initially seem, Lewis defends its truth. Lewis distinguishes two different claims. The weaker of the two claims is that, in virtue of being free, Holli is able to do something such that, if she were to do it, a law of nature would be broken. The stronger claim is that Holli is able to break a law of nature. According to Lewis, soft compatibilism requires only that the weaker of these two claims is true, and not that the stronger— and admittedly "utterly incredible"[17]—claim be true. Lewis defends the truth of the weaker claim by appealing to "a divergence miracle."[18] (It is for this reason that Lewis's view is often referred to as "local miracle compatibilism.") If Holli were to raise her hand at t_3, then some part of L that is a law of nature would have been broken prior to t_3, say at t_2. But, Lewis thinks, this miracle need not have been caused by Holli raising her hand (though he leaves it open that the miracle caused Holli to freely raise her hand). In other words, the weaker claim need not entail the stronger claim. Thus, Lewis thinks that agents do have the ability to do otherwise despite the truth of determinism in the sense that were they to do otherwise, then a divergence miracle would have taken place.[19] Thus, to relate this to the Consequence Argument discussed in Chapter 2, according to Lewis, either the "fixity of the past" or the "fixity of the laws" (or both) is false. And if Lewis is right that the Consequence Argument has a false premise, then it fails to establish the incompatibility of free will and determinism.

More recently, Jim Stone has suggested another version of classical compatibilism that, like Lewis's view, involves miracles but is stronger in that his view, unlike Lewis's, affords agents the ability to perform miracles. Stone attempts "to show that the fact that our acts are a logical consequence of the laws of nature and events in the remote past would not by itself provide a compelling reason to deny that we can do something else."[20] To put it differently, Stone argues that the mere fact that all our actions are the inevitable by-product of the conjunction of the past and the laws of nature does not entail that we lack the ability to do otherwise; it just entails that we never use this ability. If this is the case, then the truth of determinism wouldn't rule out free will in virtue of ruling out the ability to do otherwise. Stone appeals to God to refute premise (2) of the Core Argument. He begins by noting that "determinism is a thesis about nature: every event in nature is a consequence of the past and natural laws."[21] But God is a supernatural being and thus by definition is not a part of nature. Furthermore, following a long philosophical tradition, Stone understands a miracle to be a violation of a law of nature. He continues:

> It follows that there are no miracles in a deterministic universe. Nonetheless, if God exists in it, miracles are still possible. For God has the power to work miracles if he chooses and he has the power to choose, even though he never does. Such a universe is deterministic by the grace of God. Consequently, in a God-occupied deterministic universe nothing *must* happen as it does.[22]

None of this so far means that human persons have the ability to do otherwise in a deterministic universe; all it means is that even in a deterministic universe it is possible that the future be other than it will be, even holding constant the past and the laws of nature. Were God to perform a miracle, then the future would be different—and this is true even if God never does, in fact, perform a miracle. But if God were to extend the power to do miracles to human agents, or merely cooperate with them in performing a miracle, then human agents would also have the ability to do otherwise, even in a deterministic universe:

> In a God-occupied universe we may have the power to do the physically impossible: with God's help we can work miracles. ... I submit that, with supernatural assistance, we can render laws false. By enabling us to do this, God could give us the power to refrain from actions determined by the remote past and natural laws. Of course, determinism is false if ever we exercise the power. As we have seen, there can be no miracles in a deterministic universe. All that proves, however, is that in a deterministic universe we never refrain from actions determined by the remote past and natural laws. It hardly follows that we *cannot* refrain. ... If we can render laws false with God's help, we have the power to do otherwise. The universe is deterministic partly because we never do. Determinism, therefore, does not logically preclude free will.[23]

Not all versions of classical compatibilism are developed along either of these lines. In fact, the most common form of strong compatibilism, which Peter van Inwagen has labeled "conditionalism,"[24] makes no mention of miracles whatsoever. Proponents of conditionalism are strong compatibilists who embrace the alternative-possibilities condition for free will and reject premise (2) of the Core Argument by giving subjunctive or conditional accounts of the ability to do otherwise. According to such accounts, the proposition "an agent could have done other than *A*" is to be understood along the lines of "the agent would have done other than *A* if some condition *C* had been fulfilled." One way of specifying condition *C* is with "had the agent willed or chosen to do so."[25] For example, G. E. Moore writes that "[t]here are certainly good reasons for thinking that we *very often* mean by "could" merely "would, *if* so and so had chosen". And if so, then we have a sense of the word "could" in which the fact that we often *could* have done what we did not do, is perfectly compatible with the principle that everything has a cause."[26] Similarly, A. J. Ayer expresses conditionalism—as well as a commitment to *AP*— in his influential 1954 article "Freedom and necessity":

> When I am said to have done something of my own free will it is implied that I could have acted otherwise; and it is only when it is believed that I could have acted otherwise that I am held to be morally responsible for what I have done. For a man is not thought to be morally responsible for an action that it was not in his power to avoid. ... It may be said of the agent that he would have acted otherwise if the causes of his action had been different, but that being what they were, it seems to follow that he was bound to act as he did.[27]

If the ability to do otherwise is to be understood as Moore, Ayer, and other proponents of conditionalism understand it, then given that the conditional could be true even if the antecedent of that conditional were determined to be false, then having the ability to do otherwise would still be compatible with the truth of causal determinism.

However, such subjunctive accounts of the ability to do otherwise are thought by many to be a weakness in this sort of compatibilist position.[28] Though a compatibilist himself, Michael McKenna describes the situation as follows:

> Compatibilists were shouldered with the burden of crafting fancy counterfactual theories of agential ability, many of which were regarded as no more than one click away from smoke and mirrors. (And short of alchemy, smoke and mirrors is about the best one can offer.)[29]

Underlying McKenna's comments here is the following. The conditional analysis sometimes holds that an agent could have done otherwise where it is clear that the agent wasn't free. The conditional attributing to an agent the ability to do otherwise (such as "Allison would have done otherwise than *A* if *X*") could be true even when there is nothing the agent could do to fulfill the antecedent of the conditional. But if there is no way that the agent could fulfill the antecedent of the conditional, then the agent couldn't in fact do what the conditional says the agent could do. For instance, suppose that Allison falls from the deck of a cruise ship while on vacation. Her absence isn't noticed by anyone, and the ship sails on. Allison is thus stranded in the ocean hundreds of miles from the nearest land or rescue vessel. It seems that Allison can do nothing else but drown. But the following conditional is true:

Allison could do other than drown if she were a mermaid.

While one may think that this is relevantly different than the kinds of conditionals involved in conditionalism, the two are structurally parallel. This suggests that conditionalism's analysis of the ability to do otherwise will only succeed if the antecedent is fulfillable by the agent. However, if determinism is true, then whatever is used to fill in the antecedent of the conditional will be false precisely because it is determined to be false:

I could not have decided, willed, chosen or desired otherwise than I in fact did. … We will then want to know whether the causes of those inner states were within my control; and so on, *ad infinitum*. We are, at each step, permitted to say "could have been otherwise" only in a provisional sense … but must retract it and replace it with "could not have been otherwise" as soon as we discover, as we must at each step, that whatever would have to have been different could not have been different.[30]

Similarly, Hugh McCann writes that

[i]t [the conditional analysis] seems clearly to fail. For one thing, the analysis misses the target distinction almost entirely. Compulsives, addicts, people operating under duress—virtually everyone whose freedom to will differently we ordinarily view as compromised—would count by this criterion as free. Surely, if determinism is true, they would have willed differently had their strongest motives been different. Yet these are the people whose responsibility for decisions we would question, precisely *because* we think their strongest motive was too influential.[31]

It is for this sort of reason that numerous incompatibilists have argued that such accounts are "absurd"[32] or even incoherent.[33] And though a compatibilist himself, the above considerations also led John Martin Fischer to write that conditionalism "has fatal problems."[34] But even if these attempts do not work, the failure of classical compatibilism would not amount to a refutation of compatibilism. For, as we shall see in the next section, there are other compatibilist alternatives to both conditionalism and classical compatibilism in general.[35]

Frankfurt and weak compatibilism

In 1969, Harry Frankfurt published an 11-page article that has profoundly changed the debates surrounding both moral responsibility and free will. Frankfurt's aim in this trenchant article is devilishly simple: to describe an agent who is morally responsible yet lacks the ability to do otherwise, thereby showing *PAP* false and rendering the Core Argument unsound. To achieve this aim, Frankfurt gives an example in which an agent does an action in circumstances that lead us to believe that the agent has the kind of control over her actions needed to be morally responsible (i.e. she has free will). Yet unbeknown to the agent, the circumstances include some mechanism that would bring about the action in question if the agent did not perform it on her own, eliminating her alternative possibilities. As it happens though, the agent does perform the action on her own and the mechanism is not involved in any way in bringing about the action. Here is Frankfurt's scenario:

> Suppose someone—Black, let us say—wants Jones to perform a certain action [i.e., action *A*]. Black is prepared to go to considerable lengths to get his way, but he prefers to avoid showing his hand unnecessarily. So he waits until Jones is about to make up his mind what to do, and he does nothing unless it is clear to him (Black is an excellent judge of such things) that Jones is going to decide to do something *other* than what he wants him to do [i.e. other than *A*]. If it does become clear that Jones is going to decide to do something else, Black takes effective steps to ensure that Jones decides to do, and that he does do, what he wants him to do. Whatever Jones' initial preferences and inclinations, then, Black will have his way. ... Now suppose that Black never has to show his hand because Jones, for reasons of his own, decides to perform and does perform the very action that Black wants him to perform. In that case, it seems clear, Jones will bear precisely the same moral responsibility for what he does as he would have borne if Black had not been ready to take steps to ensure that he do it.[36]

Subsequently, numerous similar scenarios, many of increasing complexity, have been put forth in the literature.[37] Let us call such scenarios "Frankfurt-style-counterexamples" or *FSCs*. *FSCs*, then, purport to show that the kind of control needed for moral responsibility is compatible with the lack of the ability to do otherwise. As the scenario actually unfolds, Black does nothing precisely because Jones does the action in question. But had he been about to do otherwise, Black would have stepped in and forced Jones to do that action. So it looks like Jones is not able to do otherwise than Black wants him to do. However, since Black doesn't actually do anything (but is just "lurking in the wings", so to speak), Frankfurt claims that Black's presence doesn't undermine Jones' moral responsibility. He thus claims that such examples show that *PAP* and *AP* are false, and thus that compatibilists need not resort to conditionalism or other forms of strong compatibilism in order to reject the conclusion of the Core Argument. Commenting on the change in the debate wrought by Frankfurt's argument McKenna writes, "While some compatibilists labored mightily to make credible an account of free will that involved alternative possibilities [i.e., a version of strong compatibilism], others saw in Frankfurt's ingenious argument an elegant end-run around the most contentious element of their thesis."[38] In order to differentiate this form of compatibilism from what he refers to as strong compatibilism (and what I have been calling classical compatibilism), Campbell refers to such Frankfurt-inspired versions of compatibilism as "weak compatibilism."[39] If weak compatibilism is a defensible view, then the objections mentioned above to strong compatibilism will not be objections to compatibilism *per se*. Frankfurt-style counterexamples, then, purport to show that the kind of control required for moral responsibility is compatible with the lack of the ability to do otherwise, that is, with the falsity of AP.

Showing that *FSCs* undermine premise (1) of the Core Argument would not mean that they show that incompatibilism is false, for there might be other sound arguments the conclusion of which is the truth of incompatibilism—as Frankfurt himself is willing to admit: "Counterexamples to the Principle of Alternate Possibilities do not actually show that attributions of moral responsibility are compatible with determinism. They do go a long way, I think, to making compatibilism plausible."[40] But the success of *FSCs* would significantly change the debate regarding the Compatibility Question given the historical influence of the Core Argument. In an excellent recent discussion of the "moral of the Frankfurt-stories," John Fischer writes that

> a denial of *PAP* would seem to allow the compatibilist about causal determinism and moral responsibility [and thus also free will construed as the control condition on moral responsibility] to *side-step* the contentious and evidently intractable debates about the relationship between causal determinism and "freedom to do otherwise". ... They [that is, *FSCs*] arguably help us to reconfigure the argumentation in a way that will be advantageous to the compatibilist [by avoiding the need for the conditional analysis].[41]

That is, *FSCs* would go some distance toward showing that free will and also moral responsibility are compatible with the truth of causal determinism insofar as they would refute the Core Argument. Fischer describes *FSCs* as being part of a larger two-step argumentative strategy:

> I employ the Frankfurt-type examples as the first (but obviously important) step of a slightly more complex argument to the conclusion

that [one can have the kind of control required for moral responsibility despite lacking alternative possibilities]. ... The first step is to argue, based on the Frankfurt-type examples, that intuitively it is plausible that alternative possibilities are irrelevant to ascriptions of moral responsibility. One is supposed to see the irrelevance of alternative possibilities simply by reflecting on the examples. I do not know how to *prove* the irrelevance thesis, but I find it extremely plausible intuitively. ... The *second* step in the argument consists in asking whether causal determinism *in itself and apart from ruling out alternative possibilities* threatens moral responsibility.[42]

Fischer thinks that there is no other sound argument that shows that the truth of determinism rules out free will of the sort required for moral responsibility. But even if one disagrees with him about this second step, one should agree that *FSCs* have a significant impact on the debate over the compatibility of free will and determinism. For if *FSCs* succeed, then compatibilists will not need to defend subjunctive renderings of *AP* or embrace other variations of classical compatibilism to respond to the Core Argument, for determinism will not threaten free will simply in virtue of ruling out the ability to do otherwise. If the truth of causal determinism is incompatible with free will, it will have to be for some other reason than that suggested in the Core Argument.

Incompatibilism and alternative possibilities

Frankfurt's relatively short article has since generated an immense and complex literature. Commenting on this matter, Kadri Vihvelin writes:

> It is difficult to explain, to someone not working in this area, just how peculiar the situation is. On the one hand, Frankfurt stories, as they have come to be called, have had an impact in free will circles that is comparable to the impact of Gettier stories in epistemology. On the other hand, after over thirty years of debate and discussion, it is *still* controversial whether Frankfurt or any of his followers have succeeded in providing a genuine counterexample to *PAP*.[43]

Similarly, Stewart Goetz, himself an incompatibilist, writes that "no issue has influenced the discussion about free will more in the past thirty-five years than *PAP*."[44] Many incompatibilists, including Goetz, argue that *FSCs* fail to provide a counterexample to the alternative-possibilities condition. There are two main versions of this sort of response advocated by incompatibilists.[45] A number of incompatibilists advocate what is often referred to as the Dilemma Defense. According to the Dilemma Defense,

*FSC*s only show that the ability to do otherwise isn't required for free will if they illicitly presuppose the truth of determinism. If this is true, then to say that the agent in an *FSC* is acting freely requires assuming that free will and the truth of determinism are compatible, an assumption that the incompatibilist will insist is question-begging. The Dilemma Defense is explored in further detail in Chapter 6.

The second major incompatibilist critique of *FSC*s is what has come to be called the "Flicker of Freedom Strategy." According to proponents of the Flicker Strategy, *FSC*s fail to show that *AP* is false because *FSC*s are not instances in which the agent truly lacks alternative possibilities. Even if a counterfactual intervener such as Black eliminates some alternative possibilities (say, Jones's ability to actually do some action *X*,) there are other alternatives that Jones nevertheless retains (say, Jones's ability to *try* and do *X*.) While these remaining alternatives may only be a "flicker" of what we usually associate with the ability to do otherwise, their presence is enough to undermine Frankfurt's attempt to give a counterexample to the alternative-possibilities condition. The debate over the Flicker of Freedom Strategy is the focus of Chapter 7.

There are, however, a number of incompatibilists who accept the conclusion that *FSC*s show *AP* to be false. According to these incompatibilists, *FSC*s do show that alternative possibilities are not required for free will, but this conclusion does not, in turn, support compatibilism because incompatibilism is not committed to the requirement of alternative possibilities. These incompatibilists think there are other reasons, besides the mere elimination of alternative possibilities, why the truth of causal determinism is incompatible with free will. I return to this response in Chapter 9

CHAPTER SIX

The dilemma defense

Introduction

In Chapter 5, I introduced an influential argumentative strategy aimed at showing that the ability to do otherwise isn't required for an agent to have free will; that is, it isn't required for the agent to have the kind of control over her actions required for her to be morally responsible for those actions. The strategy, originally developed by Harry Frankfurt, is based on presenting a case where it seems that the agent lacks the ability to do otherwise but where this lack by itself doesn't show that the agent isn't free. If such Frankfurt-inspired examples work, then arguments for the incompatibility of free will and determinism based on the need for alternative possibilities (such as the Core Argument) fail. In other words, these examples claim that *AP* (the thesis that a person acts freely or exercises his free will only if he could have done otherwise) is false, and thus it is wrong to understand free will as primarily a function of being able to do otherwise than one in fact does. This chapter and the next are devoted to exploring a number of ways that incompatibilists have responded to *FSCs*. Stewart Goetz, an incompatibilist, writes that "at first glance, one cannot help but feel pulled to some degree or other toward the Frankfurtian conclusion that *PAP* is false. This is one of those cases, however, where appearances are deceiving (illusory)."[1] And, as we'll see, many incompatibilists argue that *FSCs* give us little, if any, reason to reject the view that free will requires alternative possibilities and the ability to do otherwise. One of the main strategies incompatibilists utilize here is what has come to be referred to as the Dilemma Defense.[2] This chapter is devoted to exploring the Dilemma Defense to *FSCs* and various argumentative retorts to it.

The dilemma posed

At the heart of the Dilemma Defense is the claim that *FSCs* can only show that the ability to do otherwise isn't required for free will if they illicitly presuppose the truth of determinism. Recall Frankfurt's original description from the previous chapter:

> Suppose someone—Black, let us say—wants Jones to perform a certain action [i.e. action *A*]. Black is prepared to go to considerable lengths to get his way, but he prefers to avoid showing his hand unnecessarily. So he waits until Jones is about to make up his mind about what to do, and he does nothing unless it is clear to him (Black is an excellent judge of such things) that Jones is going to decide to do something *other* than what he wants him to do [i.e. other than *A*]. If it does become clear that Jones is going to decide to do something else, Black takes effective steps to ensure that Jones decides to do, and that he does do, what he wants him to do. Whatever Jones' initial preferences and inclinations, then, Black will have his way.[3]

Black's being able to ensure that Jones does action *A* depends upon Black's ability to infallibly know what Jones is going to do—otherwise, Black may mistakenly not intervene, thinking that Jones *is* going to do *A*, and yet Jones does not actually do *A*. On such a possibility, Jones retains the ability to do otherwise. But Frankfurt doesn't specify how Black is able to have this sort of knowledge; all he says is that Black is "an excellent judge of such things." Subsequent work has attempted to fill in this lacuna.

In subsequent *FSCs*, the counterfactual intervener typically depends on the presence of some prior sign by which he knows whether or not intervention is necessary. The prior sign is what Fischer calls a "triggering event."[4] A prior sign or triggering event is one such that, if it were to occur, is part of a causal chain that leads to the event or action in question. For example, in a relatively standard *FSC*, Jones' blushing at t_1 is correlated with whether or not he will decide to *A* at t_2. If this is the case, then Black merely needs to watch to see whether or not Jones blushes at t_1 in order to know whether or not he needs to intervene in order to guarantee that Jones *A*s at t_2. However, according to proponents of the Dilemma Defense, the relationship between the prior sign and the action is problematic. Either the relationship between the prior sign and the action in question is deterministic or it is not; regardless of which of these two is true, there is a problem for the proponent of *FSCs*.[5] Assume that the relationship between the prior sign and the action is merely probabilistic. We can even assume that the correlation between the sign and the action is quite high—say, 98.7 per cent—though nothing of importance hangs on this assumption. It is Black's policy to not intervene unless required. So if Black sees that Jones is blushing at t_1, he does nothing and instead waits for Jones to A of his own accord at t_2. But on the assumption that the relationship between the prior sign and the action is indeterministic, then it is possible that Jones evidences the prior sign and still fails to do the action that Black wants him to; there is a 1.3 per cent chance that Jones blushes at t_1 and yet fails to A at t_2. Thus, even if Jones does blush, he nevertheless retains alternative possibilities with regard to whether or not he As at t_2; thus, such a version of an FSC would fail to show that the agent is acting freely and yet lacks alternative possibilities.

Let us then consider the scenario in question on the assumption that the relationship between the prior sign and the action is deterministic, that is, on the assumption that Jones' blushing is invariantly correlated with his A-ing at t_2 because there is a deterministic causal chain holding between Jones' blush at t_1 and his A-ing at t_2. In this case, Black merely needs to intervene if and only if Jones is not blushing at t_1 thereby guaranteeing without unnecessary intervention that Jones will A at t_2 no matter what. Here, the proponent of the Dilemma Defense says, is where $FSCs$ fail. For either the prior sign is itself a free action or it is not. If it is, then all the FSC has done is push the issue of whether or not the agent has alternative possibilities back from the original action in question (here, the agent's A-ing) to a prior free action (i.e., evidencing the prior sign). On the other hand, if the prior sign is *not* itself a free action, then on the present assumption that the presence of the prior sign is sufficient for the agent performing the action in question, the FSC appears to assume the compatibility of free will and causal determinism. But such an assumption in the dialectical context of critiquing the Core Argument would be begging the question against the incompatibilist proponent of that argument. That is, the incompatibilist could say that Jones is not acting freely since the blush is not a free action but its occurrence insures that Jones will do A. Thus, according to the Dilemma Defense, $FSCs$ only show that alternative possibilities are not required for free will if one assumes that determinism is true. But if it is stipulated that determinism is true in an FSC, and one also holds that the agent involved is acting freely, then one has assumed that free will and the truth of determinism are compatible. And this, the incompatibilist will insist, is question-begging.[6]

Robert Kane, Keith Wyma, Carl Ginet, and David Widerker all raise versions of the Dilemma Defense. The earliest presentation of the dilemma seems to be raised by Kane in a footnote in his 1985 book *Free Will and Values*:

The Frankfurt controller would wait to see if the agent was going to choose A on his own before intervening to make him choose A. But if the agent has sole or ultimate dominion over the choice of A, then neither the choosing of A nor the doing otherwise can be determined. This means that the Frankfurt controller cannot tell until the moment of choice itself whether the agent is going to choose *A* or do otherwise. If the controller wants to ensure that the choice of *A* is made he must act *in advance* to bring it about. But if he does this the agent will not be responsible because the agent's choice will have been controlled by the controller. Thus, if sole or ultimate dominion, and hence the indeterminist condition, are satisfied the Frankfurt controller is thwarted in his plans.[7]

Even in this early presentation of the objection, we see the idea that the assumption of indeterminism rules out the kind of predictive power needed by the Frankfurt-style controller, and that while a deterministic link would make that predictive power possible, it would do so at the expense of lack of agential responsibility. Here is how Kane develops the dilemma in a later work:

> Imagine what must be done to exercise Frankfurt control over a person's choice. The controller, Black, plans to make Jones do *A*. But he waits to see if Jones is going to do *A* on his own and only intervenes if Jones is about to do *B* instead ... [Unless we assume that the action in question is causally determined], the controller cannot know which one is going to occur beforehand unless he pre-determines one of them to occur. He can therefore wait until he finds out whether the agent will do *A* or *B*, but then it is too late to control the choice. Or he can intervene in the brain, shutting down the indeterminacy or its effects before either choice occurs, thereby determining the outcome he wants. In the latter case, the choice will be determined by the controller and the controller, not the agent, will be *ultimately responsible* for it. ... By contrast, if the controller does not intervene to predetermine the outcome and the indeterminacy remains in place until the choice is made ... then the agent, and not the controller, is ultimately responsible for it. But then it is also the case that the agent *could have done otherwise*.[8]

David Widerker raises a similar objection to *FSCs* in a series of articles. In his 1995 article "Libertarianism and Frankfurt's attack on the principle of alternative possibilities," Widerker defines an *IRR* situation as a set of "circumstances in which a person performs some action which although they make it impossible for him to avoid performing that action, they in no way bring it about that he performs it."[9] As he understands it, the point of an *FSC* is to show that the mere fact that an agent is in an *IRR* situation does not by itself entail that the agent lacks free will. Furthermore, "the success of Frankfurt's case against *PAP* depends crucially upon his ability to convince us of the plausibility of IRR [i.e. the plausibility of there being an *IRR* situation]."[10] Widerker asks us to consider an *FSC* involving an agent Jones, who is deliberating whether or not she should attempt to kill Smith. Black is the counterfactual intervener, prepared to coerce Jones into killing

Smith if Jones does not decide to do so on her own at a particular time t_2. The way that Black knows if he needs to intervene is by observing whether a prior sign, a blush, is present at an earlier time t_1. Widerker understands the central relevant features here to be the following:

1   If Jones is blushing at t_1, then, provided no one intervenes, she will decide at t_2 to kill Smith.

2   If Jones is not blushing at t_1, then, provided no one intervenes, she will not decide at t_2 to kill Smith.

3   If Black sees that Jones shows signs that she will not decide at t_2 to kill Smith, that is, sees that Jones is *not* blushing at t_1, then Black will force Jones to decide at t_2 to kill Smith; but if he sees that she is blushing at t_1, then he does nothing.

4   Jones is blushing at t_1 and decides at t_2 to kill Smith for reasons of her own.[11]

The problem with understanding an *FSC* as an *IRR* situation in this way, according to Widerker, lies in 1. If the truth of 1 is defended on the basis that Jones's blushing at t_1 is causally sufficient for her decision at t_2 or indicative of some other state that is, then the situation fails to be an *IRR* situation and the incompatibilist need not grant that the agent is acting freely. According to Widerker, "what, in my opinion, is crucial to the libertarian's conception of a free decision is that such a decision is not necessitated or determined in any way by an antecedent event or fact."[12] But if one assumes that the prior sign *is* causally sufficient for Jones' decision at t_2, then one can see why incompatibilists such as Widerker would deny the claim that Jones is deciding freely at t_2. On the other hand, if 1 is not so grounded in the blush, then the incompatibilist could "resist the contention that Jones's decision to kill Smith is unavoidable. ... Jones's power *not* to decide to kill Smith is preserved, and hence again we have not been given an example of an *IRR* situation."[13] As a result of this line of reasoning, Widerker claims that *FSCs* fail to show *AP* to be false when applied to mental actions such as choices, decisions, or volitions.[14]

Rebutting the dilemma

How might the proponent of *FSCs* respond to the Dilemma Defense as presented by Kane and Widerker? The following sections will consider two general lines of argument that have been offered in the literature. I first consider two strategies that aim at providing *FSCs* that can avoid the first horn of the Dilemma Defense—that is, they attempt to construct *FSCs* that eliminate alternative possibilities even if the truth of determinism is explicitly denied. I then consider responses that tackle the second horn of the dilemma by trying to show why the assumption of determinism isn't dialectically unfair to incompatibilism because the assumption of determinism need not be question-begging. What is interesting to note about some of these strategies is that they have been developed by incompatibilists—some of whom think that *AP* is in fact true—as well as compatibilists who, like Frankfurt, seek to undermine the Core Argument for the incompatibilism of free will and determinism, thereby indirectly supporting compatibilism.

Blockage to the rescue?

As mentioned in the previous paragraph, one general line of response to the Dilemma Defense involves the attempt to give *FSCs* that are not susceptible to the dilemma thereby showing that while some, or even many, extant *FSCs* are problematic in this way, not all *FSCs* are. If it can be shown that *FSCs* can be developed that are able to eliminate alternative possibilities without tacitly presupposing the truth of determinism, then the dilemma can be avoided. One route that some pursue in this regard is to develop *FSCs* that are based on foreknowledge rather than prior signs.[15] But doing so raises a number of philosophical questions, such as whether or not all forms of foreknowledge are analogous to causal determinism in the needed way. Given these issues, and the fact that a treatment of them would be extensive, I will not consider such issues here.[16]

In "Rescuing Frankfurt-style cases," Al Mele and David Robb attempt to show that despite the "seemingly devastating way of attacking Frankfurt style examples"[17] at the heart of the Dilemma Defense, it is nevertheless possible to give *FSCs* that are immune to the Dilemma Defense. Their aim is to offer an *FSC* that is immune to the dilemma because "a counterfactual controller's having a prior sign (Widerker) or prior knowledge (Kane) of what the agent will do is an inessential feature of Frankfurt-style cases, despite the details of Frankfurt's own case."[18] Mele and Robb begin the presentation of their *FSC* by stipulating that while certain processes and causal chains in it are deterministic, the thesis of determinism is false. They then give the following scenario:

> At t_1, Black initiates a certain deterministic process P in Bob's brain with the intention of thereby causing Bob to decide at t_2 (an hour later, say) to steal Ann's car. The process, which is screened off from Bob's consciousness, will deterministically culminate in Bob's deciding at t_2 to steal Ann's car unless he decides on his own at t_2 to steal it or is incapable at t_2 of making a decision (because, for example, he is dead by t_2). ... The process is in no way sensitive to any "sign" of what Bob will decide. As it happens, at t_2 Bob decides on his own to steal the car, on the basis of his own indeterministic deliberation about whether to steal it, and his decision has no deterministic cause. But if he had not just then decided

on his own to steal it, P would have deterministically issued, at t_2, in his deciding to steal it. Rest assured that P in no way influences the indeterministic decision-making process that actually issues in Bob's decision.[19]

In this case, Mele and Robb claim that it is plausible that Bob is acting freely and is morally responsible for his choice despite not having been able to do otherwise. They are aware that not all will be reassured by their rhetorical flourishes that such a case is coherent, particularly the claim that P (or any freedom-undermining feature) plays no role in bringing about Bob's decision at t_2. "How, one might wonder, can it happen that Bob decides on his own at t_2 to steal Ann's car, given the presence of the deterministic process we *mentioned* [i.e. given P]?"[20]

In responding to this question, Mele and Robb utilize a particular form of preemption. (Cases of preemption are cases where one causal chain leading to a particular event is preempted by another causal chain which brings about the very same event.) By their very nature, *FSCs* are cases involving preemption—that is, one causal chain sufficient for an effect produces the effect before another causal chain, which is also sufficient for the effect, is able to produce that same effect.[21] The existence of the counterfactual intervener, who is sufficient to bring about the action if the agent herself does not, is essential to the action being unavoidable. If the agent had not performed the action freely, the intervener would have brought about the very same action.[22] As Fischer and Ravizza note, "the Frankfurt-type strategy seems to *require* such preemption, since it appears to justify holding agents responsible only if the Ensuring Condition [i.e., the counterfactual intervener] is not actually efficacious in bringing about the event in question."[23] Most *FSCs*, including Frankfurt's case involving Jones and Black discussed above in relation to the Dilemma Defense, rely on a kind of preemption known as "cutting preemption": one of the causal chains involved is cut, or prevented from going through to completion, by the other, efficacious causal chain.[24] In the alternate sequence, Jones's decision to do other than A is cut by Black's forcing Jones to A. The prior sign is important to letting the counterfactual intervener know whether he needs to intervene or not by cutting the causal chain that the agent has already begun. But Mele and Robb seek to avoid using cutting preemption, instead incorporating another form of preemption known as "occurrent preemption." Douglas Ehring explains occurrent preemption as follows:

Preemptive causation also generally will include some blocking action: the main line blocks the efficacy of the alternate line. ... [In some cases of blocking,] the blocking action from the main line does not prevent the occurrence of any events in the alternate line [thereby differentiating it from cutting preemption]. The blocking action prevents the last (actual) event in the alternate line from bringing about the final effect. The efficacy of this last event is blocked, but not by preventing the occurrence of any intermediary events between that event and the final effect. Unlike in nonoccurrent preemption [such as cutting preemption], the final event in the alternate line would have *directly* caused the final effect (had it been efficacious at all). I will call this "occurrent preemption", since the main line does not block the occurrence of any *event* in the alternate line.[25]

With this distinction in mind, let us return to Mele and Robb's *FSC*. In order for their example to rule out alternative possibilities, in addition to *P*'s bringing about Bob's decision to steal Ann's car at t_2 being occurrently preempted by Bob's deciding on his own at that very same time, the case must also have a way of preventing Bob from deciding to do something else prior to t_2.[26] In other words, the case must contain a way of *blocking* alternative decisions and not just a way of having Bob's decision be preempted by the working of the failsafe mechanism.[27]

David Hunt has also developed and defended such blockage cases involving what he calls "passive alternative-eliminators." To illustrate this idea, Hunt describes an *FSC* in which the intervener (Black) wants an agent (Jones) to perform a particular action (e.g., steer his car right, rather than left, at a fork in the road thereby running over and killing Smith). Unlike more standard *FSC*s in which Black is a counterfactual intervener who only operates in the alternative sequence, in blockage cases the intervener eliminates alternative possibilities in the actual sequence but in a way that doesn't actually interfere with the agent's choice. Here is Hunt's example:

> Suppose the driving instructor [Black] can lock his wheel at a certain position to prevent the student driver [Jones] from steering beyond that range, and Black has placed a "left lock" on his steering wheel to block the possibility that Jones might take the road to the left; Jones, however, bears right at the fork and never encounters the lock. The principal difference between this kind of case and the one involving the counterfactual alternative-eliminator [as is found in Frankfurt's case] is that the passive eliminator is in place in the actual world, though the sequence of events actually productive of Smith's death never intersects with it (hence its "passiveness"). But the moral it conveys appears to be the same. A steering lock is no less effective than in Black's counterfactual resolve in ensuring that the car is going to hit Smith and that there is nothing Jones can do to avoid this outcome. Moreover, there is no less reason in this case to regard Jones as a free agent in killing Smith. The passive alternative-eliminator does not figure in the actual sequence; in its absence, Jones would have done everything the same. If these reasons support Jones's free agency in the face of a counterfactual alternative-eliminator, they equally support his free agency when a passive alternative-eliminator is at work.[28]

Hunt further suggests that similar devices can be employed to block all of the agent's alternative possibilities thereby rendering the agent unable to do otherwise in any way.[29] "There is ... no evident upper limit on the restrictions imposed by a passive alternative-eliminator. Any alternative can be passively blocked and because the alternative is eliminated passively, the actual sequence, along with Jones's free agency, is unaffected."[30] Given that passive alternative-eliminators, unlike counterfactual alternative-eliminators, do not depend upon a prior sign since they are functioning (though passive) in the actual sequence, Hunt claims that such blockage cases provide a way of sidestepping the Dilemma Defense.

It is not clear to me that Hunt is correct. Derk Pereboom has argued, convincingly I think, that blockage of this sort "makes it hard to assess moral responsibility. ... [In blockage scenarios], one's intuitions about whether the agent is morally responsible might become unstable,"[31] since it seems that complete blockage of the sort proposed by Hunt and seemingly required by Mele and Robb's case renders the action in question determined. In blockage cases, the restrictions involved *might* be relevant to the causal history of the action in question, Pereboom argues, thereby begging the question against the incompatibilist.[32] Similarly, Kane writes that in cases where all alternative possibilities are blocked by P, "this now looks like a case of determinism pure and simple."[33] And even Hunt, one of the leading proponents of such cases, is willing to grant that this criticism is plausible, even if not definitive:

By causally eliminating *all* alternatives, ... [a complete blockage case] brings it about that only [one action or decision] is causally possible. But then every state or event of possible relevance to Jones's exercise of agency is causally determined by the device, leaving no opening for the causal indeterminism critical to libertarianism.[34]

Similarly, he writes elsewhere:

While blockage cases have much to recommend them, they come with their own set of difficulties ... [which] confirms my own reticence about pushing them too strongly as definitive counterexamples to *PAP*, at least in their present form. The central difficulty is that the conditions barring Jones's access to alternative pathways and guaranteeing his decision to kill Smith must be distinguished, in some non-*ad hoc* way, from the sorts of conditions that would beg the question against incompatibilism by *causally determining* Jones's decision. ... So blockage is probably not the magic bullet for which *PAP* critics are looking.[35]

How then should we evaluate the ability of blockage cases of the sort developed by Mele and Robb and Hunt to avoid the Dilemma Defense? First, I agree with Fischer regarding the following conditional: "If the blockage cases (suitably filled in and developed) are coherent, then Kane's [and Widerker's] argument that there must be alternative possibilities in an indeterministic context in which the agent acts freely fails."[36] Nevertheless, I think that such cases are coherent only if they involve complete blockage,[37] but in such cases they presuppose that the choice or action in question was determined by something outside the control of the agent. If this is correct, then they run afoul of the second horn of the Dilemma Defense.

Non-cutting alternatives

Perhaps blockage *FSCs* can be developed in a way that does not also presuppose the truth of determinism or undermine the agent's free will and moral responsibility in some other way, but it isn't clear that this could be done. Nevertheless, I think that the Dilemma Defense fails regardless insofar as it depends on an element of existing *FSCs* which is merely accidental—namely the relationship between the prior sign and the action. This feature is not essential to *FSCs* because one can develop an *FSC* that does not contain a prior sign at all and, as such, need not illicitly presuppose determinism in order for the agent to lack the ability to do otherwise. As I show below, *FSCs* do not depend on triggering events or signs even apart from considerations of blockage. If this is true, then both horns of the Dilemma Defense can be avoided insofar as the relationship between a prior sign and the action in question is merely an accidental, rather than essential, feature of *FSCs*.

As mentioned earlier, it is the nature of *FSCs* that the agent's performing the action of her own free will is a case of preemption. The existence of the counterfactual intervener, who is sufficient to bring about the action if the agent herself does not, is essential to the action being unavoidable. Most *FSCs*, including the case of Jones and Black in the Dilemma Defense above, involved cutting preemption. Consider the following *FSC*, taken from the work of Eleonore Stump, which she calls *RCE* for "revised counterexample":

> Suppose that we replace Fischer's neurosurgeon Black with a more sophisticated neurosurgeon Grey, who uses a neuroscope sensitive to neural firings. Grey ascertains that every time Jones decides to do any of a certain range of actions—say, voting for Republican candidates—the decision to do so regularly correlates with the completion of a sequence of neural firings in Jones's brain that always includes, near its beginning, the firing of neurons a, b, c (call this "neural sequence 1"). On the other hand, Jones's deciding to vote for Democratic candidates is correlated with the completion of a different neural sequence that always includes, near its beginning, the firings of neurons x, y, z, none of which is the same as those in neural sequence 1 (call this "neural sequence 2"). ... Whenever the neuroscope detects the firing of x, y, and z, the

initial neurons of neural sequence 2, which is correlated with Jones's decisions to vote for Democrats, the neuroscope immediately disrupts the neural sequence, so that it isn't brought to completion, and activates the coercive neurological mechanism which brings it about that Jones decides to vote for Republicans. But if the neuroscope detects the firings of a, b, and c, the initial neurons in neural sequence 1, which is correlated with decisions to vote for Republicans, then the neuroscope does not interrupt that neural sequence.[38]

Now we can see exactly where the preemption takes place. Notice that if Grey's neuroscope detects the firings of the initial neurons in neural sequence 2 (i.e. neurons x, y, and z), then the neuroscope interrupts this sequence, cutting neural sequence 2 so that it is not completed. Such cutting would occur in the alternative sequence, but this is not the cutting that makes RCE a case of cutting preemption. Rather, there is also cutting that takes place in the actual sequence, making the actual sequence (in which Jones votes for a Republican without any intervention by Grey) a case of cutting preemption.

The actual cutting that makes RCE an instance of cutting preemption is subtler, and to identify it we must take a closer look at the neuroscope Grey implanted in Jones's brain. Supposedly the neuroscope is programmed in such a way that whenever Jones is in a voting situation it detects his neural firings. We must also suppose, in order to make the example work, that in such a sequence there are only two options available for Jones: to either vote Republican through neural sequence 1 or vote Democrat through neural sequence 2. If Jones had other options, such as voting for a Green Party member (which correlates with neither neural sequence 1 nor 2), then the neuroscope would not be sufficient to guarantee that Jones will vote Republican.[39] Furthermore, in order to guarantee that Jones votes Republican rather than abstaining from voting, the neuroscope must also initiate neural sequence 1 if Jones does not initiate either sequence. So, when Jones finds himself in a voting situation, either sequence a–b–c, or sequence x–y–z, or neither will fire. If the neuroscope detects either the firings of x–y–z or detects nothing, then it initiates neural sequence 1.[40] And if the presence of the neuroscope is to guarantee the completion of neural sequence 1, we must assume that the programming of the neuroscope is deterministic. If it does not detect neurons a–b–c firing, then it is programmed such that it will deterministically initiate neural sequence 1. But, in the actual scenario, neurons a–b–c do fire. Thus, the neuroscope's programming to initiate neural sequence 1 is cut, or preempted, by the firing of neurons a–b–c. So, in the actual sequence, a causal chain sufficient (i.e., the neuroscope's programming) for the action is cut. RCE, then, like most standard $FSCs$, is based on cutting preemption.

But cutting is not essential for $FSCs$. Other types of preemption will do the job. Arguing against extant counterfactual accounts of causation,

Jonathan Schaffer postulates a type of preemption that does not depend on the cutting or severing of a causal chain called "trumping preemption." Schaffer and David Lewis each give an example of trumping preemption:

> Imagine that it is a law of magic that the first spell cast on a given day match the enchantment that midnight. Suppose that at noon Merlin casts a spell (the first that day) to turn the prince into a frog, that at 6:00 pm Morgana casts a spell (the only other that day) to turn the prince into a frog, and that at midnight the prince becomes a frog. Clearly, Merlin's spell (the first that day) is a cause of the prince's becoming a frog and Morgana's is not, because laws say that the first spells are the consequential ones.[41]

> The sergeant and the major are shouting orders at the soldiers. The soldiers know that in case of conflict, they must obey the superior officer. But as it happens, there is no conflict. Sergeant and major simultaneously shout "Advance!"; the soldiers hear them both; the soldiers advance. Their advancing is redundantly caused: if the sergeant had shouted "Advance!" and the major had been silent, or if the major had shouted "Advance!" and the sergeant had been silent, the soldiers would still have advanced. But the redundancy is asymmetrical: since the soldiers obey the superior officer, they advance because the major orders them to, not because the sergeant does. The major preempts the sergeant in causing them to advance. The major's order *trumps* the sergeant's.[42]

On the assumption that trumping is a legitimate form of preemption (and I see no reason to suppose otherwise), one can construct an *FSC* based on trumping, rather than cutting, preemption.

Here then is the Trumping Case. As in *RCE*, Grey wants to ensure that Jones votes Republican. Grey also knows that acts of voting Republican strongly correlate with neural sequence 1, which contains not just neurons a–b–c, but also others. Further down and near the end of neural sequence 1, there is another neuron γ which is of an unusual type. Neuron γ has two dendrites leading into its nucleus. One is connected with the earlier neurons in neural sequence 1 (and ultimately to neurons a–b–c), while the other is hooked to a brain-stimulator implanted by Grey. Let us call the former dendrite 1 and the latter dendrite 2. If either dendrite 1 or dendrite 2 receives the appropriate neural-transmitters, γ's nucleus will send an electrical impulse down its axon leading to the completion of neural sequence 1. But γ is not just any neuron. It is constituted in such a way that, on the off-chance both dendrite 1 and dendrite 2 are stimulated by neural-transmitters at the same time, it is dendrite 1 that results in the firing of γ's axon and the completion of neural sequence 1. In other words, the stimulation of dendrite 1 *trumps* the stimulation of dendrite 2 in bringing about the completion of neural sequence 1. Grey has programmed the brain-stimulator implanted in

Jones's brain to release neural-transmitters at t_1 resulting in the completion of neural sequence 1 at t_2. The presence of the Brain-stimulator is thus sufficient to guarantee that Jones will vote Republican at t_2. As it actually happens, Jones himself brings about the firing of neurons a–b–c, which results in γ completing neural sequence 1 at t_2. Thus, even though Grey's Brain-stimulator is present and operates at t_1 to stimulate dendrite 2, it is trumped by the causal chain from a–b–c to dendrite 1.

To further see the similarity between the Trumping Case and the instances of trumping preemption given above, consider the following. In the case of Merlin and Morgana, two causal chains are each independently sufficient to bring about the effect. Let us call Merlin's spell "c_1" and Morgana's spell "c_2". In the alternate sequence (i.e., where Merlin's spell is absent), c_2 would have been the cause of the prince turning into a frog. However, in the actual sequence, both c_1 and c_2 are present, c_1 trumps c_2 and c_1 is the cause of the action. Likewise, in the Trumping Case, there are two causal chains sufficient for producing the action. We could instead call Jones's free decision to vote Republican at t "c_1" and the brain-stimulator causing Jones to vote Republican at t "c_2". Now we can see that the alternate and actual sequences parallel those of the earlier examples of trumping preemption. In the alternate sequence, c_2 causes the action in the absence of c_1. However, in the actual scenario, both c_1 and c_2 are present, but c_1 trumps c_2 and is the cause of the action. It is true that the Trumping Case appears to be different from other cases of trumping preemption in the following way: had the agent made a different choice, then the brain-stimulator would have cut the alternate neural sequence. However, the cutting of the neural sequence by the brain-stimulator in the alternate sequence would be a different case of preemption than the one involved in the Trumping Case.[43]

For those who fancy magic over science fiction, we could say that Grey enlists Merlin to cast a spell on Jones at t_1 that will cause neuron γ to fire, completing sequence 1 at time t_2 if and only if a causal chain stemming from neurons a–b–c does not arrive at γ at t_2.[44] In the actual scenario, Jones decides on his own to vote Republican, initiating the causal a–b–c chain that arrives at γ at t_2. The spell that would otherwise cause Jones to vote Republican at time t_2 is trumped by his own volition to vote Republican at t_2. The level of science fiction, or pure fiction, incorporated in an FSC does not matter. Rather, the issue is the logical possibility of constructing a scenario, however far-fetched, that meets the desiderata of showing that the freedom required for moral responsibility does not require robust alternative possibilities. And if trumping preemption is conceptually coherent, then we can construct an FSC based on it. In other words, assuming the possibility of trumping preemption, it is possible to construct an FSC based on trumping, rather than cutting, preemption. And note that in the Trumping Case, there is no prior sign that the intervener or his neuroscope must detect, thereby avoiding the challenge raised by the Dilemma Defense.[45] Furthermore, it avoids the Dilemma Defense without depending on alternative neural pathways being blocked. The Trumping Case then is immune from the criticisms discussed above that result from blocking.

Though not strictly an *FSC*, Fischer and Ravizza give an example akin to an *FSC* that, like the Trumping Case, does *not* depend on either the existence of a prior sign or blockage. They call their example "Erosion*". Comparing the Trumping Case with Erosion* further demonstrates the benefits of trumping preemption. Erosion* goes as follows:

> Betty is a double agent who has been instructed to start an avalanche that will destroy an enemy base at the foot of a large, snow-capped mountain. To accomplish her mission, Betty places dynamite in the cracks and crevices of a glacier near the top of the mountain. At t_1 she pushes the plunger detonating the explosives and starting an avalanche. The avalanche rumbles down the hill, gaining ever greater force, until some time later, say t_3, it crushes the enemy outpost. Unbeknownst to Betty and her commanding officers, however, the glacier is gradually melting, shifting and eroding. This erosion of the glacier is also causally sufficient for an avalanche that also crushes the enemy base at t_3.[46]

Unlike plain "Erosion," an earlier case in which the erosion does not actually start an avalanche because it is prevented from occurring by Betty's action at t_1, in Erosion* the "erosion actually occurs and causes a particular avalanche that crushes the enemy base at t_3 and this is sufficient for the obtaining"[47] of the effect, namely the destruction of the enemy camp. Like the Trumping Case, Erosion* is a case of overdetermination that does not involve cutting since the causal chain from the erosion to the destruction of the camp is not broken; this causal chain, like that stemming from Betty, goes to completion. In this sense, however, the Trumping Case differs from Erosion*: it is hard to see how Betty, even if her action is sufficient for the avalanche, is fully responsible for the avalanche. Two separate causal chains simultaneously bring about the destruction of the enemy camp, and Betty is only responsible for one of these causal chains. But, according to the Trumping Case, the agent is *fully* responsible for her action insofar as the only causal chain that is causally efficacious is one in which she is responsible. Erosion* is a symmetrical case of redundant causation: both candidates (Betty and the erosion) have an equal claim to being called the cause of the avalanche. In such cases, David Lewis thinks that it is "unclear whether to say that each is a cause or whether to say that neither is a cause (in which case we could still say that the combination of the two is a cause). But anyway it is out of the question to say that one is a cause and the other is not."[48] But the Trumping Case, unlike Erosion*, is not symmetric. We *can* say which of the two conditions was the sole cause of the event, namely Jones's volition. In other words, the Trumping Case is still a case of preemption, whereas Erosion* is merely a case of simultaneous overdetermination.[49] The difference between overdetermination and preemption is that in cases of the former sort, two separate causes have an equal claim to be regarded as causes of the effect, whereas in cases of the latter sort, it is clear that one *is* the cause and the other *merely would have been* the cause if the first had not.[50] Most *FSCs*, including the Trumping Case, are cases of preemption, whereas Erosion* is a case of overdetermination. Thus, the Trumping Case better serves the purpose that *FSCs* were intended for.[51] And the Trumping Case is preferable to the blockage cases considered earlier insofar as the latter cases seem to require determinism in order to avoid all alternative possibilities.

Compatibilist rejoinders

In the previous sections, I considered two ways of arguing against the first horn of the Dilemma Defense. If either of these two strategies is successful, then the Dilemma Defense fails. But there is another family of responses available to opponents of the Dilemma Defense; this strategy tackles the second horn of the dilemma by trying to show why the assumption of determinism in *FSCs* isn't dialectically unfair to incompatibilism. As mentioned earlier, this horn of the dilemma says that if the relationship between the prior sign and the choice in question is deterministic, then the assumption that the agent is choosing freely requires the assumption that it is possible to be both determined and free. Insofar as the denial of this is the hallmark of incompatibilism, assuming that it is possible to be both determined and free assumes the falsity of incompatibilism. Ishtiyaque Haji and Michael McKenna are among those who have argued against this horn of the Dilemma Defense. Haji and McKenna differentiate between two under-standings of the charge that deterministic prior-sign *FSCs* beg the question against the incompatibilist which they call the broad and narrow interpreta-tions.[52] According to the broad interpretation, such examples aim to

> persuade incompatibilists, already theoretically *committed* to a position on the compatibility of determinism and moral responsibility, that if determinism does rule out the freedom moral responsibility requires, it is *not* by virtue of ruling out alternative possibilities. The committed incompatibilist believes that a determined agent is not free or morally responsible in the first place. So if Frankfurt cases are to convince such an incompatibilist, on pain of not begging the question, [the proponent of *FSCs*] must offer a Frankfurt case that does *not* assume determinism.[53]

In other words, what is problematic about this understanding of the question-begging charge is nothing more than the assumption of the truth of determinism. And here Haji and McKenna are willing to grant that this assumption can be understood to beg the question against the incompatibilist and thus that such *FSCs* are impaled on the second horn of the Dilemma Defense.

However, they also argue that there is another way of understanding the charge that such cases beg the question. According to the narrow interpretation of the charge, the cases beg the question *"because the deterministic relation expunges alternative-possibilities."*[54] According to this latter understanding, the assumption of determinism is only indirectly question-begging insofar as the truth of determinism rules out alternative possibilities, the lack of which is incompatible with free will. "Thus, the question begging feature of the deterministic horn in this dialectical context, it is alleged, is due not to the mere fact of determinism, but rather to the fact that alternatives get ruled out for reasons other than those introduced by Frankfurt's counterfactual machinery."[55] It is this particular understanding on which Haji and McKenna think that the charge of begging the question fails.

To see why this is so, let us set aside for the moment the claim that the truth of determinism itself rules out the possibility of free will. According to the Core Argument introduced in Chapter 5, the reason why determinism is incompatible with free will is because determinism rules out alternative possibilities, which are themselves required for free will. Since we are, for the moment, setting aside whether determinism *per se* rules out the possibility of free will, we should also set aside the question of whether determinism would have to be true in order for the counterfactual intervener to rule out alternative possibilities. However, if these two issues are set aside for the moment in this way, one cannot object that it is the assumed truth of determinism in *FSCs* that begs the question against the incompatibilist. What, then, might the charge be based on? According to the proponent of the Dilemma Defense, it must be that the counterfactual intervener rules out alternative possibilities. But what *FSCs* are intended to do is to make plausible the claim that alternative possibilities are irrelevant, in and of themselves, to judging whether an agent is free and morally responsible. There are prima facie plausible prior-sign Frankfurt cases in which the counterfactual intervener, on its own, rules out alternatives. The intervener's ruling out alternative possibilities is irrelevant to any judgment concerning the agent's acting freely or being morally responsible. Thus, if this way of expunging alternatives makes no difference to judgments of free action or responsibility, then this provides some reason for thinking that the ruling out of alternatives by determinism, barring special considerations to believe otherwise, should not make a difference either.[56] And this sort of plausibility argument, Haji and McKenna claim, does not amount to begging the question.[57]

A similar argument has been put forth by John Fischer.[58] In an earlier paper,[59] Fischer suggested that indeterministic *FSCs* could be readily constructed in order to avoid the Dilemma Defense. More recently, however, Fischer has written that the Dilemma Defense is a powerful and challenging argument. I do not think that it is straight-forward that it can be defeated, and so I think that my earlier confidence that Frankfurt-type examples can exist in causally indeterministic worlds was perhaps the result of youthful optimism. But even though I do not still think that it is obvious and straightforward that there can be Frankfurt-type cases in causally indeterministic worlds, I am still strongly inclined to this view.[60]

While Fischer has come to be less optimistic than he was earlier that *FSCs* can be constructed in such a way as to avoid the first horn of the Dilemma Defense, he has come to be more optimistic regarding the second horn. According to Fischer, *FSCs* do not, by themselves, directly show that free will is compatible with the lack of the ability to do otherwise, and for the reasons canvassed above with respect to the Dilemma Defense. But according to Fischer, there is another way for the *FSCs* to succeed in refuting *AP* via a two-step argument. Here is one of Fischer's many presentations of the argument:

> First, one carefully considers the Frankfurt-type case. Upon reflection, I believe that one should conclude that in these cases the lack of alternative possibilities does not in itself ground a claim that the agent is not morally responsible for his choice and action. In other words, I think that the examples make highly plausible the preliminary conclusion that *if* Jones is not morally responsible for his choice and action, this is *not* simply because he lacks alternative possibilities. ... So the relevant (preliminary) conclusion is, if Jones is not morally responsible for his choice and action, the reason is not simply that he lacks alternative possibilities. And it does *not* appear to beg the question to come to this conclusion, even if causal determinism obtains. The first step is to argue, based on the Frankfurt-type examples, that intuitively it is plausible that alternative possibilities are irrelevant to ascriptions of moral responsibility. ... The *second* step in the argument consists in asking whether causal determinism *in itself and apart from ruling out alternative-possibilities* threatens moral responsibility.[61]

And in a more recent paper, Fischer puts it succinctly: "here is what I take to be the basic insight of the Frankfurt cases: if causal determinism rules out moral responsibility, it is not in virtue of eliminating alternative possibilities. At the most basic level, it is that simple!"[62]

Fischer's own conclusion is that the truth of causal determinism would not undermine freedom, though his reasons for this conclusion won't be discussed until later chapters. (To prefigure: we'll see in Chapter 8 why he thinks the Consequence Argument, discussed earlier in Chapter 2, doesn't establish incompatibilism; and in that same chapter, we'll see why he thinks another argument for incompatibilism fails.) Fischer thought that this two-stage argument "is highly plausible and does *not* beg the question against the incompatibilist, even on the assumption of causal determinism. Thus I believe that the use of the "prior-sign" cases can be defended against the charge of begging the question."[63] But as we shall now see, he's been forced to change his mind in response to an argument by Stewart Goetz.

Agential focus

Stewart Goetz has recently argued that the two-step strategies of Fischer, as well as Haji and McKenna, fail for the same reason that the proponents of the Dilemma Defense originally offered:

> Contrary to what Fischer claims, his two-step argument begs the question against the incompatibilist in the same way that one-step arguments do: it assumes, because it requires, the truth of causal determinism in the actual sequence of events. It requires the truth of causal determinism in order to create the *illusion* that it is the presence of something in the alternative sequence of events (e.g. Black's device) that makes it the case that Jones is not free to choose otherwise. It is only through the creation of this illusion and the fact that Black's device is not explaining Jones' actual choice that one is tempted or inclined to endorse the conclusion of the first step of Fischer's argument, which is that the lack of alternative possibilities is not sufficient for the lack of moral responsibility.[64]

Goetz's argument here requires some unpacking. Let us focus on the first of the two steps given by the compatibilist rejoinders to the Dilemma Defense. According to this step, the lack of alternative possibilities does not in itself ground a claim that the agent is not free. And why not? Presumably this would be because in the actual sequence of an *FSC*, the counterfactual intervener is both (a) causally inert (i.e., the counterfactual intervener plays no role in the unfolding of the actual sequence) and (b) sufficient, by his mere presence, to rule out the agent's alternative possibilities. This second element, (b), is what drives the intuition—or what Goetz calls the "illusion"— that his mere presence, and not involvement, cannot undermine the agent's moral responsibility. And what Goetz is claiming is that the only way for the counterfactual intervener to play this second role in the alternate sequence is if determinism were true in both sequences—for if it weren't, then the presence of Black's device couldn't ensure that the agent has no alternative possibilities, and for the same reasons claimed by the proponents of the Dilemma Defense earlier. In other words, unless determinism is assumed to be true, Black isn't able to rule out all alternative possibilities.[65] But once this point is granted, then the presence of Black and his device are not themselves necessary for establishing Jones's lack of alternative possibilities; they are instead irrelevant:

[An *FSC*] creates the appearance that it is Black's device, which is in the alternative sequence of events, that makes it the case that Jones is not free to choose otherwise. This appearance is illusory because without the obtaining of causal determinism in the actual sequence of events, the device cannot prevent Jones from making an alternative choice, and with causal determinism in the actual sequence of events it is not the device that prevents Jones from making an alternative choice. In short, if Jones is not free to choose otherwise, it is because of the occurrence of causal determinism in the actual sequence of events and not because of Black's device in the alternative sequence.[66]

More recently, Goetz has reiterated this line of argumentation:

Fischer believes that we can conclude from the first step of the argument that includes an FSC such as FSC1 that for all we know, Jones *might* be morally responsible for his choice even though he could not choose otherwise and, thus, that PAP is false. Whether it is plausible to think that he *is* morally responsible or not depends in part upon the second step in the argument which asks whether or not causal determinism *directly* or *by itself* rules out moral responsibility. ... What is one to think of Fischer's two-step argument? In the end, it is difficult to see how it advances the debate between compatibilists and incompatibilists. This is because, contrary to what Fischer claims, his two-step argument begs the question against the incompatibilist (libertarian) in the same way that one-step arguments do: It assumes, because it requires, the truth of causal determinism in the actual sequence of events.[67]

In light of this argument, Fischer has recently changed his mind about how best to respond to the Dilemma Defense. Though he grants that his earlier argument is "unsound," he still thinks that he is able "to present a refined articulation of the basic insight I have been seeking to capture."[68] He argues against Goetz's critique by presupposing agnosticism toward the claim that the truth of determinism would preclude alternative possibilities.[69] As we'll see in Chapter 8, agnosticism at this point is already part of Fischer's own view. But if the Consequence Argument discussed in Chapter 2 is correct, then this agnosticism is unwarranted.[70]

Obviously, the dialectic between proponents of the Dilemma Defense and its opponents is getting fairly complicated at this point.[71] For present purposes, we need not pursue it further. For while the various parties involved might disagree on what the relevant features of the actual sequence need to be for the agent to be morally responsible, what they all seem to agree on is that what is of central importance for whether or not the agent is acting freely is the actual sequence. The alternate sequence will be important only indirectly, that is, only insofar as the nature of the alternate sequence (such as whether or not Black's presence is sufficient to rule out alternative possibilities) indicates truths about the actual sequence (such as whether or not causal determinism is true). Furthermore, what is important for the agent's freedom, or the lack thereof, is not simply general features about the actual sequence, but specifically features about the agent in the actual sequence. One way of understanding the above dialectic between Kane and Widerker on the one hand, and Fischer, Haji, and McKenna on the other is in terms of whether or not the agent's being causally determined is a relevant feature. Regardless of how this debate is ultimately settled, I believe that a significant benefit of this debate is the increased focus on features of the agent in the actual sequence. Such features will also be central to the discussions of the Flicker of Freedom Strategy in the following chapter.

CHAPTER SEVEN

Flickers of freedom

Introduction

As introduced in Chapter 5, the "Flicker of Freedom Strategy" is the second general line of response given by incompatibilists to *FSCs*. What the Flicker Strategy aims to show is that despite what is often claimed, *FSCs* do not actually present cases where the agent is free and yet lacks alternative possibilities; thus, they fail to show that *AP* is false. In what follows, I argue that there are, in fact, two different ways to understand the Flicker Strategy, one of which is dialectically stronger than the other. According to the first version of the Flicker Strategy, it is in principle impossible for *FSCs* to show that alternative possibilities of some sort are not required for free will. This strategy, however, will not have much dialectical force against the compatibilist insofar as it presupposes the truth of incompatibilism rather than providing an argument for it. The second version of the Flicker Strategy is stronger insofar as it attempts to argue for the necessity of more robust alternative possibilities; however, it is less clear that this stronger version can be shown to withstand objections.

The flicker strategy

In response to the claim that *FSCs* show *AP* to be false, some incompatibilists seek to find previously unnoticed alternative possibilities that still exist in *FSCs*. These incompatibilists claim that if one can still find alternative possibilities that exist between the actual and alternate scenarios of an *FSC*, then the *FSC* will have failed to show that one does not need alternative possibilities in order to be free after all. Contrary to what *FSCs* claim, the argument goes, there always remain alternative possibilities and, thus, *FSCs* do not show that *AP* is false. Though himself a compatibilist and a defender of *FSCs*, it was John Martin Fischer who introduced talk of the "Flicker of Freedom Strategy" into the free will debate.[1] In his *The Metaphysics of Free Will*, which has since become one of the most influential works in the compatibilism/incompatibilism debate, Fischer describes the Flicker Strategy as follows:

> The Frankfurt-type cases seem at first to involve no alternate possibilities. But upon closer inspection it can be seen that, although they do not involve alternative possibilities of the normal kind, they nevertheless may involve *some* alternative possibilities. That is to say, although the counterfactual interveners eliminate most alternative possibilities, arguably they do not eliminate *all* such possibilities: even in the Frankfurt-type cases, there seems to be a "flicker of freedom". Thus, there is an opening to argue that these alternative possibilities (the flickers of freedom) *must* be present, even in the Frankfurt-type cases, in order for there to be moral responsibility. ... One can see that there *are* such possibilities, if one scratches the surface just a bit. And although they may not be quite the alternative possibilities traditionally envisaged, they are alternative possibilities nonetheless—and just the sort that would be ruled out ... by causal determinism.[2]

Fischer distinguishes four different ways that the Flicker Strategy could be stated:

1 The agent always has the alternate possibility of causing the prior sign or not.

2 The agent always has the alternate possibility of causing a different event-particular.

3 The agent always has the alternate possibility of agent-causing the action or not.

4 The agent always has the alternative possibility of doing the action on-her-own or not.[3]

I am not concerned here with the differences between these formulations, and thus for purposes of simplicity will present and discuss the Flicker Strategy along the lines of only one of the four options.[4] So, for example, consider an *FSC* involving agent *S*, intervener *B*, and action *A*. In the actual sequence, *S* does *A* on-her-own while *S* does *A* only as a result of *B*'s intervention in the alternate sequence. Thus, the Flicker Strategist claims there are still alternative possibilities in this *FSC*. Furthermore, it looks as if any *FSC* will necessarily contain some alternative possibilities analogous to these. As McKenna and Widerker note, "strictly speaking, Frankfurt examples do not rule out all alternative possibilities since there do exist, built right into the examples, flickers of freedom."[5]

The weak flicker strategy

Fischer grants that the Flicker Strategy is appealing; however, he does not think that it is ultimately convincing. His reasons for this will become apparent below. But Fischer's criticisms will make more sense if we first differentiate two different ways that the Flicker Strategy can be understood to be functioning in the dialectic. The present section will explore the first of these; the second will be explored in the following section.

The first way of understanding the Flicker Strategy begins by noting that the only way it would seem possible to get rid of all alternative possibilities open to the agent in an *FSC* would be to assume the truth of determinism.[6] Fischer himself admits that the truth of determinism would rule out all alternative possibilities: "For in such a world [i.e., a causally deterministic world] there cannot be even a flicker of freedom. ... Of course, causal determinism would extinguish not just a prairie fire of freedom, but also the tiniest flicker."[7] He also admits that "there are ineliminable alternative possibilities (given the assumption of indeterminism)."[8] Thus, given the Flicker Strategist's insistence on the incompatibility of causal determinism and free will, the Flicker Strategy can be understood as involving an alternative-possibilities condition of the following sort:

AP_f: an agent is free with respect to an action A at time t only if there are morally relevant alternative possibilities related to A at time t.[9]

Given that all *FSCs* involve some alternative possibilities, the Flicker Strategist might insist that AP_f is not refuted by *FSCs*.[10] In other words, the Flicker Strategist can insist that the relevant alternative possibilities condition needed by the incompatibilist is AP_f. Let us call this version of the Flicker Strategy the "Weak Strategy." Since causal determinism removes all alternative possibilities, AP_f and the Weak Strategy preserve the incompatibilist's position that free will is incompatible with the truth of causal determinism—that is, one can be free only if indeterminism is true.

According to the Weak Strategy, the alternatives remaining in an *FSC*, however minute, are relevant to free will and thus also to moral responsibility. If the falsity of determinism is relevant to free will, as the incompatibilist under consideration claims, then any alternative possibilities are also morally relevant in that they are a necessary presupposition for the agent's being free. Even if it turns out that the remaining alternative possibilities are not relevant to free will in any further way, or tell us nothing further about the nature of free will, beyond being a sign that the necessary conditions for freedom are satisfied, their absence is sufficient for the incompatibilist to claim that an agent is not free. As Alfred Mele notes, the Weak Strategy "can get significant mileage out of some flickers of freedom, given the indeterminism that those flickers require."[11] The presence of these alternative possibilities, no matter what sort of alternatives they may be, is sufficient for the falsity of causal determinism. Thus, these remaining alternative possibilities can be understood as the "flicker in the absence of which one cannot be free."[12]

According to the Weak Strategy, if one can find alternative possibilities in the actual and alternate sequences of an *FSC*, then the *FSC* will not have shown that all alternative possibilities conditions are false.[13] Given that even Fischer agrees that all *FSCs* contain some alternative possibilities, it looks like no possible counterexample can be given to AP_r. As a result, *FSCs* will not give any reason for abandoning all versions of *AP*. Furthermore, if one thinks that the falsity of an alternative-possibilities condition provides motivation for abandoning incompatibilism, as Frankfurt appears to have thought, the Weak Strategy will also undercut this reason to reject incompatibilism. So long as we keep in mind the relationship between *AP* and *PAP* discussed in Chapter 1, this same point can also be seen in the following comments by Ted Warfield:

> What in Frankfurt's work on *PAP* is supposed to support the claim that moral responsibility is consistent with causal determinism? Clearly it is the "Frankfurt stories" that are supposed to do this. Frankfurt stories … are stories that at least strongly suggest that moral responsibility is consistent with a lack of alternative possibilities. Many think that causal determinism threatens moral responsibility *precisely by* precluding alternative possibilities. So if Frankfurt cases show that the removal of alternative possibilities does not thereby remove moral responsibility, then Frankfurt stories provide at least some reason to think that R-Compatibilism [i.e., the thesis that moral responsibility and causal determinism are compatible] is true.[14]

But this is precisely what *FSCs* cannot do if the Weak Strategy holds, since *FSCs* are *not* cases in which the agent has no alternative possibilities. In order to be a counterexample to AP_r, an *FSC* would have to show that at the precise moment of the agent's action there was only one physically possible future. Of course, if the agent's action was determined, this would be sufficient for there being only one physically possible future. But, as discussed in Chapter 6, there is reason to think that determinism cannot be assumed in this way without begging the question against the incompatibilist. And it is hard to see what else would be able to eliminate all alternative possibilities.[15]

When incompatibilists put forth a version of the Flicker Strategy, it is often the Weak Strategy that they endorse. For example, both Michael Della Rocca[16] and Ted Warfield[17] appear to endorse the Weak Strategy, and Alfred Mele discusses it (though without ultimately endorsing it).[18] In fact, it looks as if the most prominent opponent of the Flicker Strategy, Fischer himself, is willing to grant that the alternative possibilities that remain will be morally significant for the proponent of the Weak Strategy. Considering an argument from Mele much to the same effect as the Weak Strategy, Fischer writes that "*if* one believes that moral responsibility requires the lack of causal determinism in the actual sequence, then the existence of alternative possibilities of any sort would be relevant (even if indirectly) to ascriptions of moral responsibility."[19] It then looks like no non-question-begging counterexample to AP_f can be given. Fischer himself countenances this possibility:

> The flicker theorist may not dispute the claim that the alternative possibilities in the Frankfurt-type examples are insufficiently robust to *ground* our ascriptions of moral responsibility. That is to say, he may not wish to argue that the existence of such alternatives in themselves supports our intuitive judgments that individuals are morally responsible for what they do. But he nevertheless may insist that alternative possibilities *must be present*, whenever an agent is legitimately held morally responsible for what he does. ... Thus, we have as yet no decisive reason to abandon the claim that moral responsibility requires the *presence* of alternative possibilities, even if the presence of these alternatives is not in itself what drives our judgments about moral responsibility. ... The flicker theorist's move could be formulated as follows. Even if the alternative possibilities are not what explain our intuitions about moral responsibility, nevertheless there may be some *other factor* which *both* grounds our responsibility ascriptions and *also* entails that there be some alternative possibility (thin and weak as it may be). And if this were so, then moral responsibility would require alternative possibilities, even thin and weak ones.[20]

Fischer apparently grants that the Weak Strategy could be used "to fan the flickers of freedom,"[21] and further admits that he has no conclusive argument against such a strategy.[22]

The robustness requirement

However, Fischer is not willing to let the debate over the flickers end here. Even if one cannot give an *FSC* that refutes AP_f, he hopes to undermine the case for incompatibilism by arguing that the remaining flickers do not pack enough "metaphysical oomph" to help establish incompatibilism. The alternative possibilities that remain in such cases, according to Fischer, are "essentially irrelevant"[23] to whether or not an agent has free will. It is this idea that is behind Fischer's requirement that the remaining alternative possibilities must be "robust" enough for the work they do in incompatibilism: "I am willing to grant to the flicker theorist the claim that there exists an alternative possibility here; but my basic worry is that this alternative possibility is not sufficiently *robust* to ground the relevant attributions of moral responsibility."[24] In a later article, he puts this same point as follows:

> I would argue that it is not enough for the critic of the Frankfurt-style examples to argue that there exist *some* alternative possibilities in these cases, no matter how flimsy or exiguous; if one grounds moral responsibility in alternative possibilities, I believe they must be *of a certain sort*.[25]

He thus disputes the claim in AP_f that the alternative possibilities that remain as pointed at by the Weak Strategy are *morally relevant*. Fischer thinks that the incompatibilist who wishes to defend *AP* must not only show that *FSCs* contain alternative possibilities, but also that the remaining alternative possibilities are relevant for free will in some way beyond *merely* insuring the falsity of determinism. Let us call this "the Robustness Requirement."[26] It is with respect to the Robustness Requirement that Fischer thinks the remaining alternative possibilities fail—the remaining flickers simply are not robust enough. Furthermore, Fischer thinks that the incompatibilist should also see the need for the remaining alternative possibilities to meet the Robustness Requirement: "If you buy into this traditional picture [according to which free will and moral responsibility require alternative possibilities], then you should also accept that the alternative possibilities must be of a certain sort—they must be sufficiently robust."[27]

There is something intuitive behind the Robustness Requirement; however, in order to evaluate its truth, we need to precisify what it is claiming.[28] How exactly should the Robustness Requirement be understood? A number of different formulations can be found in the literature. In his contribution to *The Oxford Handbook on Free Will*, Fischer writes that in order for alternative possibilities to be relevant to moral responsibility, "those alternative possibilities must contain voluntary behavior" in order for them to be a "sufficiently robust basis for moral responsibility."[29] However, given the fact that Fischer advances an actual-sequence view of free will, where an agent's having free will is solely a function of features of the actual sequence, it is strange that he would endorse an alternative-sequence view of robustness.[30] Alternatively, Derk Pereboom suggests that in order for an alternative possibility to be "robust," it must be that the agent "could have willed something other than what she actually willed such that she understood that by willing it she would thereby have been precluded from the moral responsibility that she actually has for the action."[31] In Chapter 1, I agreed that there is an epistemic requirement on free will. And while I admit it is hard to know how to specify the exact nature of this requirement, Pereboom's suggestion here regarding the epistemic feature of robustness is too demanding. An agent might be morally responsible for actions even if she fails to understand that by doing something else she could escape the moral responsibility that she actually bears; she might, for example, be *culpably* ignorant of the moral status of her relevant options. So while I agree that there is an epistemic dimension to moral responsibility, I doubt that it is as stringent as Pereboom's approach to robustness suggests.

Finally, consider the following suggestion by Michael McKenna. According to McKenna, two conditions are required for an alternative possibility to be robust:

1   The alternative must be morally significant.
2   The alternative must be within the scope of the agent's control.[32]

Presumably, while the Weak Strategy would satisfy the first of these conditions, the mere falsity of causal determinism would not mandate which of a plethora of open alternatives becomes actual is within the agent's control. Instead, there must be some feature of the agent such that by having that feature, the agent is the source for which alternative becomes actual in a free choice. McKenna's second condition thus foreshadows the debates about sourcehood that will be explored in subsequent chapters of this book. In order to avoid having to enter the issues about the nature of sourcehood at the present moment, let me use the following understanding of the Robustness Requirement for the remainder of this chapter.

> *Robustness Requirement*: an alternative possibility is "robust" only if the presence of that alternative possibility is relevant for moral responsibility in some way beyond *merely* pointing out that determinism is false.[33]

According to this understanding of the Robustness Requirement, alternative possibilities are not robust if they merely meet the aim of the Weak Strategy discussed in the previous section. Fischer would, at times, seem to agree:

> Even if the possible event at the terminus of the alternative sequence [as pointed out by the Weak Strategy] ... is indeed an alternative possibility, it is highly implausible to suppose that it is *in virtue* of the existence of such an alternative possibility that Jones is morally responsible for what he does. I suggest that it is not enough for the flicker theorist to analyze the relevant range of cases in such a way as to identify an alternative possibility. Although this is surely a first step, it is not enough to establish the flicker of freedom view.[34]

Thus, Fischer appears to think that the proponent of the Flicker Strategy needs to move beyond the Weak Strategy and show how the remaining alternative possibilities satisfy the Robustness Requirement.

The strong flicker strategy

Let us then define the "Strong Strategy" as a version of the Flicker Strategy that attempts to show that the remaining alternative possibilities can satisfy the Robustness Requirement.[35] That is, the Strong Strategy will show that the remaining alternative possibilities are relevant to the agent's responsibility. A number of incompatibilists have tried to show the relevance of the remaining alternative possibilities, and Fischer has canvassed these attempts to secure alternatives meeting the Robustness Requirement. For example, in *The Metaphysics of Free Will* he considers the notions of origination, initiation, being active rather than passive, and creativity.[36] With respect to each of these, Fischer thinks that compatibilists and incompatibilists alike can give an account of these notions, and that "there is no strong reason to opt for the incompatibilist interpretation, *apart from considerations pertaining to alternative-possibilities.*"[37] I explore the related notions of origination and initiation in further detail in the discussion of sourcehood in future chapters, where the Robustness Requirement will come up again.[38] But in this chapter I want to focus instead on a noteworthy recent incompatibilist attempt to defend the Strong Strategy, one offered by Daniel Speak.[39]

Speak doesn't make the distinction I've introduced here between the Weak Strategy and the Strong Strategy. He does, however, think there is something unsatisfactory with certain forms of the Flicker of Freedom Strategy, and I think his dissatisfaction is best seen as directed to the Weak Strategy. According to Speak, the problem with the Flicker Strategy when understood as the Weak Strategy is that

> it is satisfied with the cold coherence of incompatibilism. That is, it provides a way to vindicate incompatibilist intuitions—but in a way that can only have force for incompatibilists. ... Intuitively, we should prefer a response to the flicker argument that can, in principle, be offered persuasively to the compatibilist.[40]

Speak attempts to do this by providing a way of understanding the remaining alternative possibilities that the compatibilist could grant as morally relevant.[41]

According to Speak, what is needed beyond the Weak Strategy is to show that "these seemingly attenuated alternatives could *possibly* be relevant to our attributions of moral responsibility."[42] Speak attempts to meet this challenge and, in doing so, advances a novel version of the Strong Strategy. Speak labels the principle underlying the Robustness Requirement "the Principle of Relevant Alternatives" (or *PRA*):

> *PRA*: An alternative is relevant (i.e., it could play a role in our attribution of responsibility) only if it is one in which the agent could properly be held accountable for something.[43]

The problem with the Weak Strategy, according to Speak, is that it does not satisfy *PRA*. What the incompatibilist needs to show is that, contrary to Fischer's evaluation, *PRA* is not refuted by *FSCs* in the way that Fischer thinks. Furthermore, given that Fischer's argument against the indirect relevance of the remaining flickers is the only one currently offered by compatibilists, "the failure of this argument to establish the impossibility of relevance should be seen as *prima facie* evidence for its possibility."[44]

Speak's strategy to defend *PRA* is as follows: The agent's having the remaining alternative possibilities can be used to ground moral obligations, which *mutatis mutandis* can ground moral responsibility. If this strategy works, then the appearance that *FSCs* violate *PRA* will be "due to the way in which many formulations of Frankfurt examples obscure the existence of moral responsibility in the affected sequence."[45] In defense of *PRA*, Speak gives the following *FSC*-like example:

> Suppose Garvin is a member of our U.S. Marine Corps. On a mission in an active war zone he is captured by enemy troops. Now the leader of this rebel force had devised a wicked form of mental torture. Having also captured Garvin's close friend Johansen, the leader forcibly "connects" Garvin to a rifle aimed directly at Johansen, his finger placed lightly but unavoidably on the trigger. Now suppose the enemy leader informs Garvin that he can simply pull the trigger and have it over with, or he can wait for the initiation of an electrical impulse which will inevitably produce the same effect. Garvin's finger *will* pull the trigger, and Johansen *will* be killed … in either case. So, what ought Garvin to do? Most will grant that Garvin has a *prima facie* duty not to pull the trigger on his own.[46]

Let us stipulate that Garvin has no contravening duty to pull the trigger which outweighs his duty *not* to pull the trigger on his own. According to Speak, in such a case Garvin has a duty proper to avoid pulling the trigger on his own, and "having a duty to perform an act (or to fail to perform an act) seems to imply that one would be morally responsible for one's act should one act dutifully."[47] In the alternate sequence of this scenario in which Garvin is manipulated or coerced into shooting Johansen, he does not control his action. He shoots Johansen only because of his refusal to pull the trigger on his own. But if Garvin still has the duty not to pull the trigger on his own in the alternate sequence, then the alternate sequence is such that Garvin can be held accountable for something in it (i.e. whether or not he chooses so as to fulfill his duty) and *PRA* is fulfilled. The alternative possibilities existing in the alternate sequence are thus morally relevant, as required by the Strong Strategy. Speak concludes that scenarios like the Garvin/Johansen case "show that we can imagine scenarios with Frankfurt-style interveners in which the intervention does not cancel out all responsibility. Agents can be morally responsible in some affected sequences because they can be obligated in these sequences."[48]

What should one make of Speak's argument? The first response is to note that even if the Garvin/Johansen case does preserve *PRA*, and thus vindicates the Strong Strategy, it is not clear that all *FSCs* can be shown to preserve *PRA* in the same manner. Consider, for example, an *FSC* such as those discussed earlier in which the agent's action is prefigured by a morally neutral prior sign, such as a blush. Suppose that whether or not Jones involuntarily blushes is correlated with the action that the counterfactual intervener desires him to do. (At this point, one might be tempted to raise the Dilemma Defense, discussed in Chapter 6. In personal correspondence, Speak writes as follows: "my response to the flicker strategy presupposes that the F-cases [i.e. *FSCs*] haven't begged the relevant questions. So, I've already set aside the prior sign cases on these grounds. I'm already on board with Widerker, Kane, etc. when I introduce Garvin and Johansen." In other words, Speak appears to think that the relationship between the prior sign and the action in this *FSC* would be problematic. However, if my arguments in Chapter 6 are correct, then I do not think it is infelicitous for me to use an example involving a prior sign in order to make the present point.) Can we say that Jones has a duty to refrain from blushing? Not everyone involved in this debate thinks so. Michael McKenna, for one, argues that a blush cannot serve as the locus for moral responsibility "since, quite obviously, such an episode is not something over which a person could normally exercise any kind of control."[49] It is hard to see what such a duty not to blush involuntarily could amount to. So even if Speak has shown that some *FSCs* do not violate *PRA*, it is not clear that all *FSCs* are similar in this way. And given that *AP* is a claim about what is necessary for free will (and thus also for moral responsibility), even one *FSC* in which *PRA* is not satisfied is enough to sever the link between free will and *PRA*.[50]

Speak would not be satisfied with this response, for he claims that it is not his intention to show that every *FSC* contained obligations in the alternate sequence. Rather, his intention is to show that an alternative isn't necessarily irrelevant simply in virtue of its containing intervention. "For, if *PRA* is not violated in the obligation cases, then why think it is violated in the ordinary Frankfurt-style cases?"[51] This, he thinks, is sufficient to shift the burden of proof back to the opponent of the Strong Strategy, since the Garvin/Johansen case provides "support for the claim that these sorts of [remaining] alternatives could *possibly* play such a role."[52] One response would be to remind Speak that, on his own account, the alternate sequence satisfies *PRA* in virtue of Garvin having an obligation in that sequence. No obligation, no satisfaction of *PRA*.[53] Speak admits that his argument for the Strong Strategy is a "plausibility argument" rather than a "knock-down appeal to indubitable principles."[54] But, in cases such as the one involving a blush, it does not look plausible that the agent has the sort of moral obligation needed to ground the relevance of the alternate sequence.[55]

Nevertheless, I think one can make a more forceful objection to the Garvin/Johansen case. This more promising reply to Speak's example is to pursue a strategy that he himself suggests, namely to undermine the salience of the comparison between his case and typical *FSC*s. Speak notes two ways that his modified case differs from traditional *FSC*s. The first is that, by involving the ending of a life rather than some more mundane event of the sort often involved in *FSC*s, his modified case is "intentionally loaded from a moral standpoint."[56] Speak thinks that this modification is innocuous, and I agree.

However, the same is not true of the second way in which Speak's example differs from traditional *FSC*s. In the Garvin/Johansen case, unlike normal *FSC*s, the agent in question (i.e., Garvin) is aware of the presence of the counterfactual intervener. He knows that if he does not perform the action in question on his own, the intervener will take the needed steps to guarantee that he does what the intervener wants him to do (in Speak's example, pull the trigger). Given that there is an epistemic condition on moral responsibility, it looks as if had Garvin not known about the intervener and his ensuring mechanism, then he would not have the obligation in the alternate sequence. In response to this objection, Speak's reply is "to point out that Garvin's knowledge of the leader's power and intentions can be removed, and the result is the same. This knowledge, it seems, plays no role in our assessment of obligation."[57]

I do not think, however, that we should be so quick to dismiss the implications of Garvin's knowledge for his moral responsibility.[58] Consider the following two variants of the Garvin/Johansen case. In the first, let us call it *Variant 1*, Garvin *does not* have knowledge of the intervener's desire and ability to make him pull the trigger. Garvin refrains from pulling the trigger on his own and the intervener steps in and forces Garvin to pull the trigger, killing Johansen. In the second variant, *Variant 2*, Garvin *does* have knowledge of the intervener's desire and ability to force him to kill Johansen. That is, Garvin knows that if he does not pull the trigger by a certain time, t, then the intervener will step in at t. Garvin does not pull the trigger on his own by t, and again, as in the first variant of the story, the intervener steps in and forces Garvin to pull the trigger. *Variant 1* is like the alternative sequence of standard *FSC*s, and the standard evaluation is that Garvin is not morally responsible for Johansen's death. But the same is not true of *Variant 2*. This scenario is, at present, under-described for us to know whether or not Garvin is morally responsible. It seems to me that we are justified in withholding our moral judgment of Garvin until we find out more about Garvin's mental states. If Garvin did not desire Johansen's death, then he would not be morally responsible for Johansen's death. On the other hand, if Garvin desired Johansen's death, then knowing that the intervener would force him to pull the trigger at t (and knowing that an agent is not morally responsible for a coerced act), Garvin's desire for Johansen's death could lead him to withhold pulling the trigger on his own and yet still intentionally bring about Johansen's death via the enemy's intervention. My intuition regarding such a case is that Garvin is at least partly morally responsible for Johansen's death in *Variant 2*.[59]

Even if one does not share my intuition here, notice that if we add the same desire of Garvin's that we find in *Variant 1* to *Variant 2*, our intuitions about his moral responsibility aren't affected. Garvin's desire for Johansen's death is not appropriately connected to his pulling of the trigger to make him morally responsible. (Remember, in *Variant 1*, it is the intervener that brings about Garvin's pulling of the trigger through intervention.) This suggests that, contrary to Speak's claim, the addition of knowledge about the counterfactual intervener in his example, and the lack of such knowledge in traditional *FSCs*, may make a moral difference. For this reason, I think there is reason to think that Speak has not succeeded in offering a viable version of the Strong Strategy regarding traditional *FSCs*.

Another recent proposal comes from Brendan Larvor. Recall from above that a proposal counts as a version of the Strong Strategy if and only if it holds that the alternative possibilities remaining in a FSC are robust, that is, only if they are ones which play a role in our attribution of responsibility. Larvor thinks that Frankfurt's original case fails to present a counterexample to *PAP* not simply because the existence of the remaining alternative possibilities show that causal determinism is false, but because even in the original *FSC* "Jones has the option of not killing Smith."[60] Larvor begins by focusing on the revisability of our decisions, but the core of Larvor's criticism doesn't depend upon a close inspection of revisability. Instead, Larvor focuses our attention on the alternate sequence in which Black forces Jones to kill Smith. In this alternate sequence

> Black presses his button, initiating a reliable causal chain that ends in Smith's death. This is Black's deed. The fact that the causal chain that passes through parts of Jones's body does not make it *Jones's* deed. Jones is merely *Black's* unwilling instrument. In this scenario, it would be false to say that *Jones* kills Smith.[61]

According to Larvor, not only does Frankfurt's original *FSC* contain alternative possibilities (as proponents of the Weak Strategy hold), but it contains morally significant alternatives: in the actual sequence Jones does the deed of killing Smith, while in the alternate sequence it is Black who does it. In other words, a difference between the two sequences is who is responsible for killing Smith. This difference, he thinks, satisfies the Robustness Requirement. Furthermore, Larvor holds that "this result holds for all the various elaborations of Frankfurt's original thought experiment."[62] *FSCs* thus fail to refute *PAP*.[63]

Of course, proponents of *FSCs*, such as Fischer, will not agree that Larvor has in fact presented a successful version of the Strong Strategy. Where then does the debate surrounding this version of the Flicker Strategy stand? The first thing to note is that even if no currently developed version of incompatibilism meets the Robustness Requirement, this does not entail that forthcoming versions of incompatibilism will similarly fail. To show that no future brand of incompatibilism could satisfy the Robustness Requirement, the compatibilist would need an *in-principle* reason why no such argument could be given, and it is hard to see how this could be done without begging the question against the incompatibilist.

Dialectical considerations

In a recent paper addressing the Robustness Requirement, Michael Robinson admonishes us to keep separate two different, though obviously related, issues concerning the alternative possibilities that remain in an *FSC*:

> Perhaps the biggest problem with the robustness objection, then, is that it seems to run together two separate issues. First, do Frankfurt-type counterexamples falsify the view that moral responsibility for what one does requires alternative possibilities? [Both Robinson and I think the correct answer to this question is no.] Second, what does the mere possession of alternative possibilities add to an agent who already satisfies all the other necessary conditions for moral responsibility save the ability to do otherwise? These questions, though related, are in fact quite distinct, and answering the former does not require answering the latter. Whereas the second question has to do with whether alternative possibilities are in fact necessary for moral responsibility, the first is concerned merely with whether Frankfurt-type counterexamples show that they are not. One may wonder, of course, what the mere possession of alternative possibilities adds to an agent who already satisfies all the other necessary conditions for morally responsible agency save the ability to do otherwise. This is a fair question. It is important to see, however, that it does not directly bear on the issue of whether Frankfurt-type counterexamples are successful in falsifying PAP.[64]

I think that Robinson is exactly right here; furthermore, the distinction between the two questions is related to the difference between the Weak and Strong versions of the Flicker Strategy. How then should we understand, at this point, the relationship between the Weak and Strong Strategies and the larger compatibilism/incompatibilism debate they are a part of? I think that flicker opponents and defenders alike have often confused the two strategies (or, to be more charitable, have written in such a way that the reader could easily believe that they were confused). For example, consider Fischer's treatment of the Flicker Strategy. As we saw above, Fischer grants that the compatibilist has no definitive argument against the Weak Strategy. However, it looks to me that he is not always considering the Weak Strategy. For instance, when discussing the importance of *FSCs*, Fischer writes that "the Frankfurt-type examples have the important function of *shifting the debate* away from considerations pertinent to the relationship between causal determinism and alternative possibilities."[65] This statement will be true, however, only if one is considering the Strong Strategy insofar as the issue there focuses on the Robustness Requirement, and not the mere presence or absence of alternative possibilities. Let us then look at each version of the Flicker Strategy and their place in the compatibilism/incompatibilism debate in turn.

As noted above, the Weak Strategy and AP_f are immune to *FSCs*. However, the Weak Strategy is neither an argument for incompatibilism nor can it be used as part of a larger argument for incompatibilism. In responding to the challenge posed by *FSCs*, the Weak Strategy claims that any alternative possibilities existing due to the falsity of causal determinism are a necessary precondition for an agent being free. The Weak Strategy thus *assumes* that free will is incompatible with determinism. If the Weak Strategy were to be incorporated into an argument for incompatibilism, it would beg the question against the compatibilist. But it is not the goal of the Weak Strategy to argue for the incompatibility of determinism and free will. Rather, the Weak Strategy should be understood as follows. For one who is already an incompatibilist, the Weak Strategy means that *FSCs* do not show incompatibilism to be false in virtue of demonstrating the falsity of all alternative possibilities conditions. Thus understood, the Weak Strategy is useless in the compatibilism/incompatibilism debate except in a defensive role. Since the compatibilist rejects the incompatibility of determinism and free will, she will not be swayed by the Weak Strategy's insistence that the remaining flickers, and the indeterminism they point to, are morally relevant.

The Strong Strategy, on the other hand, would have significant relevance for the compatibilism/incompatibilism debate. A version of the Strong Strategy, that is, an incompatibilist account of alternative possibilities that meets the Robustness Requirement, would show that contrary to what Frankfurt claims to have shown, alternative possibilities are required for free will and moral responsibility. Furthermore, if a successful Strong Strategy was joined with a rejection of subjunctive accounts of the ability to do otherwise, it would constitute a formidable argument for incompatibilism. But until such a defense of the Strong Strategy can be developed, it looks as if both compatibilism and incompatibilism are defensible positions when we consider the relationship between free will and alternative possibilities, for neither has a knock-down argument against the other. How then should we understand the current state of the compatibilism/incompatibilism debate? In answering this question, it will be helpful to begin with a suggestion first advocated by Fischer over a decade ago. In *The Metaphysics of Free Will*, Fischer suggested that advocates and opponents of *AP* have reached a "Dialectical Stalemate", which he describes as follows.

> Consider a philosophical argument in which one argues for some claim
> C on the basis of a principle P which supports that claim. The proponent

of *C* may support *P* by invoking a set of examples or other considerations which provides reason for accepting *P*. But the opponent of the argument may respond that the examples are not sufficient to establish *P*; rather, all the examples establish is a weaker principle, *P´*. Furthermore, unlike *P*, *P´* does not support *C*. And the opponent of *C* does not see how one could decisively establish *P*. One reason it is so difficult is that it at least appears that one cannot invoke a particular example which would *decisively* establish *P* without begging the question in a straightforward fashion against either the opponent of *P* or the opponent of *C*. Further, it *also* seems that one cannot invoke a particular example which would *decisively* refute *P* without begging the question against the proponent of *P* or the proponent of *C*. These conditions mark out a distinctive—and particularly precarious—spot in dialectical space.[66]

And more recently, Michael McKenna has argued that a dialectical stalemate "arises when opposing positions within a reasoned debate reach points at which each side's arguments remain reasonable, even compelling, but in which argument runs out; neither can rightly claim decisively to have unseated the legitimacy of the other side's point of view."[67]

In these sorts of circumstances, Fischer thinks, further arguments would be begging the question since the two sides of the debate begin with different premises, often based on intuitions that the other side denies: "I suggest that some of the debates about whether alternative possibilities are required for moral responsibility may at some level be fueled by different intuitive pictures of moral responsibility."[68] If this is true, then perhaps it would be true to say that not much philosophical headway has been made in the past 35 years of debate begun by Frankfurt's article. It is certainly true that much is made of various and conflicting intuitions in the debate surrounding the compatibilism/incompatibilism debate. Perhaps the debate is ultimately over which set of intuitions is more plausible, in which case we should not be surprised by the lack of a clear victor. This certainly seems to be the case, for example, between the defender of the Weak Strategy and her compatibilist opponent.

Elsewhere, however, Fischer suggests that perhaps the compatibilism/incompatibilism debate is not a dialectic stalemate (or, at the least, not the *same* dialectic stalemate that it was four decades ago). In a recent argument, Fischer writes that "Frankfurt-style compatibilism does represent a genuine advance; Frankfurt has helped to shift the debates from a context in which incompatibilism has an advantage to one in which incompatibilism has no such advantage."[69] The reason for this shift was discussed earlier in Chapter 5. Prior to Frankfurt, compatibilists and incompatibilists alike defended *AP*. But while the incompatibilist's need for *AP* was rather straightforward, compatibilists were forced to give subjunctive accounts of *AP*, affirm the agent's ability to bring about the past, or do something such that a miracle was performed. If *FSCs* do show that *AP* is false, then compatibilists would have another strategy for rejecting the Core Argument for incompatibilism.[70]

Pointing towards sourcehood

In this chapter, we've seen that there is a version of the Flicker of Freedom Strategy, the Weak Strategy, which is immune to the challenge posed by *FSCs* given that such examples have alternative possibilities built into them by their very nature. However, we also saw that this version of the strategy cannot be used to argue for the truth of incompatibilism:

> Although some philosophers were initially inclined to think that such an alternative possibility was sufficient to controvert Frankfurt's claim that the counterfactual intervener provides a counter-example to the principle of alternative possibilities, there now seems to be an acceptance that such a mere alternative (or "flicker of freedom") is too insubstantial to bear the weight of moral responsibility and so cannot be called upon to rescue the principle of alternative possibilities.[71]

The alternatives at the heart of the Weak Strategy are insufficient to ground moral responsibility, since they fail to satisfy the Robustness Requirement. Granted, these alternatives entail the falsity of causal determinism, but not all indeterminism is *per se* relevant to free will. What is needed, then, to satisfy the Robustness Requirement and secure the Strong Strategy is an account of why the remaining alternatives are morally relevant beyond simply securing the falsity of determinism. As we shall see in Part III, one subspecies of incompatibilism, a view called Source Incompatibilism, thinks that the core of free will is captured by an agent being the ultimate source of her actions. And as I shall argue in subsequent chapters, the kind of sourcehood at issue here is sufficient to also satisfy the Robustness Requirement and thus provide a way of developing a new version of the Strong Strategy.

PART THREE

The importance of sourcehood

CHAPTER EIGHT

Sourcehood and compatibilism

Moving from alternatives to sourcehood

Earlier in Chapter 2, I wrote that one finds two dominant conceptions of free will in the literature. According to the first of these, free will is primarily a function of being able to do otherwise than one in fact does; this approach sees free will as rooted in an alternative-possibilities condition such as *AP*. According to the second conception, free will is primarily a function of an agent being the ultimate source of his actions and thus free will is grounded in a sourcehood condition. The distinction between these two conceptions is orthogonal to the debate between compatibilists and incompatibilists regarding whether or not the truth of determinism would *per se* preclude agents from having free will. One can find compatibilists as well as incompatibilists working primarily within the alternative-possibilities approach, as well as compatibilists and incompatibilists working primarily within the sourcehood approach. Strong compatibilists are examples of compatibilists who embrace the first of these two conceptions, while other compatibilists such as Harry Frankfurt reject the need for alternative possibilities in favor of issues of sourcehood. Similarly, Leeway Incompatibilists are those incompatibilists who think that having alternative possibilities—and thus an alternative-possibilities condition like *AP*—is at the heart of free will; Source Incompatibilists are incompatibilists who think that free will is primarily a matter of being the ultimate source of one's actions, thereby focusing on the sourcehood condition.[1]

The chapters in Part II explored issues central to *AP*: incompatibilist and compatibilist understandings of *AP*, whether *AP* functions as a premise in an argument for the truth of incompatibilism, whether or not Frankfurt cases show *AP* to be false, etc. In discussing these issues, I argued that even if I am correct that *FSCs* do not succeed in showing *AP* and Leeway Incompatibilism to be false, they do show us something important about the nature of free will. Even if alternative-possibilities are a necessary condition for free will, not all of them will be equally morally relevant; so the focus simply on their presence (or absence) will not get at the heart of the matter.[2]

There is another way of showing this same point. Imagine a possible world in which an agent is contemplating a morally significant decision: A university professor named Kelvin is contemplating whether to get out of bed on a Saturday morning and go jogging or stay in bed and watch episodes of *Dexter* on *TiVo*. Let t be the time of Kelvin's decision; let "*P*" refer to the proposition expressing the complete history of the universe prior to time t. Let "*L*" refer to the conjunction of all the laws of nature that are true in Kelvin's universe. In the actual world, where P and L are true, Kelvin carefully weighs his options and decides at t to get out of bed and go jogging. Consider also another world, *Beta*; as in the actual world, P and L are true in *Beta*, that is, both *Beta* and the actual world have identical histories and are governed by the same laws of nature. In world *Beta*, Kelvin also weighs his options. At t, the very moment where in the actual world Kelvin decides to go jogging, God smites Kelvin dead (let this be a lesson to slothful university professors). Furthermore, let us stipulate that *Beta* and the actual world are the only two possible worlds compossible with P and L; this then is what John Fischer calls a Fischer-scenario: a scenario in which the agent dies in all of the alternative sequences open to him but one.[3]

Despite being in a Fischer-scenario, alternative possibilities remain at t: Kelvin can either decide to go jogging or he can die. There is thus leeway with regard to his future. Insofar as the truth of determinism would mean that there are not multiple open futures at t, Leeway Incompatibilists think that having the alternative possibilities available to Kelvin would satisfy some minimal alternative-possibilities condition, thereby satisfying a necessary condition for free will.[4] But consider a particular strain of Leeway Incompatibilism, which might be called "Naïve Leeway Incompatibilism." The Naïve Leeway Incompatibilist claims that it is *solely in virtue of* having such alternative possibilities, however miniscule or flimsy, that an agent satisfies the control condition for moral responsibility. In other words, on this view having any kind of alternative possibility would be sufficient for free will. To the best of my knowledge, no one actually endorses Naïve Leeway Incompatibilism in the literature, and (I think) for good reason. Even if Kelvin meets the other necessary conditions for moral responsibility, the alternative possibilities that he has in this case are not of the right sort to ground free will. It would be ludicrous to claim that Kelvin is acting freely solely in virtue of having the following alternative possibility: God could have smitten him at that very instant.

The problem with Naïve Leeway Incompatibilism is that it does not address the need for the agent involved to have control over which alternative possibility becomes actual in order to be morally responsible. Surely moral responsibility requires not just alternative possibilities but also, as Timothy

O'Connor puts it, the ability for the agent in question to "determine which tendency will come to fruition on a particular occasion."[5] Or to put the point in a slightly different way, Naïve Leeway Incompatibilism is plagued by the "chance" or "Luck" objection often raised against various forms of incompatibilism: the *mere possibility* of something else happening outside of the agent's control would undermine, rather than bolster, the kind of control necessary for moral responsibility.[6] As Fischer noted in an early paper on incompatibilist responses to Frankfurt-cases, "[f]or the agent to have control, in the relevant sense, there must be an alternate sequence in which the agent does otherwise as a result of an *appropriate sort* of chain of events."[7] A similar thread came up in Chapter 7 when discussing compatibilist responses to the Weak Flicker Strategy: the mere existence of alternative possibilities does not entail the moral relevance of such alternatives beyond indicating that causal determinism is false.

So in order to avoid the problem that besets Naïve Leeway Incompatibilism and show that the agent's remaining alternative possibilities are more directly relevant to her free will, the Leeway Incompatibilist is going to need to develop a way for the resolution of the leeway to be under the control of the agent in some appropriate way. Insofar as it is an incompatibilist theory, whatever it is about the agent in virtue of which she controls what alternative possibility becomes actual will have to be something that is not causally determined by anything outside of her. Most often, the language used at this point is that of the agent being the "source" of the action, or the action "originating" in the agent in some particular way, or the agent "initiating" the choice, or the outcome "ultimately" being up to the agent. This suggests that to avoid the apparent absurdity of Naïve Leeway Incompatibilism, the incompatibilist will have to appeal to some notion of "source" or "origination" at the heart of free will. However, to do that is to enter into discussions of the second general approach to free will and the realm of Source Incompatibilism. Derk Pereboom's work is an excellent example of just such an approach:

> I oppose a type of incompatibilism according to which the availability of alternative possibilities is the most important factor for explaining moral responsibility, and accept instead a variety that ascribes the most significant explanatory role to the way in which the agent actually produces the action. In metaphysical terms, the sort of free will required for moral responsibility does not consist most fundamentally in the availability of alternative possibilities, but rather in the agent's being the causal source of her action in a specific way.[8]

The remaining chapters of this book will explore issues surrounding sourcehood in greater detail.

Before turning to issues of sourcehood, however, one final observation regarding *AP* is worth making. As is apparent to those familiar with the free will literature from the past three decades or so, a significant amount of it focuses on the need for alternative possibilities, the importance of being able to do otherwise, how to respond to Frankfurt-type scenarios, etc. In recent years, however, much of the literature has begun to focus more directly on the issues of "sourcehood," "ultimacy," and "origination." One might think that this suggests that philosophers have traditionally thought that having alternative possibilities is more fundamental for free will than issues of sourcehood. While I think this suggestion is mistaken, I do think that the issues explored in the previous chapters of this book are important for helping to shift the focus off the mere presence of alternative possibilities toward a more metaphysically robust kind of agency.[9]

Two compatibilist accounts of sourcehood

I argued earlier that even if *FSCs* are not ultimately successful in refuting *AP*, they do give us reasons to think that the mere having of alternative possibilities is not what lies at the heart of free will. And while I argue for a version of Source Incompatibilism in subsequent chapters, the belief that free will is primarily a function of an agent being the source of her choices in a particular way is not unique to incompatibilism; as noted earlier, there are also compatibilist readings of the sourcehood requirement. In fact, the Core Argument for incompatibilism that utilizes *AP* as a key premise as well as Harry Frankfurt's critique of *AP* can both be seen as suggesting the need to focus on the source of an agent's choices. Instead of understanding free will to be a function of an agent having access to alternative possibilities, Frankfurt and other critics of *AP* suggest that we need to focus on features of the actual sequence.[10] Frankfurt, for example, advances a hierarchical account of freedom of the will.[11] According to his early position, a person has free will (or what Frankfurt calls "freedom of the will") if he has second-order volitions in the actual sequence—that is, if he has a desire that certain other of his desires actually move him to action—and if those second-order volitions mesh with his first-order desires.

> *A* wants the desire to *X* to be the desire that moves him effectively to act. It is not merely that he wants the desire to *X* to be among his desires by which, to one degree or another, he is moved or inclined to act. He wants this desire to be effective—that is, to provide the motive in what he actually does.[12]

On this view, for example, Allison freely decides to take her dog for a walk in the park if she desires to go for a walk with her dog, and she desires that the previously mentioned desire be the reason why she actually goes for a walk. Note that agents can have second-order desires even if they are in *FSCs*. Returning to the example involving Black and Jones, Jones may desire to do *X* and desire that desire to move him to action even if Black is waiting in the wings to cause Jones to do *X* if he doesn't do it on his own. So, on Frankfurt's account, having free will is primarily a function not of having alternative possibilities but of having that choice's source be located in the agent in a particular way—namely if the first-order volition meshes with the agent's second-order desire for the first-order desire to become a volition. This way of understanding free will gives a strong reason for thinking that Jones, the agent in an *FSC*, *is* choosing freely when he chooses to do *X* on his own. As Fischer notes about the actual sequence of *FSCs*, "it seems irresistible to say that the individual is the source of his behavior, given that the fail-safe device does not actually intervene (and is thus a merely *counterfactual* intervener). He is the source of his behavior."[13] But Jones is not the source of his action in the alternate sequence in which Black coerces Jones (through whatever the effective steps are) to choose *X*. In this case, Black is the source of Jones's choice and thus Jones isn't choosing freely. This, I think, gives an intuitive initial notion of the sourcehood condition (*SC*) that might be expressed as follows:

> *SC*: A person chooses freely only if he is the source (or originator or initiator) of his choice.

SC helps capture the following intuitions regarding an agent's choices:

> My choices should depend on facts about *me*!
> *I'm* the one who made it happen.
> It's in virtue of *my* activity that the world is changed.[14]

Of course, the difficulty comes in trying to spell out the particular way that an agent must be the source of his choice in order for that choice to be free. This is precisely why both incompatibilists and compatibilists have their own understandings of *SC*, just as they have their own readings of *AP*. This leads to the need for further investigation regarding exactly what it means to be the "source" of one's choices as expressed in *SC*. In the remainder of this chapter, I present and criticize two influential compatibilist accounts of sourcehood. The objections leveled against these two accounts will point us in the direction of an incompatibilist understanding of sourcehood, one that I think is at the very heart of free will, and which I explore in greater detail in Chapter 9.

Frankfurt's approach to sourcehood

One influential compatibilist understanding of *SC* can be seen in Frankfurt's account of freedom of the will. As indicated above, Frankfurt thinks that "the enjoyment of a free will means the satisfaction of certain desires—desires of the second or higher orders."[15] Thus, for Frankfurt, just as freedom of action is being able to do what one wants to do, freedom of the will is being able to have the kind of will that one wants to have. It is for this reason that Frankfurt's account is often called a "structural" or "hierarchical" account, since he understands freedom of the will to be primarily a function of having a certain kind of structural or hierarchical mesh between one's first- and second-order desires and volitions. And since having the will one wants to have is independent of whether one could have had a different will, Frankfurt's account isn't based on an alternative-possibilities condition such as *AP*.

A natural way of understanding Frankfurt's view at this point is as involving a certain kind of sourcehood condition, which might be put as follows: a person wills freely only if he wills in a way that is consistent with a second-order desire. But given the importance of the second-order desire in adjudicating which of a set of conflicting first-order desires becomes the agent's first-order volition, it is natural to ask what adjudicates among conflicting second-order desires. For instance, what if Allison is divided at the level of her second-order desires; perhaps she wants both her desire to take her dog for a walk and her conflicting desire to stay at home and nap to become her will. If the solution to this conflict is to be found in a third-order desire, then we are off on a potentially infinite regress of ordered desires. Though she has a view which, in many ways, is similar to Frankfurt's, Susan Wolf raises a worry that hierarchy by itself cannot account for free will:

> First of all, even if there is no *logical* limit to the number of levels of reflection or depth a person may have, there is certainly a psychological limit—it is virtually impossible imaginatively to conceive a fourth- much less an eight- order, desire. More importantly, no matter how many levels of self we posit, there will still, in any individual case, be a last level—a deepest self about whom the question "What governs it?" will arise, as problematic as ever.[16]

In response to this sort of objection to his hierarchical account of free will, Frankfurt utilizes a notion of "wholeheartedness". Robert Kane nicely captures Frankfurt's view here as follows:

> Persons are "wholehearted" when there are no conflicts in their wills [at the various levels of desires] and they are not ambivalent about what they want to do. Ambivalent persons, by contrast, are of two (or more) minds about what they want to do and cannot make up their minds. Reflection on our desires stops, says Frankfurt, when we reach desires to which we are wholeheartedly committed and to which we have no ambivalence. It is not arbitrary, he insists, to identify with such wholehearted desires

because they are the desires with which we are "fully satisfied" and we have no "active interest" in bringing about a change in them.[17]

Wholeheartedness, for Frankfurt, does not require the complete absence of conflicts among an agent's desires. Rather, Frankfurt understands that an agent can be wholehearted even if his desires conflict so long as he decisively identifies with one of these desires and separates himself from the other. As Frankfurt puts it, "the conflict between the desires is in this way transformed into a conflict between one of them and the person who has identified himself with its rival."[18] Thus, in answer to Wolf's question "What governs the hierarchy?", Frankfurt holds that the agent in question does in virtue of endorsing wholeheartedly a particular level of desire past which there is no more conflict in the agent's volitional structure. We might thus understand Frankfurt's view as involving the following sort of condition:

> *Frankfurt's Condition*: A person chooses freely only if he chooses in a way that is consistent with a second-order desire that he wholeheartedly identifies with—that is, if the source of that volition is a desire with which the agent unwaveringly aligns himself.

From this condition, we see that Frankfurt grounds freedom of the will in the agent's choice originating in his volitional structure in a particular way. Not only is free will internal to the agent's volitional structure, but it more specifically involves the source of the agent's first-order volitions being located in those second-order desires with which he identifies.

Nevertheless, there is reason to think that wholehearted identification cannot ground free will for reasons relating to manipulation. Before turning to the objection, however, a few words are in order about manipulation. When I speak of manipulation in this chapter, I mean something along the lines of what Robert Kane calls "nonconstraining control," whereby

> the controllers do not get their way by constraining or coercing others against their wills, but rather by manipulating the wills of others so that the others (willingly) do what the controllers desire. The controlled agents consequently do not feel frustrated or thwarted. They act in accordance with their own wants, desires or intentions. Yet they are controlled never-theless by others who have manipulated their circumstances so that they want, desire, or intend only what the controllers have planned.[19]

So understood, manipulation is more than mere influence by another. Whether or not a particular case of influence by another amounts to a case of manipulation or not and, if so, in virtue of what particular features, are complicated questions. Nevertheless, I believe that the following case is fairly obviously a case of responsibility-undermining manipulation.

Consider a case involving Allison and her manipulative husband, Hal, who is a master hypnotist. Suppose that Hal hypnotizes her and that, as a result, Allison finds herself with the desire to make Hal his favorite dessert every night. However, this desire is implanted in her psychological hierarchy by her husband via hypnosis. Furthermore, Hal also causes Allison to have the second-order desire to have her first-order desire to bake become her will. And in case Allison has any conflicting first-order desire not to bake, as part of his plan Hal also causes her to wholeheartedly identify with those other desires that he has implanted in Allison's psychological hierarchy. It looks then that Allison has been manipulated into identifying with a particular second-order desire. In such an instance, even though Allison's desire to make dessert for her husband meshes with her volitional structure, it does not originate in that volitional structure since the mesh is solely the result of external manipulation. According to Frankfurt's account, Allison would enjoy freedom of the will in such a case despite all of the relevant desires being implanted via hypnotism. Frankfurt himself countenances such a possibility:

> The only thing that really counts is what condition I am in. How I got into that condition is another matter. If I'm in the condition where I'm doing what I want to do and I really want to do it, i.e. I decisively identify with my action, then I think I'm responsible for it. It makes no difference how it came about that that is the case. ... If the person is wholehearted in the action, let us say performs the action because he wants to perform it and the desire to perform it is a desire that he really wants to have and there's no reservation, there's no imposition, no passivity: the person is completely, fully, wholeheartedly identified with what's going on. What more could there be? What more could you want? That's all the freedom that's possible for human beings to have, in my opinion. ... What accounts for the fact that he's completely whole-hearted is no longer relevant. The only important consideration is that he is doing exactly what he wants to do and he's totally satisfied with doing this.[20]

In an earlier article, Frankfurt writes that "the degree to which his choice is autonomous and the degree to which he acts freely do not depend on the origin of the conditions which lead him to choose and to act as he does."[21] And more recently, he's been more explicit that manipulation of this sort need not undermine freedom and responsibility:

> [a] manipulator may succeed, through his interventions, in providing a person not merely with particular feelings and thoughts but with a new character. That person is then morally responsible for the choices and the conduct to which this character leads. We are inevitably fashioned and sustained, after all, by circumstances over which we have no control.

The causes to which we are subject may also change us radically, without thereby bringing it about that we are not morally responsible agents. It is irrelevant whether those causes are operating by virtue of the natural forces that shape our environment or whether they operate through the deliberative manipulative designs of other human agents.[22]

But surely the kind of manipulation under consideration would undermine, rather than give rise to, free will. Even Al Mele, who is sympathetic to much of Frankfurt's compatibilist view, finds this aspect of it "difficult to accept."[23] Although Frankfurt is willing to bite the bullet here, I think the size of this particular bullet gives us sufficient reason to look elsewhere for a satisfactory account of sourcehood.[24]

Fischer and Ravizza's approach to sourcehood

A second influential compatibilist account of free will based on sourcehood can be found in the work of John Martin Fischer and Mark Ravizza.[25] Fischer and Ravizza call their view "semi-compatibilism"; by this they mean that the truth of causal determinism is *compatible* with moral responsibility even if causal determinism ends up being *incompatible* with a certain kind of freedom.[26] Fischer and Ravizza differentiate between two kinds of control: guidance control and regulative control. Regulative control involves having control over which of a number of genuinely open possibilities becomes actual; we can thus think of regulative control as fundamentally linked with *AP*, discussed earlier. Fischer thinks that "it's natural to think that we need alternatives in order to be responsible."[27] Nevertheless, for reasons discussed in earlier chapters, Fischer and Ravizza think that *FSCs* and other similar considerations show that this kind of control is *not* required for free will. Yet there is another kind of control that they think *is* required, namely guidance control; as we'll see below, their understanding of guidance control can be understood as a form of sourcehood.

Fischer and Ravizza's discussion of guidance control is extensive, but we can focus here on the two central aspects that they think are needed for an agent to have guidance control. "Guidance control of one's behaviors has two components: the behavior must issue from one's own mechanism, and this mechanism must be appropriately responsive to reasons."[28] The responsiveness that Fischer and Ravizza take to be required here requires that the agent "act on a mechanism that is regularly receptive to reasons, some of which are moral reasons."[29] This means that the volitional structure that results in the agent's choices manifests an understandable pattern of recognizing moral reasons for choosing in various ways. Such an agent "recognizes how reasons fit together, sees why one reason is stronger than another, and understands how the acceptance of one reason as sufficient implies that a stronger reason must also be sufficient."[30] Furthermore,

Fischer and Ravizza think that the agent's volitional structure must also be reactive to those reasons in the right kind of way.

> In the case of reactivity to reasons, the agent (when acting from the relevant mechanism) must simply display *some* reactivity, in order to render it plausible that his mechanism has the "executive power" to react to the actual incentive to do otherwise.[31]

The second requirement for guidance control is that the agent takes responsibility for the reasons-responsive mechanism that results in his choices; that is, that the mechanism is *his own* or one for which he has taken responsibility. This feature of Fischer and Ravizza's view marks an important difference between their understanding of the kind of free will required for moral responsibility and that considered earlier from Frankfurt. Recall that on Frankfurt's view, all that is needed is the right sort of hierarchical mesh among an agent's desires, including wholehearted identification; it was this feature of Frankfurt's account that led to the earlier objection that his account was faulty insofar as he thinks manipulation didn't undermine control. Fischer is sensitive to this worry:

> I think that manipulation cases are a compatibilist's dirty little secret. Compatibilists don't like to admit that this is a problem. ... [But] we compatibilists have to deal with this. In my view, honestly, Harry Frankfurt really has not addressed this problem. He has discussed it in different ways and in different places and it doesn't add up to much.[32]

One can think of Fischer and Ravizza's ownership requirement as an attempt to avoid the problems regarding manipulation besetting Frankfurt's account.[33] For Fischer and Ravizza, "the *mere existence* of a mesh is *not* sufficient for moral responsibility; the *history* behind the mesh is also relevant."[34] In addition to having the right kind of mesh within his volitional structure, the history of that mesh must include the agent's taking responsibility. This involves three related elements:

> Taking responsibility involves three elements. First, the agent must see that his choices have certain effects in the world—that is, he must see himself as the source of consequences in the world (in certain circumstances). Second, the individual must see that he is a fair target for the reactive attitudes as a result of how he affects the world. Third, the views specified in the first two conditions—that the individual can affect the external world in certain characteristic ways through his choices, and that he can be fairly praised and/or blamed for so exercising his agency—must be based on his evidence in an appropriate way.[35]

Putting these various elements together, we can understand Fischer and Ravizza's view as follows:

Fischer/Ravizza's Condition: a person chooses freely only if he chooses as he does (i) because of an appropriately reasons-responsive mechanism and (ii) he sees that mechanism as his own in an appropriate way.

We might think of these two aspects as respectively insisting on the agent having the right kind of mesh and the right history behind that mesh. Taken together, these two aspects clearly mark it as a sourcehood approach—or as Fischer often puts it, an "actual-sequence" approach to free will and moral responsibility.[36]

Fischer and Ravizza's account has been called "the most plausible compatibilist account of freedom" (and this by an incompatibilist!).[37] Nevertheless, I think that it fails to provide a satisfactory account of sourcehood. There are a number of extant criticisms of Fischer and Ravizza's account, but I want to focus on one that is particularly pressing in the context of the present chapter.[38] This problem, raised also by a number of others, is that it appears that even on Fischer and Ravizza's view an agent could be manipulated into satisfying all the components of the control condition for moral responsibility.[39] One might think that in the earlier story of Allison and Hal, Allison already meets these components. It isn't clear that she does, given that the case, as presented earlier, is under-described at a few points. But the example can be modified so that Allison does satisfy *Fischer/Ravizza's Condition*.

Consider a modification of the earlier case involving Allison and her husband Hal. As in the earlier case, Allison's husband, Hal, implants desires in her volitional structure via hypnosis (or via a neuroscope he's purchased from Frankfurt's *Neurostimulators Inc.*). Suppose that Hal wants his father-in-law to die because he stands to inherit a considerable sum of money from her father's estate. However, Hal doesn't want to wait for the money, as he owes his bookie for unpaid gambling debts. So he hypnotizes his wife into killing her father. Such a case could be described in such a way that Allison satisfies all of *Fischer/Ravizza's Condition*, thereby having free will on their account, although plausibly Allison should not be thought to be free in virtue of the manipulation involved. Suppose that when Allison is deliberating about their financial situation, Hal causes her to have a certain reasons-responsive mechanism of the sort that Fischer and Ravizza think is required for guidance control—that is, he induces in her a volitional structure that is different from the one that she previously had. This new reasons-responsive mechanism is so sensitive to their financial demands that it judges that killing her father to receive the inheritance immediately is the preferable action; nevertheless it satisfies the first half of *Fischer/Ravizza's Condition*. In addition, during the process of hypnosis Hal also causes her to take ownership of this new mechanism thereby also fulfilling the second half of their condition as well. Because of the inputs from her husband, Allison sees herself as the source of the choices that result from this newly implanted volitional structure, believes that she is responsible for how she chooses on the basis of this new structure in appropriate circumstances, and believes this on the basis of the evidence that she has at the time. Allison acts on the bases of these reasons and kills her father for the inheritance. It appears that in such a case, Allison would meet all the requirements that Fischer and Ravizza think are required for guidance control despite the fact that her meeting all these requirements is the result of her being hypnotized or otherwise manipulated by her husband. Interestingly, Frankfurt thinks Fischer and Ravizza's view is susceptible to this kind of objection:

> Fischer and Ravizza seek to insulate their account of moral responsibility against the possibility that someone who is manipulated by another person might be wrongly held to be morally responsible for what he does. It seems to me that ... an agent who is being manipulated in ways that undermine moral responsibility can, according to the criteria that Fischer and Ravizza provide, act on a mechanism that is both suitably reasons-responsive and the agent's own. Thus ... their criteria do not satisfactorily identify the conditions upon which moral responsibility depends.[40]

But there is good reason to think that in this case Allison would not have the kind of control over her choices required for her to be morally responsible for killing her father since all of the relevant factors are the product, not ultimately of Allison herself, but of her being hypnotized by her husband, Hal.

Fischer and Ravizza consider this sort of case. In *Responsibility and Control*, they begin by noting how their view, unlike Frankfurt's, can easily account for the agent's non-responsibility in some manipulation cases: "On our approach, an agent need not be held morally responsible for acting on certain moderately reasons-responsive mechanisms that have been 'implanted': these mechanisms are not the agent's own."[41] They then go on to consider more complex manipulation accounts, such as that above involving Allison and Hal:

> But it is conceivable that a different sort of manipulation takes place, in which the agent's taking responsibility itself is somehow electronically implanted. That is, it is conceivable that the individual's view of himself as an agent and an apt candidate for the reactive attitudes be electronically implanted. Does our account of taking responsibility (and moral responsibility) imply that such an agent must be considered morally responsible?[42]

Not surprisingly, Fischer and Ravizza argue that the answer to this question is "no". The reasoning they provide to justify this answer is as follows:

> Earlier, we specified the third condition on taking responsibility as follows: the agent's view of himself must be based on his evidence in

an appropriate way. Obviously, this is abstract and schematic. This condition is intended (in part) to imply that an individual who has been electronically induced to have the relevant view of himself (and thus satisfy the first two conditions on taking responsibility) has *not* formed his view of himself in the appropriate way. But the relevant notion of appropriateness must remain unanalyzed.[43]

That is, Fischer and Ravizza think that there is something about coming to take responsibility for one's mechanism, even if done on the basis of evidence, that is not done in the appropriate sort of way if done as the result of manipulation. But short of analyzing what "appropriateness" amounts to in this context (a failure which one respondent calls "a serious lacuna in their account"[44]), it is difficult to see how the third condition amounts to any more than the stipulation that "the relevant self-conception must emerge from the agent's unmanipulated experience of his own agency."[45] Apart from a mere stipulation that the agent cannot be manipulated, the case of Allison and her husband Hal above give reason to think that *Fischer/Ravizza's Condition* for sourcehood fails.[46]

Derk Pereboom has also advanced a related critique of Fischer and Ravizza's view. Pereboom advances the following case as a counterexample to *Fischer/Ravizza's Condition*:

Case 1
Professor Plum was created by neuroscientists, who can manipulate him directly through the use of radio-like technology, but he is as much like an ordinary human being as is possible, given this history. Suppose these neuroscientists "locally" manipulate him to undertake the process of reasoning by which his desires are brought about and modified—directly producing his every state from moment to moment. The neuroscientists manipulate him by, among other things, pushing a series of buttons just before he begins to reason about his situation, thereby causing his reasoning process to be rationally egoistic. Plum is not constrained to act in the sense that he does not act because of an irresistible desire—the neuroscientists do not provide him with an irresistible desire—and he does not think and act contrary to character since he is often manipulated to be rationally egoistic. His effective first-order desire to kill Ms. White conforms to his second-order desires. Plum's reasoning process exemplifies the various components of moderate reasons-responsiveness. He is receptive to the various pattern of reasons, and his reasoning process would have resulted in different choices in some situations in which the egoistic reasons were otherwise. At the same time, he is not exclusively rationally egoistic since he will typically regulate his behavior by moral reasons when the egoistic reasons are relatively weak—weaker than they are in the current situation.[47]

(More on this case below.) Pereboom's evaluation of this case, with which I am sympathetic, is that Plum is neither free nor responsible because of the manipulation, despite meeting Fischer and Ravizza's compatibilist sourcehood requirement. According to Pereboom, "Plum's actions would seem to satisfy all the compatibilist conditions [provided by Fischer and Ravizza's account] ... But, intuitively, he is not morally responsible because he is determined by the neuroscientists' activities, which are beyond his control."[48] He thus concludes that "taking responsibility in conjunction with moderate reasons responsiveness appears not to generate a sufficient condition for moral responsibility,"[49] contrary to Fischer and Ravizza's view.

In his response to Pereboom's example, Fischer somewhat surprisingly concedes that Plum *is* morally responsible for his killing of Ms. White. What Fischer denies is that Plum is morally blameworthy for killing Ms. White:

> Moral responsibility, as Ravizza and I understand the notion, is more abstract than praiseworthiness or blameworthiness: moral responsibility is, as it were, the "gateway" to moral praiseworthiness, blameworthiness, resentment, indignation, respect, gratitude, and so forth. Someone who is morally responsible is an *apt candidate* for moral judgment and ascriptions of moral properties. ... Someone becomes an apt candidate or target—someone is "in the ballpark" for such ascriptions and attitudes— in virtue of exercising a distinctive kind of control ("guidance control"). But it does not follow from someone's being an apt target or candidate for moral ascriptions and attitudes that any such ascription or attitude is justifiable in any given context. After all, an agent may be morally responsible for morally neutral behavior. Further, an agent can be morally responsible, but circumstances may be such as to render praise or blame unjustified. Once the distinction between moral responsibility and (say) blameworthiness is made, it is natural to suppose that Professor Plum is morally responsible for killing Ms. White, even if he is not blameworthy (or not fully blameworthy) for doing so.[50]

Fischer is certainly right that an agent can be morally responsible for an action and fail to be morally blameworthy for that action, as is the case when the action is a morally good action and the agent is morally praiseworthy rather than blameworthy. But it isn't clear how an agent could be morally responsible for a morally wrong action (by virtue, in part, of exercising the appropriate kind of control over that action) and fail to be morally blameworthy for that action. Perhaps Plum could be exercising the kind of control over his action needed for moral responsibility (i.e. Plum has free will) but fails to meet one of the other conditions for moral responsibility; one such example would be if Plum was non-culpably ignorant of some relevant feature of his action. But this isn't what Fischer is claiming either.

What Fischer appears to be saying is that an agent such as Plum could meet all the criteria for moral agency with respect to a particular morally wrong action and yet fail to be morally blameworthy for that action. He then uses this distinction to negate the charge that an agent like Plum could be manipulated into being morally blameworthy for an action. But unless he can give us a better account of why Plum, in this particular case, fails to be blameworthy despite being morally responsible, it appears as if the *Fischer/Ravizza Condition* can be met in *Case 1* involving Plum, thus implying moral blameworthiness, despite significant and plausibly responsibility-undermining manipulation.[51]

It thus looks like the two leading compatibilist approaches to sourcehood face problems in dealing with manipulation cases. Insofar as one thinks that agents who are manipulated in this way are not free, one must look for a different account of sourcehood.

Manipulation arguments

Suppose that the arguments above are sound; that is, suppose that Frankfurt and Fischer and Ravizza fail to expound an acceptable account of sourcehood which is compatible with the truth of determinism. This, in itself, would not mean that a satisfactory compatibilist account could not be given, for there remains the possibility that some other compatibilist view would be able to exclude from morally responsible agency those agents who have been manipulated in these problematic ways. And if such an account could be given, then the arguments earlier in this chapter will have failed to show that no satisfactory compatibilist account of sourcehood can be given. Enter Derk Pereboom and Alfred Mele. Both advocate arguments which aim to show not only that compatibilist accounts of sourcehood fail for reasons of manipulation but also that the truth of causal determinism would threaten free will and moral responsibility for the very same reasons.

Pereboom's 4-case argument

Pereboom's argument serves as a powerful argument for the truth of Source Incompatibilism. The central idea of Pereboom's argument is that

> an agent's non-responsibility under covert manipulation generalizes to the ordinary situation [on the assumption of the truth of determinism]. If I am right, it will turn out that no relevant difference can be found among these cases that would justify denying responsibility under covert manipulation while affirming it in ordinary deterministic situations.[52]

Pereboom's argument is based on four cases, the first of which was introduced above:

Case 1
Professor Plum was created by neuroscientists, who can manipulate him
directly through the use of radio-like technology, but he is as much like
an ordinary human being as is possible, given this history. Suppose these
neuroscientists "locally" manipulate him to undertake the process of
reasoning by which his desires are brought about and modified—directly
producing his every state from moment to moment. The neuroscientists
manipulate him by, among other things, pushing a series of buttons
just before he begins to reason about his situation, thereby causing his
reasoning process to be rationally egoistic. Plum is not constrained to
act in the sense that he does not act because of an irresistible desire—the
neuroscientists do not provide him with an irresistible desire—and he
does not think and act contrary to character since he is often manipulated to be rationally egoistic. His effective first-order desire to kill Ms.
White conforms to his second-order desires. Plum's reasoning process
exemplifies the various components of moderate reasons-responsiveness.
He is receptive to the various pattern of reasons, and his reasoning
process would have resulted in different choices in some situations in
which the egoistic reasons were otherwise. At the same time, he is not
exclusively rationally egoistic since he will typically regulate his behavior
by moral reasons when the egoistic reasons are relatively weak—weaker
than they are in the current situation.[53]

As noted previously, Pereboom argues that despite satisfying *Fischer/
Ravizza's Condition*, Plum is not morally responsible for his killing of
Ms. White because of the manipulation enacted by the neuroscientists.
Pereboom then argues that the same responsibility-undermining features of
this case can be found in other cases, including deterministic cases which
do not involve manipulation. He concludes that both manipulation and the
truth of determinism would equally undermine free will and moral responsibility. This is clearly an incompatibilist conclusion.
  Pereboom's second case takes the responsibility-undermining manipulation and moves it back temporally in the life of the agent, making the
manipulation indirect rather than direct:

Case 2
Plum is like an ordinary human being, except that he was created by
neuroscientists, who, although they cannot control him directly, have
programmed him to weigh reasons for action so that he is often but not
exclusively rationally egoistic, with the result that in the circumstances in
which he now finds himself, he is causally determined to undertake the
moderately reasons-responsive process and to possess the set of first- and

second-order desires that results in his killing Ms. White. He has the general ability to regulate his behavior by moral reasons, but in these circumstances, the egoistic reasons are very powerful, and accordingly he is causally determined to kill for these reasons. Nevertheless, he does not act because of an irresistible desire.[54]

Pereboom claims that the temporal difference between these first two cases cannot account for why Plum would be morally responsible in Case 2 but not in Case 1. In both of these cases, the fact that Plum is causally determined to choose as he does by the neuroscientists undermines his moral responsibility. In Case 3, Pereboom replaces Plum's "creation" by neuroscientists in Case 2 with more common, but necessitating, moral training:

Case 3
Plum is an ordinary human being, except that he was determined by the rigorous training practices of his home and community so that he is often but not exclusively rationally egoistic (exactly as egoistic as in Cases 1 and 2). His training took place at too early an age for him to have had the ability to prevent or alter the practices that determined his character. In his current circumstances, Plum is thereby caused to undertake the moderately reasons-responsive process and to possess the first- and second-order desires that result in his killing White. He has the general ability to grasp, apply, and regulate his behavior by moral reasons, but in these circumstances, the egoistic reasons are very powerful, and hence the rigorous training practices of his upbringing deterministically result in his act of murder. Nevertheless, he does not act because of an irresistible desire.[55]

Again, Pereboom claims that the difference between Case 2 and Case 3 is irrelevant to whether or not Plum is morally responsible. Insofar as he thinks that Plum is not morally responsible in Case 2 (in turn, because he is not responsible in Case 1), Pereboom concludes that the manipulation in Case 3 is also responsibility-undermining.

Finally, Pereboom considers a case in which Plum's volitional hierarchy does not directly involve manipulation by some other agent or set of agents, but is instead simply the result of non-intentional deterministic processes:

Case 4
Physicalist determinism is true, and Plum is an ordinary human being, generated and raised under normal circumstances, who is often but not exclusively rationally egoistic (exactly as egoistic as in Cases 1–3). Plum's killing of White comes about as a result of his undertaking the moderately reasons-responsive process of deliberation, he exhibits the specified organization of first- and second-order desires, and he does not act because of an irresistible desire. He has the general ability to

grasp, apply, and regulate his behavior by moral reasons, but in these circumstances the egoistic reasons are very powerful, and together with background circumstances they deterministically result in his act of murder.[56]

Pereboom thinks that the non-responsibility of Cases 1–3 generalizes to Case 4 as well, insofar as there are no factors relevant for free will and moral responsibility in one case but not in another. According to Pereboom, "no relevant difference can be found among these cases that would justify denying responsibility under covert manipulation while affirming it in ordinary deterministic circumstances, and [that] this would force an incompatibilist conclusion."[57] Pereboom then concludes that these four cases show that free will and moral responsibility are incompatible not only with manipulation but also with the truth of causal determinism:

> The best explanation for the intuition that Plum is not morally responsible in the first three cases is that his action results from a deterministic causal process that traces back to factors beyond his control. Because Plum is also causally determined in this way in Case 4, we should conclude that here too Plum is not morally responsible for the same reason. … Plum's exemption from responsibility in Case 1 generalizes to his exemption from responsibility in Case 4.[58]

Pereboom's argument provides a way of extending the failure of sourcehood from manipulation cases such as those mentioned above in the discussion of Frankfurt's and Fischer and Ravizza's views to all compatibilist accounts, thereby arguing that compatibilists cannot give a satisfactory account of sourcehood. One way of understanding Pereboom's generalization strategy, which I'll call "Pereboom's Two-Step Strategy," involves the following two aspects.[59]

Pereboom's Two-Step Strategy:

(i) *manipulation undermining claim*: argue that in cases of overt manipulation, the agent fails to be the proper source of his action in the way required for free will and moral responsibility, and

(ii) *similarity claim*: argue that causally deterministic cases are relevantly similar, with respect to the agent's failure to be the proper source of his actions, to cases of overt manipulation.[60]

These same two steps can be found in another type of manipulation argument.

Mele's zygote argument

Alfred Mele also develops an argument against compatibilist accounts of free will centered on manipulation. (However, it should be noted that Mele's official position regarding the Compatibility Question is "agnostic autonomism," which he defines as the conjunction of agnosticism regarding the compatibility of free will and determinism with the belief that there are autonomous human beings.[61]) Mele's argument follows the same two-step pattern I identified in Pereboom's 4-case argument. First, Mele constructs a case which aims to show that certain kinds of manipulation would undermine an agent's freedom and responsibility:

> Diana creates a zygote Z in Mary. She combines Z's atoms as she does because she wants a certain event E to occur thirty years later. From her knowledge of the state of the universe just prior to her creating Z and the laws of nature of her deterministic universe, she deduces that a zygote with precisely Z's constitution located in Mary will develop into an ideally self-controlled agent who, in thirty years, will judge, on the basis of rational deliberation, that it is best to A and will A on the basis of that judgment, thereby bringing about E. … Thirty years later, Ernie is a mentally healthy, ideally self-controlled person who regularly exercised his powers of self-control and has no relevant compelled or coercively produced attitudes.[62]

Mele suggests that even compatibilists would deem that Ernie does not freely A given the manipulation that Diana performed on the zygote that would become Ernie.[63] This is step one, as seen above. The second step is then to claim that a causally deterministic case is similar, with respect to the agent's failure to be the proper source of his actions, to the case involving the manipulation of Ernie:

> Compare Ernie with Bernie, who also satisfies [a set of] compatibilist sufficient conditions for free action. The zygote that developed into Bernie came to be in the normal way. A major challenge for any compatibilist who claims that Ernie A-s unfreely whereas Bernie A-s freely is to explain how the differences in the causes of the two zygotes has this consequence. Why should that historical difference matter, given the properties the two agents share?[64]

Of course, these arguments are not uncontroversial.[65] Since the argument proceeds in two steps, there are two general ways to resist its conclusion. First, one might reject the manipulation-undermining claim, and deny that manipulation undermines free will. Following Michael McKenna, we shall call these "hard-line replies" to manipulation arguments. Second, one could concede that manipulation undermines free will, but then deny the similarity claim. Such responses are called "soft-line replies". In what follows, we'll examine each of these two claims in more detail to see what the prospects for hard-line and soft-line responses are.[66]

I start with the manipulation-undermining claim. According to these sorts of manipulation arguments, manipulation undermines freedom if, as a result of that manipulation, the agent's "action results from a deterministic causal process that traces back to factors beyond his control."[67] One way of understanding the claim that manipulation would undermine freedom construed as rooted in a sourcehood condition is that in such cases there would be a causal chain originating outside the agent which was sufficient for bringing about the action in question. Let us consider an example—I'll use the example of Allison and her husband introduced above, though Pereboom's Professor Plum and Ms. White would also work equally well. Given Hal's hypnotic handling of Allison's agential aspects, Hal and his manipulating mechanism are causally sufficient for Allison's decision to kill her father.[68] Furthermore, while this causal chain which results in Allison's decision to kill her father crucially involves aspects of her agential structure (since Hal causes Allison to have a certain reasons-responsive mechanism that she has taken ownership of), the origin of that causal chain is temporally located prior to its inclusion of her agential structure. In other words, there is a part of the causal chain which is sufficient to bring about her decision despite the fact that the entirety of this part of the causal chain is external to her agential structure.

Abstracting away from this particular example, let us define a causal chain x being *externally sufficient* for agent A's decision to d if the following conditions are all met:

1 There is a proper part of x, let's call it y, involving A's agential structure which is causally sufficient for A's decision to d.

2 There is a proper part of x, let's call it z, which does not involve A's agential structure.

3 z is temporally prior to y.

4 z is causally sufficient for y.

These four conditions in the definition of an externally sufficient causal chain capture why a manipulated agent would fail to be morally responsible for a particular decision if manipulation causally necessitates the decision in question. In other words, these conditions jointly claim that a choice cannot be a free choice if there exists an externally sufficient causal chain for that choice, thereby supporting Pereboom's manipulation-undermining claim. But a further condition needs to be added to these four. To see why, suppose that Allison strongly desires to kill her father for the inheritance, but knows that she is likely to falter in carrying out this desire ("It is my father after all; maybe I shouldn't," she might think). So she enlists her husband Hal to ensure that she will not waver in carrying out her desire via his manipulative mechanisms. We thus have a modification of Odysseus binding himself to the mast. Taking such a step ensures that the agent will exercise her freedom in a particular way, rather than undermining the agent's freedom. So to allow for this sort of possibility, let us add a fifth condition to the above definition of the external sufficiency of a causal chain:

5   There is no proper part of x which is temporally prior to z, involves A's agential structure, and is causally sufficient for z.

In cases of manipulation where the manipulation is brought about by an externally sufficient causal chain as defined here, it is plausible that the agent fails to be free—and thus fails to be morally responsible—precisely *because of* the satisfaction of conditions 1 through 5. So Pereboom's manipulation-undermining claim is a claim that an agent's decision is free and one for which she can be morally responsible only if the causal chain that actually leads to that decision is such that it is not an externally sufficient cause for that choice. If something along these lines is the right way to construe the sourcehood condition, then the manipulation-undermining claim is preserved and hard-line responses will fail.

Moving on to soft-line replies to manipulation arguments. Such responses reject the similarity claim, according to which causally deterministic cases are similar—with respect to the agent's failure to be the proper source of her actions—to manipulation cases. As we saw above, it looks as if it is possible to generate a manipulation case which satisfies all the conditions on free will that a compatibilist would give. (And here we again encounter Fischer's unsatisfactory response to Pereboom's case 4 that we discussed above.) Though a compatibilist himself, Michael McKenna has admitted that soft-line replies are doomed to failure.[69] If the satisfaction of conditions 1 through 5 is what undermines the agent's free will in cases of manipulation, the truth of determinism would likewise entail the satisfaction of these five conditions. For if causal determinism is true, then there is a proper part of the distant past which is causally sufficient for Allison's decision to do x but doesn't include Allison's agential structure given that it is temporally prior to her existence. On the assumption of the truth of determinism, there would be a part of the past that initiates a causal chain that would be externally sufficient for all of Allison's decisions (given the laws of nature).

Understanding free will as requiring the absence of any externally sufficient causes for a free decision thus explains both steps of Pereboom's generalization strategy.[70] Pereboom's argument, when coupled with the argument that free will is primarily a function not of having alternative possibilities or the ability to do otherwise but of being the source of one's choices and actions in a particular way, thus leads to Source

Incompatibilism. The conjunction of these two arguments is that Source Incompatibilism is true. In the following chapter, I want to further explore Source Incompatibilism, particularly its relationship with the alternative-possibilities condition *AP* as discussed earlier in this volume.

CHAPTER NINE

Sourcehood, incompatibilism, and alternatives

Source incompatibilism

The first use of the term "Source Incompatibilism" to refer to the view in question is from Michael McKenna, though the view is older than the name.[1] Eleonore Stump argues that Augustine developed and defended it in the fourth century,[2] and others suggest that the view was endorsed by a number of figures in the medieval scholastic period.[3] The explicit contrast between Source Incompatibilism and Leeway Incompatibilism, however, first appears in John Fischer's 1982 "Responsibility and control." There, Fischer describes the position as "a radical departure from the conventional incompatibilist approach."[4] According to Fischer, an incompatibilist can agree with "the kernel of truth in Frankfurt's example ... that responsibility attributions are based on what happens in the actual sequence"[5] without having to agree with the compatibilist that agents can be morally responsible even if causal determinism is true. Fischer elaborates this as follows:

> There are two ways in which it might be true that one couldn't have done otherwise. In the first way, the actual sequence compels the agent to do what he does, so he couldn't have initiated an alternate sequence; in the second way, there is no actual-sequence compulsion, but the alternate sequence would prevent the agent from doing other than he actually does. Frankfurt's examples involve alternate-sequence compulsion; the incompatibilist about determinism and responsibility can agree with Frankfurt that in such cases an agent can be responsible even while lacking control [i.e., the ability to do otherwise], but he will insist that, since determinism involves *actual-sequence* compulsion, Frankfurt's examples do not establish that responsibility is compatible with determinism.[6]

Although Fischer doesn't use the term "Source Incompatibilism," the quotation strongly suggests that he has something along the general lines of "sourcehood" or "origination" as a necessary condition for moral responsibility in mind.

Through a series of papers beginning in 2001, McKenna has cemented the term "Source Incompatibilism" into the current taxonomy of positions. According to McKenna:

> The source incompatibilist agrees with Frankfurt as to the unimportance of alternative possibilities, but disagrees with those inclined to work towards compatibilist conclusions by building upon Frankfurt's argument. Source incompatibilists hold that determinism *does* rule out free will. But it does so, not because it rules out alternative possibilities, but instead, because, if true, the sources of an agent's actions do not originate *in* the agent but are traceable to factors outside her.[7]

Again, one sees that a notion of "origination" or "ultimacy" is at the heart of Source Incompatibilism. As McKenna has more recently written, "the core [source] incompatibilist thought is that an agent is the ultimate cause of his action only if he contributes some necessary ingredient to it that cannot be traced back to causally sufficient conditions obtaining independently of his."[8]

Manipulation arguments of the sort discussed in the previous chapter by Pereboom and Mele give reason to think that incompatibilist approaches to sourcehood are better than their compatibilist counterparts. Unlike compatibilist views, Source Incompatibilism requires that the source of a free action cannot have sufficient causal antecedents that are external to the agent in question; it instead requires that those factors that are outside the agent's volitional structure are not sufficient for the agent's choosing in a particular way. It is for this reason that free will requires the falsity of causal determinism, even if the mere falsity of determinism doesn't ground the agent's freedom and responsibility.[9] But there are two significant challenges facing Source Incompatibilism at this point, both of which are related to the indeterminism that it claims is necessary for free will. I shall deal with one of them presently; the second challenge, which is more pressing, is the topic of the final chapter.

A hostage crisis

John Fischer objects to Source Incompatibilism (and, indeed, to incompatibilism in general) in that it requires certain theories about the physical world to be true in order for free will to exist—namely, it requires the falsity of the thesis of causal determinism. And insofar as we do not currently know whether or not causal determinism is true, the incompatibilist cannot know whether or not we are free. With his usual flair, Fischer describes the delicacy of this situation as follows:

> I could certainly imagine waking up some morning to the newspaper headline, "Causal Determinism Is True!" (Most likely this would not be in the *National Enquirer* or even *People*—but perhaps the *New York Times* ...) I could imagine reading the article and subsequently (presumably over some time) becoming convinced that causal determinism is true—that the generalizations that describe the relationships between complexes of past events and laws of nature, on the one hand, and subsequent events, on the other, are universal generalizations with 100 percent probabilities associated with them. And I feel confident that this would not, nor should it, change my view of myself and others as (sometimes) free and robustly morally responsible agents. ... The assumption that we human beings—most of us, at least—are morally responsible agents (at least sometimes) is extremely important and pervasive. In fact, it is hard to imagine human life without it.[10]

But if the incompatibilist becomes convinced that determinism is true, she would have to give up her beliefs that agents are free and morally responsible in order for her beliefs to be consistent. In contrast, the compatibilist does not face this problem:

> A compatibilist need not give up this assumption [that we are at least sometimes free and morally responsible], even if he were to wake up to the headline, "Causal Determinism is True!" (and if he were convinced of its truth). ... A compatibilist need not "flipflop" in this weird and unappealing way.[11]

Elsewhere, Fischer explains that compatibilism's impunity at this point is a significant point in its favor: "One of my main motivations for being a compatibilist is that I don't want our personhood and our moral responsibility, as it were, to hang on a thread, or to be held hostage to the possible scientific discovery that determinism is in fact true."[12] Thus, as compared with incompatibilism, compatibilism is able to reconcile freedom with a greater range of scientific discoveries. Let us call this the "Held-Hostage Objection" to incompatibilism. What should the incompatibilist think of this objection?

It will be helpful at this point to differentiate between two different kinds of compatibilists. The first of these not only thinks that free will is compatible with the truth of determinism but further insists that free will is incompatible with the falsity of determinism. One sees this position reflected, for example, in R. E. Hobart's article "Free will as involving determination and inconceivable without it," discussed earlier in Chapter 2.[13] As indicated there, Hobart argues that any indeterminism related to choice and action would be detrimental to moral agency. Hobart writes:

> Such absence of determination, if and so far as it exists, is no gain to freedom, but sheer loss of it; no advantage to the moral life, but blank subtraction from it. ... Freedom is something that we can attribute only to a continuing being, and he can have it only so far as the particular transient volitions within him are determined.[14]

And another compatibilist from the first part of the twentieth century, P. H. Nowell-Smith, expressed a similar view: "the clearest proof that it [incompatibilism] is mistaken or at least muddled lies in showing that I could not be free to choose what I do *unless* determinism is correct. ... Freedom, so far from being incompatible with causality implies it."[15] Note, however, that this form of compatibilism is just as susceptible to flip-flopping and the Held-Hostage Objection as is incompatibilism. If incompatibilism is problematic in that discovering the truth of determinism would rule out free will, this particular form of compatibilism would face the parallel problem if science were to discover that determinism is false. Few contemporary compatibilists embrace this position; in fact, it is doubtful that even Hobart accepted it. It is hard to see, for example, how the presence of indeterminism restricted to some distant corner of the universe would undermine free will on Earth.

Thus, the Held-Hostage Objection would at most favor another kind of compatibilism, namely a form of compatibilism which holds free will to be compatible with both the truth *and* the falsity of determinism—a form of compatibilism which is sometimes referred to as a "free will either way" account. Dan Speak has referred to this reason for preferring this kind of compatibilism to both Hobartian compatibilism and libertarianism as "the resiliency intuition."[16] According to this intuition, "our self-conception as morally responsible agents should be understood to possess a certain kind of stability. It should not be too easily undermined or too readily threatened by at least certain possible ways the world could turn out to be. It should, in short, be resilient."[17] It is this intuition which is at work in Fischer's story, above, regarding the *New York Times* headline. There is a spectrum of positions the compatibilist could embrace here, depending on how much indeterminism one thinks is compatible with free will, and where such indeterminism could be located without undermining freedom. One might think, for example, that free will is compatible with the falsity of determinism so long as the indeterminism is not found in the volitional structure of the agent (or, perhaps, so long as it is not found in particular parts of the agent's volitional structure). Here the compatibilist faces a trade-off. On the one hand, the wider she sees the scope of freedom undermining indeterminism to be, the more her view of free will is held hostage to the possible future discoveries of science. On the other hand, the more she thinks that free will is compatible with both determinism and indeterminism, the less motivated will be the Luck Objection to libertarianism, which holds that indeterminism undermines rather than supports freedom by making the agent's choices "simply the result of luck". (The Luck Objection is discussed in greater detail in the next chapter). If one thinks that free will is compatible with both determinism and indeterminism at a wide range of places causally relevant to a particular action, the less dialectical force the Luck Objection will carry—for if indeterminism *per se* doesn't undermine free will, then the driving intuition behind the Luck Objection will be undercut.[18]

Before ending this discussion of the Held-Hostage Objection, it should be admitted that incompatibilism is committed to the idea that our having free will *is* dependent upon certain truths about the order and functioning of the world and, as such, is dependent upon certain scientific discoveries. If, as I've argued above, free will requires incompatibilist sourcehood, the discovery that the conjunction of the past and the laws of nature entails all of an agent's actions and choices is precisely the kind of discovery that would undermine freedom insofar as it would mean that the source of the agent's actions and choices are not located in the agent in the way mentioned earlier. Instead, there would be *externally sufficient* conditions for all of the agent's actions. Hence, the incompatibilist will be forced to admit that the discovery of the truth of determinism would entail that agents lack free will (and thus also moral responsibility).[19] However, all plausible accounts of free will are also subject to some similar empirical constraints. If, for example, we were to discover that a particular agent suffered from certain forms of mental illness or neuro-pathology or that she had been the victim of neurological or psychological manipulation, then many compatibilists as well as incompatibilists would grant that the agent was not free. So the view of ourselves as free agents isn't indifferent to potential scientific discoveries regardless of one's view about the compatibilism/incompatibilism debate. Fischer admits as much when he says, "this is of course not to say that these basic views [of ourselves as free and morally responsible] are resilient to *any* empirical discovery—just to this sort of discovery [i.e. the truth of determinism]."[20] There are, of course, differences between these potential discoveries and the potential discovery of the truth of determinism.[21] The former would affect only those who suffer from those afflictions, while the latter is global in scope and—if incompatibilism is true—would mean that all actual agents lack free will. These differences should not be overlooked; but the point here is simply to note that compatibilist views are not wholly resilient to empirical discoveries. What is needed is for the compatibilist proponent of this objection to differentiate between those empirical discoveries that would undermine free will from those that do not.[22] Nevertheless, it's true that, as indicated above, incompatibilism is committed to the idea that our having free will *is* dependent upon certain truths about the nature of the world and its causal laws in a way that most compatibilist views are not.[23]

Two kinds of source incompatibilism

As mentioned in Chapter 5, many compatibilists were quick to embrace Frankfurt's argument against *AP*, and it is not hard to see why. Recall, also from Chapter 5, the Core Argument:

(1) Free will requires the ability to do otherwise.

(2) If causal determinism is true, then no agent has the ability to do otherwise.

(3) Therefore, free will requires the falsity of causal determinism.

The conclusion of this argument is that compatibilism is false. But if Frankfurt has been successful in showing the first premise of the argument to be false, then the compatibilist can easily deny the conclusion of the Core Argument without having to embrace a version of strong compatibilism, which involves the ability to do otherwise, even given the truth of determinism. It is this fact, I believe, that goes a long way toward explaining the degree to which compatibilists have attempted to defend Frankfurt-style counterexamples.

What is more surprising, however, is the effect that *FSCs* have had on some incompatibilists. Most incompatibilists think that some version of *AP* must be true in order for incompatibilism to be true. One reason for this is that some think that *AP* and incompatibilism go hand in hand. For example, William Hasker says that alternative possibilities are "crucial" for the incompatibilist's position and says that the abandonment of *AP* "would force either a redefinition of libertarianism [and thus also incompatibilism more generally] or an outright capitulation to compatibilism."[24] However, not all incompatibilists think that they need to embrace *AP*. This is one reason to differentiate between the two fundamentally different kinds of incompatibilism introduced in Chapter 2—Leeway Incompatibilism and Source Incompatibilism. Both Leeway Incompatibilism and Source Incompatibilism agree that the truth of causal determinism would be sufficient for the lack of moral responsibility, but they differ in terms of what *is* most fundamentally required for moral responsibility. In the rest of this chapter, I will argue that despite the fundamental difference between Leeway Incompatibilism and Source Incompatibilism in terms of what they take to be central to free will, the need for alternative possibilities is not ultimately separable from Source Incompatibilism.

It will be helpful, at this point, to distinguish between two subcategories of Source Incompatibilist positions. The reason for this is that some Source Incompatibilists do think there is an alternative-possibilities condition for free will; what makes them Source Incompatibilists, however, is that the source condition is more "fundamental" or "important" in some sense for free will (and thus also for moral responsibility). This is true, for example, of the views held by Robert Kane and Derk Pereboom.[25] However, there are other Source Incompatibilists who think that an agent could be the required kind of source of her action even if she has no alternative-possibilities whatsoever. Eleonore Stump[26] has such a view, as do Linda Zagzebski[27] and David Hunt.[28] For these Source Incompatibilists, it is not the case that the sourcehood condition is simply more fundamental than the alternative-possibilities condition; according to them, there is no required alternative-possibilities condition for free will and moral responsibility at all.

Let us then differentiate between "Narrow" and "Wide" versions of Source Incompatibilism.[29] Narrow Source Incompatibilists will be those who think that an agent having free will with respect to some action A is a matter of the agent being the proper source of A, and that being the proper kind of source doesn't require alternative possibilities at all. The term "narrow" here is intended to capture the idea that, on this view, alternative possibilities are outside of the scope of what is required for moral responsibility. Those incompatibilists who reject all AP principles are thus Narrow Source Incompatibilists. Wide Source Incompatibilists, on the other hand, take a broader, more inclusive approach to free will. These incompatibilists insist that what is most fundamental to free will is ultimacy or sourcehood, but still maintain that there is some AP-like condition that is also true insofar as it is implied by the sourcehood condition, and that in virtue of this alternative possibilities of some sort are a necessary condition for having free will.[30] Exactly how these alternative possibilities are related to free will according to the Wide Source Incompatibilist is a complex issue for numerous reasons, not least of which is the debate surrounding the "Robustness Requirement" discussed in Chapter 7.[31]

Incompatibilism without *AP*

In this section of the present chapter, I examine the writings of leading Narrow Source Incompatibilists in order to investigate the claim that sourcehood requires no commitment to AP. In particular, I examine the writings of Eleonore Stump and argue that, despite her claims, she is committed to a version of AP. If this is correct, it will show that her version of Narrow Source Incompatibilism is an unstable position. I think that this discussion will also go some distance to showing that all Source Incompatibilists are in a similar position regarding the need for some AP-like principle, although I will not consider other Narrow Source Incompatibilist views in detail. This will then lead to a discussion about the relationship between the sourcehood condition and the alternative-possibilities condition in the remainder of the chapter.

Stump's modified libertarianism

Eleonore Stump is perhaps the best known among the Narrow Source Incompatibilists. She defends a position she calls "modified libertarianism," and claims that it can be found in such medieval figures as Augustine and Aquinas. Stump defines modified libertarianism as assent to the following two claims:

> (L1′) an agent acts with free will, or is morally responsible for an act, only if the act is not *ultimately* causally determined by anything outside the agent,

and

> (L3) an agent acts with free will, or is morally responsible for an act, only if her own intellect and will are the sole ultimate source or first cause of her act.[32]

Stump differentiates modified libertarianism from "common libertarianism" in that the latter accepts, and the former rejects, an additional criterion:

> (L2) an agent acts with free will, or is morally responsible for an act, only if he could have done otherwise.[33]

This third criterion is rather obviously a form of *AP*. According to Stump, "what reflection on queer Frankfurt-style examples ... shows us is that the association between the presence of an alternative possibility and the ability to do what we really want holds only for the most part."[34] Stump elaborates this point in a later paper:

> Nothing in the argument has the implication that libertarian free will is never accompanied by alternative possibilities. It may be true that in most cases in which an agent acts with free will or is morally responsible, the agent can do otherwise. What Frankfurt-style counterexamples show is only that the ability to do otherwise isn't essential to a free action or an action for which the agent is morally responsible. ... Frankfurt-style counterexamples are successful against *PAP*; but ... the libertarian has nothing to fear from them.[35]

Despite her ultimate rejection of *AP*, Stump understands the intuitive pull that it has on the incompatibilist. After all, it certainly seems that there are alternatives remaining in an *FSC*:

> In the actual sequence the victim does some act *A* on his own, as it were, and in the alternate sequence he is caused to do *A* by the counterfactual

intervener. Consequently, it seems that there is an alternative possibility open to the agent after all. He can do *A* on his own, or he can fail to do *A* on his own. Defenses of *PAP* based on this feature of *FSCs* are not so easily dismissed.[36]

Despite its initial appeal, however, Stump thinks that this defense of *AP*—which is a version of the Flicker of Freedom Strategy discussed at greater length in Chapter 7—fails. Stump thinks that the Flicker Strategy fails because it is either "confused and leads to counter-intuitive results; or ... it is possible ... to construct an *FSC* in which there is no flicker of freedom at all. Either way, the Flicker of Freedom strategy is ineffective against *FSCs*.[37]

The particular version of the Flicker Strategy Stump considers is based on the distinction between an agent doing an action on her own in the actual sequence and the agent doing that action as the result of some coercive mechanism in the alternate sequence. Stump agrees that there is an important distinction between these two sequences at this point, and that the distinction is relevant to ascriptions of moral responsibility. However, she does not think this is enough to save *AP* from the challenge posed by *FSCs*. According to her, the Flicker Strategy depends on two assumptions, both of which she thinks ought to be rejected. These assumptions are:

(i) the agent's doing an action-on-his-own must be something that the victim does, that is, it must be an action,

and

(ii) the agent's doing an action-on-his-own must be a distinct act from his doing that act.[38]

If these two assumptions were true, it would follow that *FSCs* fail to undermine *AP* since the agent would have alternative possibilities for action. In the actual sequence, the agent does an action, namely the action that is "the agent doing an action, *W*, on-her-own," while the alternate sequence does not include this action. It, instead, contains a numerically distinct action, namely "the agent doing the act in question, *W*." According to Stump, both of these assumptions are necessary for the Flicker Strategist's case:

If doing *W*-on-his-own weren't an *action* that the victim does, then there wouldn't be something the agent does in the actual sequence but omits to do in the alternative sequence, as the flicker of freedom proponents argue. And if doing *W*-on-his-own weren't different from doing *W*, then what the victim does in the actual and the alternative sequence would be identical, and the victim wouldn't have alternative possibilities available to him.[39]

However, Stump thinks that neither of these assumptions should be granted. To see why, consider some action W, and the agent's doing-W-on-her-own, which Stump calls action O. The two assumptions above can then be understood as

(i´) O must be an action,

and

(ii´) O must be a distinct action from W.

And while Stump thinks that willings and choosing can be actions and that causal-genesis accounts of act-individuation are false (more on this below), she nevertheless thinks there is good reason to reject both (i´) and (ii´).

Regarding (i´), Stump thinks "it isn't clear that it makes sense to take O as an action at all, and there are counterintuitive consequences of doing so."[40] Stump asks us to consider an *FSC* in which the agent does O in the actual sequence and does W in the alternate sequence. Now consider an analogue to this *FSC* in which the two sequences are reversed; in this case, the agent does W in the actual sequence and does O in the alternate sequence. If the agent in the *FSC* has alternative possibilities, then he should have the same two alternative possibilities in the analogue case, the only difference being that the possibility for action available to the agent in the actual sequence of the *FSC* is the possibility available to him in the alternate sequence in the analogue and vice versa. Stump thinks it "clearly false" that in the analogue the agent has alternative possibilities for action:

> In the actual sequence [of the analogue] ... [the agent] would be entirely within his rights in claiming, afterwards, that he couldn't have done otherwise than he did, and he wouldn't be moved to rescind that claim by our insistence that there was an alternative possibility for his action in the alternative sequence in which he does O.[41]

What the analogue case shows us, Stump thinks, is that taking "doing W-on-one's-own" as an action leads to counterintuitive results and ought to be rejected. But if (i´) is rejected, then (ii´) must be rejected as well for if "doing W-on-one's-own" is not an action, then *a fortiori* it cannot be a numerically different action than doing W. Both assumptions that were needed for the Flicker Strategy to show that the agent in an *FSC* still could have done otherwise, according to Stump, are false.

For those who are not persuaded by her argument that "doing W-on-one's-own" is not an action, Stump proposes a different strategy for undermining the Flicker Strategy; she believes that one can construct an *FSC* in which there is not even a flicker of freedom based on her understanding of the correlation between volitions and neural sequences in the brain. Stump is intentionally vague about the exact nature of this corre-lation in order to accommodate any position in the philosophy of mind except what she calls "Cartesian dualism." By Cartesian dualism, Stump is not thinking primarily of any position that Descartes himself may or may not have held. Rather, she means those views in the philosophy of mind that reject any correlation between neural states and volitional states.

Given the assumption that Cartesian dualism is false, that is, given that all volitions are correlated *in some way or other* with a neural sequence in the brain, Stump suggests constructing an *FSC* based on the neural sequence correlated with doing W-on-one's-own:

> We can construct one *FSC* in which the counterfactual intervener desires not just some act *W* on the part of the victim but also the further act *O* [i.e. doing W-on-one's-own], as well as the act of doing O-on-his-own if there is such an act, and any further iterated acts of doing on one's own. We can stipulate that the counterfactual intervener controls all these acts in virtue of controlling the firings of neurons in the neural sequences correlated with each of these acts. If the victim doesn't do all these acts, the coercive neurobiological mechanism will produce them. In such a *FSC*, there are no alternative possibilities for action of any sort on the part of the victim.[42]

It is important to note what this example shows about Stump's under-standing of *AP*. As shown in Chapter 6, it is not the case that an *FSC* can be given in which there are *no* differences at all between the actual sequence and the alternative sequence; so this cannot be what Stump means by "eliminating all alternative possibilities." Rather, what Stump's example shows us is that *FSCs* should not be understood as eliminating all alter-native possibilities *simpliciter* but as eliminating all alternative possibilities regarding numerically distinct actions (i.e. in both the actual and alternate sequence of this *FSC*, the agent does O, which is doing-W-on-one's-own). In other words, the principle that Stump thinks *FSCs* undermine is one akin to the following:

> AP_a: an agent is free with respect to an action *A* at time *t*, only if she could have done an action numerically distinct from *A* at time *t*.[43]

And while I concur that there might be good reason to think that this principle is shown to be false by *FSCs*, I think that more needs to be said about how the numerically same action can occur in both sequences on Stump's view.

Given Stump's commitment to a Thomistic understanding of the relationship between the will and the intellect in freedom, it is perplexing that Stump thinks that the numerically same action could occur in both the actual and the alternate sequences, which her response to *FSCs* depends on.

According to Stump's Thomistic understanding, the will is a faculty that cannot be acted on with efficient causation by anything other than itself, even by the agent's own intellect. For this reason, it does not seem possible that the counterfactual intervener in an *FSC* could produce the same act of willing in the alternate sequence that the agent produces herself in the actual sequence. Discussing an *FSC* based on characters from Dostoyevsky's novel *The Possessed*, Stump writes:

> Even if it were coherent to suppose that one agent, say Verkhovensky, could directly produce some reasoning in the mind of another, such as Stavrogin, that reasoning would not be Stavrogin's but rather Verkhovensky's (or at any rate a product of Verkhovensky's reasoning). If Verkhovensky continuously produced thoughts in Stavrogin, then Stavrogin would have ceased to be a person and would instead be something like Verkhovensky's puppet. ... An agent's second-order volitions cannot be produced by someone else.[44]

Elsewhere, Stump notes that

> Aquinas, for example, thinks that the essence of freedom is that the agent's own mental faculties, her intellect and will, are the ultimate sources of any free act, and not something outside the agent. ... A free action (mental or bodily) [can] not be caused by something external to the agent.[45]

If the intervener were to cause the agent to do an action, either through bypassing her intellect or overriding her will, then the action would not be one that originated in the agent's own intellect and will. In one sense then, the action in the two sequences would not be the same; the action in the actual sequence would be an act originating in the agent's own intellect and will, while the act in the alternate sequence would be one that originated in the intervener's intellect and will.

Stump explicitly rejects causal-genesis accounts of action individuation, which are accounts of actions according to which all the causes of an action are essential to it. In virtue of this, she thinks it is possible for the numerically same action to occur in both sequences.[46] However, exactly how this is supposed to happen is unclear. I, for one, find it difficult to see how the actions in the two sequences could be numerically identical since they are the products of different intellects and wills. If the intervener bypasses the agent's own intellect and will in the alternate sequence, then it seems as if the alternate sequence will contain a different action. Yet, in order for an *FSC* to be an example of a situation in which the agent is morally responsible without having the possibility of performing a different action, both sequences must contain the same action. But how this is possible is not clear on Stump's account. When does the intervention in the agent's brain make it no longer that agent's action, and thus, *a fortiori*, no longer the same action? And how can the intervener intervene at the neural level without bypassing the agent's intellect and will, which are correlated with her neural firings?

However, even if Stump can satisfactorily address these concerns, there is still a flicker lurking in her account of free action. To see how, let us return to her evaluation of the Flicker Strategy. Stump thinks that the Flicker Strategist is correct in pointing out that the difference in the actual and the alternate sequences is important for freedom and moral responsibility:

> There is something right about the claim made by the proponents of the flicker of freedom defense of *PAP*, that there is an important difference between an agent's doing an act on his own and his doing it because he is caused to do so by an external intervener. As I have been at pains to argue, the difference is not a difference between different actions the agent does, as the flicker of freedom proponents suppose. Rather, the difference has to do only with *how* the agent does what he does. Even if the victim in a *FSC* has the same act of will *W* in the actual and the alternative sequence, there nonetheless remains a difference in *how* the victim wills what he does. He is causally determined to an act of will *W* in the alternative sequence, but not in the actual sequence. In the alternative sequence, the ultimate cause of what the victim wills is the intervener; in the actual sequence, it is the victim himself.[47]

In another place, Stump insists that every *FSC*

> leaves it up to the victim whether the act in question is done by the victim without coercion or is done as caused by the intervener. Consequently, although it is not up to the victim whether or not he does the act in question, it is evident that the *mode* of the action is up to the victim. ... The one and only act open to the victim can be caused by the intervener or brought about by the victim of his own accord, and which of these modes is the one by which the act is done depends on the victim.[48]

In other words, Stump thinks that the actions in the actual and alternate sequences are the numerically same act; what differs in the two sequences is "only the mode of the action, which is caused by the agent in the actual sequence but not in the alternative sequence."[49] Stump agrees with the proponent of the Flicker Strategy that this difference is relevant to the ascription of moral responsibility. However, she writes, "it is hard to see that this is a defense of *PAP* against *FSCs*, since on this flicker of freedom argument, the agent is not able to act otherwise that he does."[50] These comments show that, for Stump, the mode of an act is not essential to the act. What is up to the agent isn't whether or not a particular action occurs, but whether or not the agent is blameworthy for that action. Thus, while she rejects AP_a, it appears that she would accept the following principle:

AP_m: an agent is free with respect to action A at time t only if she has alternative possibilities regarding the mode of action A at time t.

Since even in an *FSC* the agent does have alternative possibilities regarding the mode of the action, *FSC*s do not rule out AP_m. In the actual sequence of any *FSC*, the mode of the action is up to the agent in the requisite manner. If an agent is coerced into doing an action, as in the alternate sequence, then the action is not freely performed by the agent (and thus is not one for which the agent is morally responsible). Furthermore, since Stump is a Source Incompatibilist, she thinks that the truth of causal determinism would mean that the agent wouldn't be the proper source of the mode of an action in the way required by AP_m.

It is interesting to note the similarities between AP_m and AP_f introduced in chapter 7. Recall that AP_f was defined there as follows:

AP_f: an agent is free with respect to an action A at time t only if there are morally relevant alternative possibilities related to A at time t.

If the agent has alternative possibilities regarding the mode of the action, that is, if it is up to the agent whether the act in question is done freely or only as the result of coercion, then there are alternative possibilities of some sort related to that action (since coercion undermines free will.) In other words, AP_m seems to entail AP_f. In fact, AP_m is simply a slightly stricter version of AP_f, since AP_m insists that the relevant alternative possibilities related to the action just are the modes of the action. Thus, although Stump rejects one understanding of the Flicker Strategy, her insistence on the importance of the mode of the action can be understood as a different version of the Flicker Strategy. If determinism were true, then there would be no alternative possibilities regarding either the action itself or the mode of the action; there would be no alternative possibilities at all. But the mode of the action is relevant to ascriptions of freedom and moral responsibility. According to Stump, "it is up to [the agent] whether or not he does what is blameworthy. But it need not be up to Jones in virtue of the fact that alternative possibilities for action [i.e. numerically distinct actions] are open to him."[51]

It looks then as if the mode of an action is the sort of alternative that, while it need not involve a numerically distinct action, is relevant to freedom and moral responsibility nonetheless. For this reason, I think that Stump's view is best understood as involving an alternative-possibilities condition such as AP_m. This condition need not insist on distinct actions in the actual and alternate sequences, but only on some alternative possibilities (such as the action's mode) which are morally relevant. But then it looks as if Stump's "modified libertarianism" is best understood not as a version of Narrow Source Incompatibilism, given what she says about the Flicker Strategy, but instead as a version of Wide Source Incompatibilism.

A criticism and rejoinder

Though I will not pursue the project here, I think that a similar line of argument could be given against other versions of Narrow Source Incompatibilism.[52] Since all incompatibilists insist on indeterminacy at some point in the causal history of an action, they also need there to be some alternative possibilities between the actual and alternate sequences of an *FSC*. These alternatives may not be numerically distinct actions; they may indeed be very "weak" or "flimsy"—but they are needed nonetheless. It might be helpful to think of the presence of alternative possibilities as a verifying or indicating condition for the satisfaction of the sourcehood condition, even if their presence isn't what itself satisfies the sourcehood condition. The presence of alternative possibilities obviously won't be a perfect indicator of the satisfaction of the sourcehood condition, insofar as the former doesn't entail the latter. The presence of alternative possibilities thus verifies that, as things actually stand, it is possible that the sourcehood condition is satisfied. Though he rejects this view, John Fischer captures it nicely:

> So one reason someone might insist on the importance of even exiguous possibilities—mere flickers of freedom—would be as *indicators* of something in the actual sequence—the lack of causal determinism. Some philosophers have argued then that even though access to alternative possibilities does not in itself explain or ground moral responsibility ascriptions, it is a necessary condition of such attributions.[53]

But when the need for alternative possibilities is understood in this rather limited way, their presence is sufficient for the truth of AP_f as well as necessary for the satisfaction of the more fundamental sourcehood condition.

Seth Shabo has recently criticized the argument given above that Stump's "modified libertarianism" in fact commits her to an alternative-possibilities condition.[54] If Shabo's criticism is correct, then it will call into question not just my evaluation of Stump's view but also the larger claim about Narrow Source Incompatibilism in general. According to Shabo, my response "exploits concessions she [i.e. Stump] need not have made"[55]; he goes on to argue that the Source Incompatibilist can indeed avoid any *AP* condition thereby preserving Narrow Source Incompatibilism as a viable alternative to Wide Source Incompatibilism. Shabo raises two primary objections. The first of these is that AP_f (and, likewise, AP_m) doesn't have the motivational force that AP_a does, because it is not clear whether the former principle "has any real application outside the narrow confines of these highly artificial scenarios [i.e., outside of *FSCs*]."[56] In other words, he thinks that the alternative-possibilities condition that I endorse above merits consideration *only* in Frankfurt-style counterexamples, and thus has no independent motivation for accepting it.

This criticism is far from decisive. As Shabo himself grants, if AP_a were true, then this would entail the truth of AP_f precisely because AP_f is such a weak alternative-possibilities condition. Thus, whatever considerations count in favor of a fairly strong alternative-possibilities condition such as the one that historically has been at the focus of free will debates, I can see no reason why those very same considerations wouldn't also count in favor of the weaker alternative-possibilities condition. Perhaps the reason why the stronger condition has received more attention than its weaker analogue is that in many discussions, the former was more intuitive. However, this doesn't mean that we lack good reason for revising an intuitive principle in the light of new considerations, particularly if the revised principle can do the same argumentative work as the original (e.g., by serving as a premise in the Core Argument) but is immune to certain counterexamples that the original cannot avert. Apart from considerations such as *FSCs*, perhaps we would have no reason to think that the relevant alternative-possibilities condition for free will requires morally relevant alternatives and not morally relevant *and* numerically distinct alternative actions. However, even if I were to grant this, I do not see why this should count against AP_f. Instead, I think that what the recent attention to the Frankfurt-cases have shown is that it was really something akin to AP_f that was at issue all along. Furthermore, if I am right that AP_f is fundamentally intertwined with sourcehood, then this would give further reason to think that AP_f has application and plausibility beyond simply considerations of *FSCs*.

The second, and more substantial, objection that Shabo raises to my argument is that AP_m (and thus also the more general AP_f) admits of two different interpretations. On the weaker of the two, AP_m might be plausible but is not strong enough to sustain the Flicker Strategy; on the stronger of the two readings, AP_m is strong enough to do the work I suggest above but lacks credible support of its own. The two versions of AP_m that Shabo differentiates are as follows:

PAP_m1: an agent is morally responsible for her action only if it was possible that she perform that action under a different mode.[57]

and

PAP_m2: an agent is morally responsible for her action only if it was up to her whether to perform that action under a different mode.[58]

Shabo admits that *FSCs* cannot refute PAP_m1 insofar as all *FSCs* are built around an actual sequence in which the agent is acting freely and is morally responsible, and an alternate sequence in which the agent is neither acting freely nor is morally responsible. However, Shabo contends that although such a weak alternative possibilities condition is perhaps *a* necessary condition for free will and moral responsibility, it is too weak to be an interesting necessary condition. Instead, while PAP_m2 is strong enough to be an interesting necessary condition, he thinks that *FSCs* can show it to be false:

> Let us return to Fischer's blush case. If Jones is *able* to decide under Black's impetus to vote Republican (as opposed to its merely being *possible* that he so decides), he can plausibly be said to have a robust alternative, one that could be thought to ground his actual responsibility. Since, however, the blush is completely involuntary, Jones lacks this ability.[59]

It should be obvious at this point that Shabo's argument is intimately connected with both the Dilemma Defense, discussed in Chapter 6, and the Flicker of Freedom Strategy, discussed in Chapter 7. As I argued there, the dilemma that Kane and Widerker, among others, raise against *FSCs* can be avoided—for *FSCs* can be constructed which avoid the objectionable features that give rise to the dilemma (namely, the prior sign and its relationship with the agent's purportedly free action). However, as argued in Chapter 7, even if it cannot be shown that the remaining alternative possibilities satisfy the Robustness Requirement—that is, even if it cannot be shown that they are relevant for free will and moral responsibility beyond merely pointing out the falsity of determinism—they are sufficient for showing the falsity of causal determinism. This is a point that Stump, as an incompatibilist, would no doubt grant. Furthermore, I have also argued that the remaining alternative possibilities need not *ground* the agent's free will in order to be relevant to her free will. In fact, as I have argued, what does ground an agent's free will is *not* the satisfaction of an alternative-possibilities condition, but rather the satisfaction of a sourcehood condition. And what I have tried to argue in this chapter is that *if* the incompatibilist agrees that free will is primarily a function of sourcehood, then she should also grant that some minimally weak alternative possibilities condition is also true insofar as it is entailed by the sourcehood condition. In other words, the Source Incompatibilist should be a Wide Source Incompatibilist.

Shabo appears to think that in order to show that Stump's view (and other purported Narrow Source Incompatibilist views) does, in fact, carry with it an alternative-possibilities condition, I need to show her view requires more leeway than what follows from the action being causally undetermined:

Now if the leeway incompatibilist is to have an interestingly different position, she must say one of two things. Either she must say that Jones' action's being causally undetermined entails more substantial leeway (affording greater control) than one might think, *or* she must say that less substantial leeway, though consistent with an action's being causally undetermined, is sufficient for moral responsibility. What the leeway incompatibilist *cannot* say is that the leeway that follows from an action's being causally undetermined is as limited as the source incompatibilist says it is, but that it nonetheless sustains the traditional link between responsibility and the freedom to do otherwise.[60]

As the discussion in Part III of this book indicates, I do not think that the incompatibilist's position should be rooted in an agent's having leeway, the presence of alternative possibilities, or an alternative-possibilities condition. So I have no interest in defending Leeway Incompatibilism over Source Incompatibilism. But as I've argued here, the Source Incompatibilist should admit that her commitment to the sourcehood condition also carries with it a commitment to some alternative-possibilities condition, even if it is a very weak one which insists on no more leeway that the sourcehood condition's requirement of the falsity of causal determinism already secures.

The relation between sourcehood and alternatives

I have argued that sourcehood is at the heart of freedom and thus at the heart of responsibility and agency in general. In fact, as I argued in Chapters 6 and 7, I think that this is one of the central lessons of *FSC*s. In this respect, I agree with John Fischer when he writes that "the moral of the Frankfurt Stories is that acting freely (and being morally responsible) is a matter of how the actual sequence unfolds."[61] However, I disagree with Fischer when he further concludes that *FSC*s also show that whether or not the agent in question has "genuine metaphysical access to alternative sequences"[62] is not relevant at all to free will. For if, as I have argued, a satisfactory account of sourcehood requires the falsity of determinism and such an account of sourcehood would also entail the satisfaction of an alternative possibilities condition, then the two issues will not ultimately be separable in this way. In fact, if the argument for Source Incompatibilism in Chapter 8 holds, then it could be used to underwrite a version of the Strong Flicker Strategy introduced in Chapter 7. Recall that what differentiates the Strong Strategy from the Weak Strategy is that the former shows how the alternative possibilities remaining in an *FSC* are relevant for free will beyond *merely* insuring the falsity of determinism. If among the differences between the actual and alternate sequences of an *FSC* is the fact that the agent only fulfills the sourcehood condition in the actual sequence, then this will be a morally relevant difference.

In an earlier paper, Al Mele has already suggested that an incompatibilist response to *FSCs* along the lines of the Flicker Strategy could be motivated by concerns of sourcehood in just this way. Though not an incompatibilist himself (he is, as mentioned in the previous chapter, "officially agnostic about the truth of compatibilism"[63]), Mele says that the incompatibilist can argue that having alternative possibilities is "valuable as a logically necessary condition of one's being an indeterministic initiator."[64] In response to the need for the present alternative possibilities to satisfy the Robustness Requirement, Mele continues that incompatibilists

> may reply that nonrobust alternative possibilities, rather than *grounding* correct ascriptions of moral responsibility, are only part of the grounding mix. They may claim that the possession of at least nonrobust alternative possibilities is necessary for moral responsibility because it is necessary for indeterministic initiation, and that the latter is required for moral responsibility.[65]

In other words, if the remaining flickers are due to the presence of sourcehood in the actual sequence but not the alternate sequence, then they will be morally relevant beyond just showing that causal determinism is false. Furthermore, we see that such alternatives are not playing the "magical" role that Fischer repeatedly attributes to them: their mere presence doesn't transform a case of non-responsibility into a case of responsibility.[66] Instead, insofar as the flickers are the result of the agent satisfying the sourcehood condition only in the actual sequence, they merely result from what does ground freedom and responsibility: sourcehood. It is sourcehood which simultaneously grounds freedom and also provides morally relevant alternative possibilities. It is for this reason that Fischer is wrong in saying that "the flicker theorist contends that our moral responsibility always can be traced back to some suitably placed flicker of freedom; our responsibility is *grounded in and derives from* such alternative possibilities."[67] What Fischer calls "the problem of alchemy" only arises if one thinks that non-robust flickers *ground* free will. However, if the remaining flickers are themselves rooted in sourcehood, then it is the sourcehood condition that is grounding free will.

More recently, Fischer seems to allow for the legitimacy of this view on the relationship between the remaining flickers and sourcehood. In a recent article, he grants

> that merely adding this sort of alternative possibility could not *in itself and apart from indicating something about the actual-sequence* make a difference to the agent's moral responsibility. ... It seems to me that the *only* way that the existence of alternative scenarios of this sort could help to explain or ground moral responsibility would be in virtue of pointing to something (indicating something) about the *actual sequence*.[68]

And in an even more recent article, he again considers that the fact that causal determinism rules out alternative possibilities could be directly irrelevant to freedom and responsibility, even though the determinism itself *is* relevant insofar as it "issues in lack of "sourcehood," in a sense relevant to moral responsibility."[69] It is in just this way that the Wide Source Incompatibilist thinks that the remaining alternative possibilities are related to free will and, in turn, moral responsibility. In his recent book on free will, Stewart Goetz argues in just this way:

> It is true that the advocate of PAP believes that the lack of the freedom to choose otherwise *is sufficient for* the lack of moral responsibility, and in that sense the latter obtains simply because of the former. It is incorrect, however, to assume that a person who affirms PAP believes that the lack of moral responsibility obtains simply because of the obtaining of the lack of the freedom to choose otherwise in the sense that the obtaining of the latter *by itself*, i.e. apart from what *explains* it, *explains* the obtaining of the former. ... On this view, then, what the advocate of PAP believes is that when an agent is not morally responsible because he is not free to choose otherwise, he lacks moral responsibility *not* simply because he is not free to choose otherwise but because he is not free to choose otherwise *because of causal determinism* in the actual sequence of events. ... Given source incompatibilism, I believe that while the lack of an alternative possibility at the point of choice does not *explain* the lack of moral responsibility ..., it is nevertheless a *necessary condition* of, and in that sense not independent of, both causal determinism and the lack of moral responsibility.[70]

If the arguments in this chapter are correct, then an agent can only be free and responsible if she is the source of her actions in a way that requires the falsity of determinism (and the lack of manipulation). But if these conditions are met, then the agent will also have alternative possibilities for action.

At numerous places in the preceding pages, I have granted that the mere having of alternative possibilities is not the fundamental issue involved in free will, and that such alternatives do not ground moral responsibility. We also see, however, that having certain sorts of alternative possibilities is both a result of fulfilling the sourcehood condition and an indicator that that condition might be met in the actual sequence. Thus, like other Wide Source Incompatibilists, I do not think that one can completely separate the source condition from the alternative-possibilities condition.[71] As a result of this, the debates regarding *AP* and *FSCs* are still important for free will.

There is thus an element of what Fischer refers to as "an alternative-possibilities framework" to the approach to free will that I defend. Nevertheless, I think that Wide Source Incompatibilism remains an "actual-sequence approach" to free will and moral responsibility insofar as an agent being the source of her actions in the actual sequence is the most funda-mental requirement for free will and moral responsibility. Wide Source Incompatibilism is an actual-sequence approach in much the same way that Fischer's account of guidance control is an actual-sequence account. Recall from Chapter 8 that on Fischer's view, moral responsibility requires a reasons-responsive mechanism that is sensitive to reasons for acting in alternative sequences:

> Under circumstances in which there are sufficient reasons for the agent to do otherwise and the actual type of mechanism operates, three condi-tions must be satisfied: The agent must take the reasons to be sufficient, choose in accordance with the sufficient reasons, and act in accordance with the choice.[72]

Despite the appeal to alternative sequences in this way, Fischer's view is still an actual-sequence-based account insofar as the role the alternative sequences play is indicating something about the nature of the actual sequence (more specifically, that the agent in the actual sequence is reasons-responsive). Something parallel is true for Wide Source Incompatibilism. On this view, the mere presence of alternative possibilities is important, not in and of itself, but rather insofar as their presence can indicate something about the actual sequence, namely that in the actual sequence the agent might fulfill the sourcehood requirement.[73] That is, on both views, what happens in other possible worlds is relevant to the agent's freedom in virtue of specifying something about the actual sequence.[74] The following words, which Fischer uses to describe his own view, are also true of the view that I have developed in this book: "the purpose of the assessment of ranges of non-actual possibilities is to establish the nature of the properties that are in fact (actually) exemplified in the sequence of events leading to the behavior under consideration."[75] The primary difference between Fischer's view and my own is that I think that the sequence of events leading to a free choice or action must be such that causal determinism is false. This requirement is the guiding principle behind actual-sequence, or source, incompatibilism.

However, nothing argued for to this point entails that we *do* have free will. For one, I have not argued that causal determinism is false. As indicated earlier in Chapter 1, I take the truth or falsity of causal determinism to be an empirical claim. But even if it were to be shown that determinism is false, that wouldn't mean that we do have free will—for the falsity of causal determinism is only a necessary, rather than sufficient, condition for moral responsibility. What would still need to be shown is that the indeterminism present contributes in some way to freedom and responsibility rather than detracts from it, for there is a powerful argument that indeterminism in the causal history of our choices and actions would render them "lucky" rather than under our control. This is what I referred to earlier as the Luck Objection to incompatibilism; and issues of luck will be the focus of the final chapter.

CHAPTER TEN

Incompatibilism and luck

Taking stock

I want to begin this final chapter by briefly surveying some of the terrain that has been traversed in the preceding chapters. The opening chapter introduced many of the terms and issues that are at work in contemporary philosophical debates about free will and moral responsibility, which subsequent chapters have explored in further detail. Chapter 2 explored the Compatibility Question and the answer both compatibilists and incompatibilists give in response to it. Chapter 2 also drew our attention to two different basic approaches to free will: *free will as having the ability to do otherwise* and *free will as being the source of one's actions*. Chapter 3 explored various forms of revisionism which are offered as alternatives to compatibilism and incompatibilism; I argued that the two leading revisionist accounts of free will are best understood as kinds of compatibilism. Part I ended, in Chapter 4, with a discussion of the ways one might argue for or against the existence of free will. The focus throughout part II was on the relationship between free will and alternative possibilities. Chapter 5 discussed the Core Argument for incompatibilism, and the two leading compatibilist responses to it. Some forms of compatibilism, called "strong compatibilism," reject the Core Argument by claiming that agents can still have alternative possibilities even if determinism is true. Other compatibilists, inspired by Harry Frankfurt, claim that alternative possibilities are not needed for free will and moral responsibility. Chapters 6 and 7 continued the examination of the alternative possibilities condition (*AP*) and Frankfurt-style scenarios (*FSCs*); each concluded that it is best not to think of free will as primarily a function of having alternative possibilities or the ability to do otherwise.

Part III turned toward source-based approaches to free will. Chapters 8 and 9 explored free will as primarily a function of being the source of one's choices and actions in a particular way. More specifically, and more controversially, they also argued that the most promising account of sourcehood is one according to which agents cannot be the source of their choices and actions in the way required for moral responsibility if causal determinism is true. The conjunction of the central arguments thus far is that Source Incompatibilism is true. If the central thrust of this book could be distilled into a short passage, it would look remarkably like the following quotation from Robert Kane:

> [The] exclusive focus on alternative possibilities in debates about compatibility is a mistake. The fact that these debates have tended to stalemate over differing interpretations of *can*, *power*, *ability*, and "could have done otherwise" is a symptom of a deeper problem— namely, that *AP* alone provides too thin a basis on which to rest the case for incompatibilism: the Compatibility Question cannot be resolved by focusing on alternative possibilities alone. This does not mean that alternative possibilities have no role to play in free will debates, as some compatibilists would have us believe. But it does mean that their role is more complicated than is generally recognized.[1]

Given that Kane is also a Source Incompatibilist, it is not surprising that I am sympathetic with this passage. Furthermore, as discussed at the end of the previous chapter, I think that Kane is also correct in thinking that sourcehood cannot be completely separated from alternative possibilities. Like him, I think that the satisfaction of the sourcehood condition will entail the satisfaction of an alternative-possibilities condition.

However, as also discussed in the previous chapters, there are a number of significant challenges to the existence of free will. Perhaps the most pressing of these is what I have already referred to as the Luck Objection. I think that luck presents a serious challenge to the existence of free will, and this final chapter will focus on that threat. However, we shall see that luck is a problem not just for incompatibilists, but for both incompatibilists and compatibilists alike.

The luck objection

One of the most common objections raised against incompatibilist views of free will is "the Luck Objection." However, there is no single objection that goes by this moniker; rather, the Luck Objection is best thought of as a family of related objections. Here are three recent versions of the Luck Objection against incompatibilist accounts of free will:

> Another frequently heard objection to indeterministic free will is precisely that undetermined free choices must *always* amount to mere

random choices, like flipping a coin or spinning a wheel to select from among a set of alternatives. Perhaps there is a role for random choices in our lives—for sometimes settling choices by a coin flip or spinning a wheel—when we are indifferent to the outcomes. (Which movie should I see tonight when I like both available options?) But suppose that *all* our free and responsible choices—including momentous ones, like whether to act heroically or treacherously, to lie to a friend, or to marry one person rather than another—had to be settled by random selection in this way. Such a consequence, according to most philosophers, would be a reduction to absurdity of the view that free will and responsibility require indeterminism.[2]

Agents' *control* is the yardstick by which the bearing of chance or luck on their autonomy and moral responsibility is measured. Luck (good or bad) becomes problematic when it seems significantly to impede agents' control over themselves. ... To the extent that it is causally undetermined whether, for example, an agent intends or decides in accordance with a better judgment that she made, the agent may seem to lack control over what she intends or decides.[3]

Suppose that Peg is deliberating about whether to tell the truth about a certain matter. She judges that she (morally) ought to tell the truth, though she recognizes and is tempted to act on reasons of self-interest not to. She decides to tell the truth, and her decision is nondeterministically caused, in an appropriate way. ... Everything prior to the decision, including everything about Peg, might have been exactly the same, and yet she might have made the alternative decisions. Peg in some other possible worlds, or some of her counterparts, are exactly the same up to the moment of decision but decide not to tell the truth. It is a matter of luck, it is said, that Peg decides to do what she judges to be morally right. To the extent that some occurrence is a matter of luck, the argument continues, it is not under anyone's control. The indeterminism in the process of her decision is thus said to diminish Peg's control over the making of her decision (in comparison with an otherwise similar deterministic case, in which the indicated luck would be absent).[4]

Though they have differences, these arguments all seem to share a central core. Dan Speak has recently offered the following argument as a distillation of the core of various versions of the Luck Objection:

(1) Indeterminism just is (or entails) luck.
(2) Luck just is (or entails) lack of control.
(3) Control is necessary for freedom and responsibility.
(4) Therefore, indeterminism is incompatible with freedom and responsibility.[5]

Because this argument so neatly captures what is at the core of the Luck Objection, a response to the former will hereafter be construed as a response to the latter. In what follows, I will refer to this argument as the "Distilled Luck Objection," or *DLO*.

Two kinds of luck

Note that the above formalism of the *DLO* will be valid only if "luck" as used in premise (1) means the same thing as "luck" as used in premise (2); that is, only if the argument doesn't equivocate. In this section, I want to raise some reasons for thinking that the above version of the argument outlined by Speak does equivocate. (Insofar as Speak doesn't endorse the argument, I'm not claiming that he equivocates. Rather, I'm claiming, as he does in his article, that this understanding of the Luck Objection equivocates.) To begin with, I want to differentiate two ways that "luck" can be understood.[6] On the one hand, saying that an event was "lucky" or "the result of luck" could mean nothing more than that the event in question was not causally determined to happen by the conjunction of previous events and the laws of nature. On this view, luck is synonymous with indeterminacy. This is the sense of "luck" at work in premise (1) of *DLO*. Alternatively, luck could also be understood to be any feature of an event which is sufficient by its mere presence to undermine an agent's control over the occurrence of that event. This is how the term "luck" is used in (2) of *DLO*. In order to avoid confusing these two senses of the term luck, I will refer to the first of these two views as "indeterministic luck" and will refer to the second as "control-undermining luck." I want to suggest that these two understandings of luck are not clearly synonymous or even co-extensive. If I'm right that there is a difference in scope between these two understandings of luck, then without an argument the all indeterministic luck entails control-undermining luck, *DLO* will be invalid.

Lest the reader think that no one endorses an argument along the lines of *DLO*, consider the following comments by A. J. Ayer:

[Indeterminism] does not give the moralist what he wants. For he is anxious to show that men are capable of acting freely in order to infer that they can be morally responsible for what they do. But if it is a matter of pure chance that a man should act in one way rather than another, he may be free but he can hardly be responsible. ... Either it is an accident that I choose to act as I do or it is not. If it is an accident, then it is merely a matter of chance that I did not choose otherwise; and if it is merely a matter of chance that I did not choose otherwise, it is surely irrational to hold me morally responsible for choosing as I did. But if it is not an accident that I choose to do one thing rather than another, then presumably there is some causal explanation in my choice: and in that case we are led back to determinism.[7]

Ayer seems to be arguing along the lines of *DLO* insofar as he says that a non-determined choice is "a matter of pure chance" for which it is "surely irrational to hold the agent responsible." That is, he appears to think that every instance of indeterministic luck will also be an instance of control-undermining luck, and that any indeterminism undermines an agent's control by its very presence. To put this point a slightly different way, he seems to think that it is the indeterminacy involved in the causal history of our decisions or actions which *per se* erodes an agent's control insofar as indeterminism just is randomness or control-undermining chance. This is the central thrust of *DLO*. As Speak points out, (1) and (2) jointly entail:

(5) Indeterminism just is (or entails) lack of control.[8]

Ayer seems to agree to endorse this claim; but as Speak correctly notes, once "this central claim is made explicit, it should be obvious that the libertarian is completely within her rational rights to deny it."[9]

The libertarian will deny (5) because she thinks not all indeterministic luck is control-undermining luck. For starters, the two aren't clearly synonymous. As Robert Kane notes,

"Chance" and "luck" are terms of ordinary language that carry the meaning of "its being out of my control". So using them already begs certain questions. Whereas "indeterminism" is a technical term that merely rules out *deterministic* causation, though not causation altogether. Indeterminism is consistent with nondeterministic or probabilistic causation, where the outcome is not inevitable. It is therefore a mistake (in fact, one of the most common in debates about free will) to assume that "undetermined" means "uncaused" or "*merely* a matter of chance". ... These further meanings of "luck" and "chance" do not follow *from the mere presence of indeterminism.*"[10]

Given that the two terms do not mean the same thing, unless these two understandings of luck can be shown to nevertheless be co-extensive, then *DLO* will be invalid.

There are, of course, cases in which indeterminism does diminish an agent's control in various ways. Think, for example, of a standard roulette wheel with 36 numbered pockets alternating between red and black and one green 0 pocket. If the operation of the wheel is truly indeterministic, then the player does not have the kind of control to ensure the ball will land on Red 29. However, to illustrate why not all indeterministic luck necessarily undermines control in the same way, consider the following three examples. The first comes from Robert Kane:

A husband, while arguing with his wife, in a fit of rage swings his arm down on her favorite glass-top table intending to break it. ... Suppose that some indeterminism in his outgoing neural pathways makes the momentum of his arm indeterminate, so that it is undetermined whether the table will actually break right up to the moment when it is struck. Whether the husband breaks the table is undetermined and yet he is clearly responsible, if he does break it. (It would be a poor excuse to offer his wife, if he claimed: "Chance did it, not me." Though indeterminism was involved, chance didn't do it, he did.)[11]

According to Kane, such a case shows that an "agent can be held responsible for an action even though the action was undetermined."[12] In this example, the indeterministic luck is located in the agent's ability to turn his volition (here, his volition to hit the table) into a particular external action (actually breaking the table). Given that the indeterminacy doesn't enter into the agent's volition, he is responsible for that volition even if he doesn't succeed in breaking the table. Furthermore, he also is responsible for breaking the table if he succeeds in doing so in virtue of being responsible for the volition that resulted in that action.

We can, however, back the indeterministic luck up so that it figures into the volition itself, as illustrated by the following example. Suppose that Tom is a military commander who is willing to torture a captured prisoner of war. Tom and his forces have captured 17 members of the opposing army. Although Tom is willing to torture each of these individuals, he only needs to torture one to get the information he seeks about the location of the enemy base. (Whatever his other character flaws, Tom prefers not to torture people needlessly.) So Tom creates a device which he affectionately calls "the Wheel of Torture." The Wheel of Torture operates like an indeterministic roulette wheel; however, instead of having 37 numbered pockets, the Wheel of Torture has only 17 pockets, each marked with the name of one of the prisoners of war. Tom's volition is to torture whichever person whose name is on that pocket that the ball lands in. Tom spins the Wheel of Torture and (unfortunately for prisoner Pete), the ball lands in the pocket bearing Pete's name. Tom, on the basis of his previous intention and the indeterministic workings of the Wheel of Torture, thus indeterministically forms the volition to torture prisoner Pete. In this case, Tom is morally responsible not just for his volition to torture someone or other but also for his volition to torture prisoner Pete given that the ball landed in Pete's pocket, despite the fact that this latter element involves a measure of indeterministic luck. Tom's use of this indeterministic apparatus does not mean that the reactive attitudes are inappropriately applied to Tom's torturing Pete the prisoner any more than the indeterminism involved in the first example exculpates the husband.

The third case locates the indeterminacy even earlier in the volitional process. Consider, then, the case of Laurel, who is torn between two incommensurable courses of action. Laurel wants to do X and also wants to do Y, but she knows that choosing to do X would preclude her from doing

Y and vice versa. While she sees good reasons for each of these courses of action, it isn't obvious to her which of these it would be better for her to pursue, and which set of reasons will ultimately win out over the other is not determined by anything prior to her actual decision. However, were she to decide to choose *X*, then she would see this as a volition for which she has good reasons and which is the result of her own volitional structure. She would embrace the choice as something that she had done and would see it as a reflection of her own agency. Similarly, if she were to choose *Y* instead, she would feel the same way about this choice. As Kane describes such cases,

> [n]ote that, under such conditions, the choice the woman might make either way will not be "inadvertent", "accidental", "capricious", or "merely random" (as critics of indeterminism say) because the choice will be *willed* by the woman either way when it is made, and it will be done for *reasons* either way—reasons that she then and there *endorses*. ... When she decides, she endorses one set of competing reasons over the other as the one she will act on. But *willing* what you do in this way, and doing it for *reasons* you endorse, are conditions usually required to say something is done "on purpose", rather than accidentally, capriciously, or merely by chance. Moreover, these conditions taken together ... rule out each of the reasons we have for saying that agents act, but do not have *control* over their actions.[13]

Taken together, these three examples provide reason to think that some instances of indeterministic luck fail to be instances of control-undermining luck. So while Source Incompatibilism holds that indeterminacy is needed in the causal history of a free choice or action, its presence *in and of itself* need not be seen as undermining the kind of control that is at issue in debates about free will. And as Stewart Goetz has recently argued, the further "inward" one pushes the indeterminism in this way, the more the resolution of that indeterminacy is teleological given the connection between the agent's volition and her reasons.[14] If what the agent chooses to do is a function of the agent's reasons, as Kane and Goetz suggest, then there isn't reason to think that the mere presence of indeterministic luck in the agent's volitional faculties undermines the agent's control.

Control-undermining luck as moral luck

According to the previous section, not all indeterministic luck amounts to control-undermining luck, and the mere presence of indeterminism need not lead to a lack of agential control. It is still possible, however, that libertarians face a problem with respect to control-undermining luck in their accounts of freedom. What is worrisome here is that libertarians face a problem with respect to what Thomas Nagel has called *moral luck*. According to Nagel, moral luck is involved "where a significant aspect of what someone does depends on factors beyond his control, yet we continue to treat him in that respect as an object of moral judgment."[15] Insofar as this definition doesn't mention the falsity of determinism, such a definition understands luck along the lines of control-undermining luck and not indeterministic luck. He differentiates four kinds of luck that might be at work in moral luck:

Resultant luck: luck in the way one's actions and projects turn out;

Causal luck: luck in how one is determined by antecedent circumstances;

Circumstantial luck: luck in the kinds of problems and situations one faces;

Constitutive luck: luck regarding the kind of person you are, where this is not just a question of what you deliberately do, but of your inclinations, capacities, and temperament.[16]

Resultant luck primarily deals with the relationship between one's volitions and actions. Nagel gives the example of a driver who is guilty of a minor degree of negligence, such as failing to have his brakes checked recently. If he is unlucky enough to have a child run out in front of him while he's driving and he hits the child, he experiences resultant luck insofar as what happens (i.e. his hitting the child) doesn't depend on his volitions given that he has no control over whether a child will run into the path of his car. "From the point of view which makes responsibility depend on control, all this seems absurd. How is it possible to be more or less culpable depending on whether a child gets into the path of one's car?"[17] While I think there are legitimate questions that need to be answered regarding resultant luck, insofar as my primary interest is in free will, I'll set aside such cases of luck in what follows.[18]

Consider next causal luck. If determinism is true, then it looks as if everything that an agent does, including her volitions, is subject to causal luck insofar as everything the agent does is determined by antecedent circumstances. For the compatibilist, such luck by itself cannot be sufficient to undermine the agent's freedom and responsibility, for this is precisely what makes her a compatibilist. So if moral luck is to be problematic for the compatibilist, it must be circumstantial or constitutive luck, or a combination of the two, that generates the problem. But insofar as the libertarian holds that freely performed decisions are not deterministically caused, she won't face this problem.

Of these, constitutive luck seems to be the more problematic for present purposes for both sides of the compatibilism/incompatibilism debate, particularly for those who endorse source-based accounts of responsibility, as I've argued we should. Constitutive luck—luck with respect to an agent's inclinations, capacities, and temperament—is more "internal" to the agent than are the circumstances that an agent faces. Furthermore, many of the circumstances that an agent finds herself in can be traced back to previous decisions for which her constitution plays a significant role. Suppose, for example, that given her current temperament and inclinations, it is not possible for Allison to resist eating a gluttonous amount of chocolate from her pantry. Insofar as there being chocolate in her pantry is a necessary condition of her gluttonous action, circumstantial luck might also be involved in whether or not she acts immorally on this occasion. But the fact that there is presently chocolate in her pantry is itself a result of her inclinations and temperament when she went to the store on the previous day, for the very same desire for chocolate that leads her to eat it also helps explain why she purchased the chocolate that is now in the pantry. Of course, her gluttonous disposition could itself be at least partly explained by her previous acts of chocolatey indulgence, which in turn depended on her even earlier dispositions.[19] So even if the entirety of Allison's act of gluttony on this occasion cannot be explained by constitutive luck, some of the circumstantial luck present will itself be the by-product of constitutive luck. Nagel himself considers such a position: "We may admit that if certain antecedent circumstances had been different, the agent would never have developed into the sort of person who would do such a thing [that is, commit murder]; but since he *did* develop (as the inevitable result of those antecedent circumstances) into the sort of swine he is, and into the person who committed such a murder, *that* is what he is blamable for."[20] Levy thinks that the compatibilist can avoid the problem of distant luck by rejecting the need for a historically sensitive account of the sourcehood requirement. In Chapter 8, however, I argued that ahistorical compatibilist views, like Frankfurt's, face what looks to me to be insurmountable problems with respect to manipulation arguments. Even Michael McKenna, a compatibilist, says that denying the relevance of history in this way is not so much a bullet as "a mortar shell."[21] I think that these kinds of considerations should lead compatibilists to endorse a historically sensitive source-based account of free will, like that offered by Fischer and Ravizza, rather than a history-insensitive account, like Frankfurt's. It is only the former kind of compatibilist view that requires the agent not only to *be* a certain way, but also to have *come to be* that way in a particular way.

The real problem with luck

The literature on the Luck Objection to libertarianism is vast, and I cannot treat it all in detail here.[22] In this section, I want to consider what I think is a representative articulation of the worries regarding control-undermining luck advocated by Neil Levy. Levy begins by trying to get clear exactly what luck amounts to: "Since some of these debates, in particular those in which freedom is the focus, turn on arguments concerning whether a certain class of events is a matter of luck we need to focus on luck itself to resolve them. We cannot rest content with a pretheoretical or intuitive notion of luck."[23] As I counseled above, Levy suggests that luck—of the control-undermining sort at issue here—should be distinguished from what I termed indeterministic luck. (His term for indeterministic luck is "metaphysically chancy," where an event is metaphysically chancy if and only if it is "the product of an indeterministic process."[24]) Levy doesn't think that the mere presence of indeterministic luck is always sufficient for control-undermining luck, though he thinks that some events can be so chancy that they're also lucky.[25] Furthermore, he thinks that indeterministic luck also fails to be necessary for control-undermining luck, for there are kinds of luck which can undermine freedom and responsibility but which don't require the falsity of determinism. Compare two possible worlds in which an agent, Alex, has the same set of inclinations, capacities, and temperament. The first of these two worlds, let us call it W_1, is deterministic; and the second of them, W_2, is indeterministic. The mere truth or falsity of causal determinism wouldn't mean that Alex is constitutively lucky in one of these possible worlds but not in the other. So we see that an agent might be constitutively lucky even if she doesn't face indeterministic luck. So indeterministic luck (or, in Levy's terminology, metaphysically chancy) not only isn't sufficient for control-undermining luck, but it isn't necessary either.

With this distinction between luck and chanciness in mind, Levy presses the Luck Objection to libertarianism as follows:

> Standard event-causal libertarianisms and agent-causal libertarianism fail to secure sufficient control to ground moral responsibility because the acts or decisions that are, on these accounts, the locus of moral responsibility are not acts (or decisions; from now on I suppress this disjunct for ease of exposition) over which the agent exercises sufficient control. Whenever an agent acts with direct freedom, on these accounts, either more than one such act was causally open to the agent, or the agent must be the ultimate source of their action (depending on whether the account is a "leeway" or a "sourcehood" libertarianism). On either view, the agent must control the action. Now, though the conceptions of control demanded by source and leeway views are somewhat different ..., they fail because on either kind of libertarianism, it is a matter of luck that the agent chooses, or is the source of, the action he actually performs.[26]

Earlier in Chapters 7 through 9, I've expressed my own preference for Source Incompatibilism over Leeway Incompatibilism. Particularly in the beginning of Chapter 8, I argued that the alternative possibilities that indeterminism introduces don't by themselves amount to the kind of control needed for moral responsibility. I agree with Levy that Leeway Incompatibilist views are problematic given that there is no requirement that the resolution of the indeterminism is something that the agent controls. What is needed, as I put it in Chapter 8, is for the resolution of the indeterminism to be up to the agent in some way, which is exactly what source-based views require. So in what follows, I'm going to focus on source-based libertarian views.

Development and free will

Broadly speaking, Source Incompatibilism holds that an agent freely chooses only if it doesn't originate in a causal chain that is externally sufficient for the agent's choice, as defined earlier in Chapter 8. And in Chapter 9 I argued, against Narrow Source Incompatibilism, that satisfying the sourcehood condition on free will entails satisfying at least a weak alternative-possibilities condition. Even if sourcehood doesn't require numerically distinct actions to be open to the agent at the time of her choice, it does require that the agent have some morally relevant alternative-possibilities. This is why I think that a satisfactory account of sourcehood will entail the satisfaction of an alternative possibilities condition, and that the two issues are not ultimately separable. Despite this connection between sourcehood and alternative possibilities, I do not think that meeting the sourcehood requirement at a particular time t entails having alternative-possibilities at t. Elsewhere, I've argued that the Source Incompatibilist can maintain that an agent need not have alternative-possibilities open to her at the very moment of every choice.[27] Her volitional or agential structure at a particular time can be such that she simply sees no reason at all in choosing a particular course of action, even if there is nothing external to her agential structure which prevents her from making such a choice. This is why leeway is not always necessary. But source incompatibilists do not simply endorse the negative thesis that leeway is not always necessary. They are also committed to the thesis that agents are only free if their choices have their source in their agential structure. And, I contend, this connection between an agent's present agential structure and her choice can be used to respond to the worries about control-undermining luck.

John Kronen and Eric Reitan articulate well this point about an agent's volitional structure: an agent's "moral character influences, often decisively, what one does or does not do. In other words, one's moral character gives rise to motives for actions, the totality of which excludes some actions, permits others, and necessitates still others."[28] What Kronen and Reitan are presupposing here is that for an action to be free, that action needs to be something that the agent did for a purpose or reason. Freely performed actions, on this view, are teleological, and the achieving of that *telos* serves as a purpose or reason for why the agent did that action. Moreover, as R. Jay Wallace points out:

> It is important to our conception of persons as rational agents ... that [their] motivations and actions ... are guided by and responsive to their deliberative reflection about what they have reason to do. Unless this guidance condition (as we might call it) can be satisfied, we will not be able to make sense of the idea that persons are genuine agents, capable of determining what they shall do.[29]

If the agent has no motivation or desire at time t to perform a particular action A—that is, if she then sees no reason *at all* in performing that action—then she will not freely choose at t to A. In fact, I think that the following conditional, which makes the stronger claims that the agent cannot choose at t to A, is true:

> If an agent's agential structure at time t is such that she sees no reason for X-ing, then there is no possible world in which she has that agential structure and freely chooses to X at t.

In what follows, I'll refer to the kind of impossibility at work in the above conditional as "psychological impossibility"—if an agent sees no reason for X-ing at a particular time, then it is psychologically impossible that she freely choose to X at that time.[30] Taken to its extreme, this conditional suggests why agents don't always have to have alternative possibilities available to them at the moment of choice, even according to Wide Source Incompatibilism. An agent could act freely at a time even if it is psychologically impossible for her to do any other action at that time. Suppose, for example, that the agent has reasons at t for freely doing Y and sees no reason at all for not doing Y (and that no Frankfurt-style intervener is waiting in the wings to force her to Y if she doesn't choose to Y on her own). In this case, the agent's freedom to choose Y does not entail that she has alternative possibilities at t. But, of course, if she is to be responsible for having the agential structure which make her unable to not freely choose Y, she would have had to have alternative possibilities at some point in her past (for reasons discussed in Chapter 8).

The above conditional about psychological impossibility helps ward off Levy's concern about present luck, "luck at or around the moment of (putatively) free action or decision."[31] Given the connection between an agent's volitional structure, her reasons, and what she chooses to do, it's not as if an agent's volition is indifferent to her present agential structure. Following Levy, we can understand present luck as luck at the moment of choice, holding everything fixed about the agent in question. Understood in this way, present luck is plausibly the kind of luck that is particularly problematic for Leeway Incompatibilism insofar as it locates free will primarily in the having of alternative possibilities.

But if the Source Incompatibilist has a view, like that sketched above, according to which an agent's choice depends on her agential structure, then present luck will be diminished. Levy writes that "the objection from present luck ... can be avoided only by facing down constitutive luck; by successfully defending an account of moral responsibility upon which how an agent came to have his values, beliefs, and desires is irrelevant to whether he is responsible for actions motivated by or expressive of these values, beliefs, and so on."[32] This much is, I think, surely right. Source Incompatibilists already think that agents are only free if their choices have their source in the agent, and the connection between an agent's present agential structure and her choice can be used to respond to the worries about control-undermining luck.

However, this point about agential structure is not sufficient to free the Source Incompatibilist from all aspects of the Luck Objection. The Source Incompatibilist who wants to affirm the existence of free will here faces a dilemma: either purportedly free agents have always had their agential structure, or they have not. If they have—that is, if such agents existed infinitely into the past and always had the numerically same agential structure that they presently have—then the libertarian needs to give an account of how such an agent can meet the sourcehood condition. On the other hand, if the libertarian is trying to give an account of how finite agents with a temporally limited past can be free, then she needs to be able to give a developmental story about how a finite agent can develop an agential structure which avoids the problem of control-undermining constitutive luck and is sufficient for free will. I don't think this development question has received sufficient attention in the contemporary literature.[33] If the libertarian is interested in human agents' free will, then her answer to the developmental question will have to take seriously issues from developmental psychology. One can see pretty quickly how giving such an account will be a difficult task. This is one reason why, in the first edition of this book, I never committed myself to the existence of free will.[34] And this is the issue that I think is most pressing for libertarians to address. What all this shows is that a full account of the nature of freedom and responsibility will need to consider issues that arise is developmental psychology and respects the constraints of Source Incompatibilism. But that, unfortunately, is a project for another book.

Incompatibilism, but maybe not libertarianism

Let us briefly take stock before closing. I earlier argued that people should prefer source-based accounts of free will to leeway-based accounts. I also argued that we should be incompatibilists, rather than compatibilists. Hence, I'm a proponent of Source Incompatibilism. However, I've also indicated that the biggest challenge facing source-based views is giving an account of the way in which an agent can develop from a non-free and non-responsible agent into a free and responsible agent—how a person can overcome the constitutive luck regarding the building blocks of her moral character. Developing such an account will be a difficult project, and one which I've not successfully done, nor even attempted. This is, in my view, a serious lacuna in the libertarian's position.

However, it's also worth noting that this lacuna does not undermine incompatibilism *vis-à-vis* compatibilism, for compatibilists face their own problems of luck. If the worry about luck is that "people cannot be morally assessed for what is not their fault, or for what is due to factors beyond their control"[35]—as compatibilists often charge libertarians—it looks like the compatibilist herself faces a significant problem of luck all her own. As Nagel himself forcefully puts the point:

> If one cannot be responsible for consequences of one's acts due to factors beyond one's control, or for antecedents of one's acts that are properties of temperament not subject to one's will, or for the circumstances that pose one's moral choices, then how can one be responsible even for the stripped-down acts of the will itself, if *they* are the product of antecedent circumstances outside of the will's control? The area of genuine agency, and therefore of legitimate moral judgment, seems to shrink under this scrutiny to an extension-less point. Everything seems to result from the combined influence of factors, antecedent and posterior to action, that are not within the agent's control. Since he cannot be responsible for them, he cannot be responsible for their results.[36]

For those compatibilists who think that determinism is true (or more strongly like Hobart, that the truth of determinism is required for the existence of free will), there is the problem of what Alfred Mele refers to as "remote deterministic luck":

> Incompatibilists want to know how agents can be morally responsible for actions of theirs or perform them freely, if, relative to their own powers of control, it is just a matter of luck that long before their birth their universe was such as to ensure that they would perform those actions. How, they want to know, is agents' *remote deterministic luck* compatible with their exercising *MR* freedom-level control in acting?[37]

The worry that Mele is expressing here is that if determinism is true, then an agent's actions are causally necessitated by the conjunction of past states of affairs and the laws of nature—that is, they are the result of remote deterministic luck and not under the control of the agent. The argument behind this worry (which Mele himself doesn't ultimately endorse) is intimately connected with the Consequence Argument, discussed earlier in Chapter 2. It's not my intention to reenter that debate here in these closing pages;

rather, the present point is to show that worries about luck don't favor compatibilism.

As noted earlier, most contemporary compatibilists are "free will either way theorists"; that is, they think that we can have free will if determinism is true (this is what makes them compatibilists) but also if determinism is false. In a recent paper, Manuel Vargas refers to compatibilists who think that free will is compatible with both determinism and indeterminism as "supercompatibilists."[38] For these compatibilists, the truth or falsity of determinism is irrelevant to free will. If it turns out that determinism is false, these supercompatibilists will face the exact same problem of luck that libertarians face. According to Vargas,

> the considered position of most contemporary compatibilists ought to be one that does not deploy the Luck Problem objection. After all, it would be an inelegant piece of self-sabotage to argue for compatibility with determinism and indeterminism, while also arguing that indeterminism (which could be widespread) has some general freedom- and/or responsibility-undermining feature.[39]

Such compatibilists should hope, instead, that there is an acceptable developmental account of moral agency that is compatible not only with the truth of determinism, but also with its falsity. Regardless of whether it's supercompatibilists or libertarians who develop such an account, the other group will likely be able to employ the same response to the Luck Objection.[40]

This conclusion that luck is just as much a problem for these compatibilists as it is for libertarians will provide little comfort to most incompatibilists. For while Impossibilism is technically a version of incompatibilism insofar as it holds that one cannot be both determined and free, most incompatibilists think that we are free and morally responsible agents. And so I hope to see libertarians and supercompatibilists alike working toward a psychologically respectable account of the development of moral agency and free will. Despite our other differences, this is a task that we should work on together.

FOR FURTHER READING

As the bibliography at the end of the book indicates, the contemporary philosophical literature on free will is voluminous. And new is constantly appearing; as this volume goes to press, I'm aware of no fewer than five books that are scheduled to appear in print in the next year that I would engage with here if they were already out. The reader interested in further exploring any particular topic I've discussed is encouraged to follow the footnote trail. My aim here isn't to be exhaustive, but rather to point towards what I think are the most helpful and approachable texts that someone interested in free will might want to pursue upon completion of the present volume.

General overviews

Kane, Robert (2005). *A Contemporary Introduction to Free Will*. New York: Oxford University Press. This is one of the best introductory texts presently available. Kane provides an excellent and balanced treatment of most aspects of the contemporary debates about free will.

Kane, Robert, ed. (2011). *The Oxford Handbook of Free Will*, 2nd ed. Oxford: Oxford University Press. This recently updated and expanded collection is probably the best single-volume collection available. The volume's introduction offers a fairly comprehensive survey of the recent free will debates. While the volume introduces all of the central issues, it is written at a higher level of sophistication than the other introductory texts mentioned here.

Levy, Neil and Michael McKenna (2009). "Recent work on free will and moral responsibility." *Philosophy Compass*, 4.1, 96–133. This article is a thorough and even-handed discussion of six current debates in the free will literature. It is an excellent source for those already familiar with the basics of the debates and wishing to find information on recent work.

Watson, Gary, ed. (2003). *Free Will*, 2nd ed. Oxford: Oxford University Press. Watson's collection is probably the best collection of seminal papers from the past three decades. Nearly every paper included is a classic in the literature.

Books advocating specific positions

Fischer, John Martin (2006). *My Way: Essays on Moral Responsibility*. New York: Oxford University Press. A collection of many of Fischer's central papers on free will and moral responsibility, constituting a presentation and extended defense of semicompatibilism.

Fischer, John Martin, Robert Kane, Derk Pereboom, and Manuel Vargas (2007). *Four Views on Free Will*. Philosophy. Malden, MA: Blackwell. This book is a debate between four of the leading scholars on free will, each advocating a distinct position: compatibilism, event-causal libertarianism, hard incompatibilism, and revisionism. The book covers the major arguments for and against these views, but provides little coverage of other views.

Goetz, Stewart (2009). *Freedom, Teleology, and Evil*. London: Continuum. Goetz's book is an impressive defense of a non-causal libertarian view of free will. It is rich in careful analysis and argument, particularly as it relates to the problem of luck, the Dilemma Defense, *FSCs*, and the teleological nature of free choice.

Kane, Robert (1996). *The Significance of Free Will*. Oxford: Oxford University Press. This book by Kane is the most sophisticated defense of an event-causal libertarian view. Kane argues that free will is grounded in "ultimate responsibility" (which is a kind of sourcehood), which requires the falsity of determinism.

Pereboom, Derk (2001). *Living Without Free Will*. Cambridge, UK: Cambridge University Press. Pereboom's book develops the influential "four-case argument" against compatibilism. Pereboom also argues for the contingent non-existence of free will, and describes how many of our social practices (e.g. punishment) need to be modified as a result.

van Inwagen, Peter (1983). *An Essay on Free Will*. Oxford: Oxford University Press. This is a significant and influential book arguing for the incompatibilism of free will and determinism. It is perhaps best known for its role in delineating and defending the Consequence Argument.

The problem of luck

Levy, Neil (2011). *Hard Luck: How Luck Undermines Free Will and Moral Responsibility*. Oxford: Oxford University Press. Levy raises the Luck Objection to both compatibilist and incompatibilist views. His book is the most forceful luck-based challenge to free will I've seen.

Mele, Alfred (2006). *Free Will and Luck*. New York: Oxford University Press. Mele offers a thorough treatment of issues of luck as they relate to free will. He also develops both an incompatibilist and a compatibilist view that he thinks can withstand the threat luck raises to free will. This book also contains a forceful presentation of the "zygote argument" against compatibilism.

NOTES

Chapter One

1 Manuel Vargas (forthcoming b), 1 in manuscript.

2 David Hume (1975), 95.

3 Susan Wolf (1990), vii.

4 Richard Taylor (1976), 293. For a dissenting view, see Robert Audi (1974), 10–14.

5 See, among others, Joseph Campbell (2011), Robert Kane (1996) and Laura Waddell Ekstrom (1998).

6 See, for instance, Peter van Inwagen (1983), 155ff. Richard Taylor offers a stronger position, namely that one *cannot* deliberate unless one thinks that the future is open. See Richard Taylor (1983). For critical discussion of these sorts of arguments, see Tomis Kapitan (1986) and John Martin Fischer (2006b), particularly sections 2 and 3.

7 See, for instance, John Martin Fischer (2006d), 21–4 and chapter 5 (pp. 106–23). Because he thinks that determinism rules out alternative possibilities and regulative control, Fischer must hold, as he does, that the ability to make a difference is *not* a value of moral responsibility. Fischer elaborates on the notion of narrative as it relates to free will in John Martin Fischer (2005a). There, for instance, he writes: "The value of acting freely, or acting in such a way as to be morally responsible, is the value of self-expression. This value is a kind of aesthetic value, or akin to an aesthetic value. When I act freely, I "make a statement", and the value of my free action is the value of writing a sentence in the book of my life (my narrative), rather than the value of "making a difference" (of a certain sort) to the world" (Fischer, 2005a, 380). See Chapter 8 in this book for a further discussion of Fischer's view.

8 John Martin Fischer (2006d), 29. See also John Searle (2001), 62ff.

9 For an excellent discussion of the origins of philosophical reflection on free will, see Michael Frede (2011).

10 See, for example, Augustine (1993).

11 Saul Smilansky (2006), 29.

12 Manuel Vargas (2010b), 61. For different senses of moral responsibility that are not at issue in the present volume, see Derk Pereboom (forthcoming).

13 Peter Strawson (1962). See also the discussions in Paul Russell (1995) and Leonard Kahn (2011) for other versions of reactive attitudes views. R. Jay

Wallace's (1994) is the most extensive discussion and development of this approach to the nature of moral responsibility.

14 Peter Strawson (1962), 195 and 190.

15 Ibid., 190.

16 Michael McKenna (2005a), 166.

17 For a further treatment of this view and its connection with our moral practices, see Manuel Vargas (2000b).

18 Michael Zimmerman (1988), 38.

19 Ibid., 39. Ledger views differ on their relationship with the truth of causal determinism. Ish Haji, for instance, argues that judgments of deontic morality such as "right," "wrong," "ought," "ought not" are incompatible with the truth of causal determinism, but that marks in the ledger involving "good" and "bad" are compatible with the truth of causal determinism. See Ishtiyaque Haji (2002). In contrast, Derk Pereboom argues that moral responsibility is incompatible with the truth of determinism, but that the truth of determinism is nevertheless compatible with the judgments of deontic morality. See Pereboom (2001).

20 Marina Oshana (1997), 77.

21 Ibid., 74f. Oshana's paper also contains a critique of the reactive attitudes view. Cf. John Martin Fischer (2006d), chapter 10.

22 F. H. Bradley (1961), 44.

23 John Martin Fischer (2006d), 194.

24 Joseph Campbell (2011) also describes the moral condition on moral responsibility: "a person is morally responsible for an act only if the act is or was morally right or morally wrong. ... No one doubts this condition" (33f). There may well be other conditions required for moral responsibility as well, such as an authenticity condition.

25 Peter van Inwagen (1989), 419.

26 For a discussion of some of the issues involved, see Timpe (forthcoming b).

27 Susan Wolf (1990), 7.

28 Peter van Inwagen (1983), 162. For similar statements, see Manuel Vargas (2007a), 128 and Derk Pereboom (2007b), 200.

29 Robert Kane (2005), 6. See also Robert Kane (2002a), 10 for a similar discussion. Gary Watson also distinguishes between "self-determination (or autonomy) and the availability of alternative possibilities" (Watson (1987), 145).

30 John Martin Fischer (1999a), 99.

31 Peter van Inwagen (1983), 162. Elsewhere, van Inwagen writes "[I]t seems to be generally agreed that the concept of free will should be understood in terms of the *power* or *ability* of agents to act otherwise than they in fact do" (Peter van Inwagen, 1975, 188). As we shall see later, however, the exact relationship between free will and alternative possibilities is a contested issue; it is better, in my view, not to prejudge their relationship by defining the former in terms of the latter.

32 Randolph Clarke (2003), 3.

33 In short, "guidance control involves two chief elements; mechanism ownership and reasons-responsiveness. An agent exhibits guidance control of an action insofar as the action issues from the agent's own, 'moderately reasons-responsive' mechanism" (John Martin Fischer (2006), 196). For more on this view, see the discussion in Chapter 8 below.

34 John Martin Fischer (2005b), 145.

35 See Thomas Hobbes (1994), chapter XIV.

36 Rogers Albritton (2003), 411.

37 Guus Labooy (2002), 184.

38 Robert Kane (2002a), 9.

39 Bertrand Russell (1914), 221.

40 The "state of the world at the moment in the past" must exclude the temporally relational facts about the world (such as "being one-hundred years before 2092") in order for determinism not to be a tautology. As van Inwagen says, "if it were not for this restriction, 'the state of the world' could be defined in such a way that determinism was trivially true. We could, without this restriction, build sufficient information about the past and the future into each proposition that expresses the state of the world at an instant, that ... determinism would be a mere tautology" (Peter van Inwagen 1975, 186).

41 David Lewis (1973), 559.

42 Galen Strawson suggests that "it is an *a priori* truth that determinism cannot be proved false" even though it could be proved true (Galen Strawson (2000), 154f).

43 See, for instance, the discussion in Campbell (2011), 83.

44 Randolph Clarke (2002), 377. For a different evaluation, see Ted Honderich (2002b), 71ff.

45 For an introduction to some of the issues here, see Chapters 3 and 4 in Robert Kane (2002c).

46 Ted Honderich (2002b), 5.

Chapter Two

1 Libertarianism about the nature of free will should be kept distinct from the view in political philosophy which goes by the same name.

2 R. E. Hobart (1934), 1.

3 R. E. Hobart (1934), 2 and 13.

4 A recent interdisciplinary collection on free will does contain an essay defending this literal Hobartian position: "So we do have free will in a deterministic universe. Indeterminism, on the other hand, makes free will impossible. ... To the extent that determinism is true, we humans do indeed have something that we all innately feel and believe that we have: free will. In

this most important sense, determinism makes free will possible" (John Baer 2008, 309).

5 See, for instance, R. E. Hobart (1934), 17.

6 Manuel Vargas has recently referred to this kind of compatibilist view as "supercompatibilism"; see Vargas (forthcoming a), 4 in draft. For a further discussion of supercompatibilism, see also Chapter 10 below.

7 John Martin Fischer (2007a), 44–7.

8 John Martin Fischer (2000), 323. See also John Martin Fischer (1999), 129 and (2006b), 183. For another presentation of this worry, see Manuel Vargas (2007), 141f. Fischer grants that there are other empirical discoveries that would threaten our view of ourselves as free and responsible agents; see, for instance, John Martin Fischer (2008a), 169.

9 Susan Wolf (2003), 376. In a recent paper, Eddy Nahmias gives some experimental evidence to support that this is in fact what is going on; see Nahmias (2011).

10 Philippa Foot (2002), 62.

11 Laura Waddell Ekstrom (2002), 310.

12 Laura Waddell Ekstrom (2000), 57.

13 Robert Kane (1999), 218. More recently, however, Kane seems to have toned down his estimation, now writing that incompatibilism is the view "many ordinary persons have in mind" (Kane 2007a, 7).

14 J. P. Moreland (2009), 41.

15 For a brief discussion of this emerging trend, see Joshua Knobe (2004) and (2007).

16 See, for instance, Eddy Nahmias et al. (2006), Shawn Nichols and Joshua Knobe (2007), and Joshua Knobe (2007). Excellent overviews of experimental work on free will can be found in Tamler Sommers (2010) and Eddy Nahmias (2011). Also note that experimental philosophy has itself been the focus of much philosophical criticism. See, for instance, Ernest Sosa (2007) and Manuel Vargas (2007a). I do not think the current studies have settled the issue about folk-intuitions—but I do think that they have shown that things are not nearly as clean-cut as Ekstrom and Kane seem to think.

   Finally, lest the reader think that only incompatibilists appeal to intuitions, note that in Harry Frankfurt's seminal article about the Principle of Alternate Possibilities, discussed in greater length in later chapters, Frankfurt himself appeals to "our moral intuitions" (Harry Frankfurt 1969, 830)—as have many compatibilists in his footsteps.

17 William Lycan (2003), 109. See also David Chalmers (1996), 96: "In general, a certain burden of proof lies on those who claim that a certain description is logically *impossible*. ... If no reasonable analysis of the terms in question points towards a contradiction, or even makes the existence of a contradiction plausible, then there is a natural assumption in favor of logical possibility." A similar methodological principle is also endorsed by Jonathan Bennett (1984).

18 For an interesting discussion of related issues, see Chapter 3 in Peter van Inwagen (2006).

19 For a different, and less optimistic, treatment of the epistemic issues in deciding whether or not two properties are compatible, see Peter van Inwagen (1977), particularly 382–6.

20 Kadri Vihvelin (2008), 306f. For a similar claim about compatibilism as the default position, see Michael Nelson (2011), 36–40. However, for a different view of the dialectical burden, see Michael McKenna (2010). McKenna offers a different analysis of the dialectical burdens according to which compatibilism doesn't fare quite as well as Vihvelin and Nelson think, insofar as compatibilists must show that the "conventional wisdom that the deterministic worlds are inhospitable places to suppose one would find free will in the first place" fails (431).

21 For a discussion of various ways to argue against the existence of free will, see Chapter 4.

22 The only exception that I'm aware of is Neil Levy; see Levy (2009).

23 For an introduction to these issues, however, see Helen Beebee, Christopher Hitchcock, and Peter Menzies (2010), particularly parts II and III.

24 For a discussion of the differences among incompatibilist views on this issue, see Randolph Clarke (2002), 362ff.

25 Other incompatibilists "require that a free decision or other free action have no cause at all" (Clarke (2002), 356). For a discussion of noncausal accounts, in addition to Clarke 2002, see Ginet (1990), Goetz (2009) and Pink (2011).

26 Ned Markosian (1999), 259.

27 Ned Markosian (1999), 268.

28 Ned Markosian (1999), 270. In a more recent paper, Markosian has argued that all compatibilists *ought* to be agent-causalists; see Markosian (2012).

29 Ned Markosian (1999), 273f.

30 Those interested in this literature would do well to begin with Ned Markosian (2012), Timothy O'Connor (2011), and Randolph Clarke (2011).

31 See especially Peter van Inwagen (1975) and (1983). For an excellent discussion of the history of the Consequence Argument, see Joseph Campbell (unpublished). Those interested in the Consequence Argument should also begin with Daniel Speak (2011). According to Speak, the Consequence Argument "does not seem to be a single argument but instead an argument form or schema that can be filled out in various ways" (Speak (2011), 116).

32 Peter van Inwagen (1983), 56.

33 For whether all versions of the Consequence Argument involve a transfer principle, see Joseph Campbell (unpublished), section 4b.

34 Peter van Inwagen (1983), 56.

35 Peter van Inwagen (1983), 56.

36 For an excellent discussion of the relationship between the various formulations of the Consequence Argument, see Joseph Campbell (unpublished) and Daniel Speak (2011).

37 The third argument is introduced on pages 93ff of Peter van Inwagen (1983).

38 Peter van Inwagen (1983), 93.

39 See Chapters 5 and 7. For a related discussion, see also Tomis Kapitan (2011).

40 For a challenge to the validity of α, which is sometimes described as "entirely uncontroversial" (Eleonore Stump and John Martin Fischer (2000), 53), see Stephen Kearns (2011).

41 Peter van Inwagen (1994), 95ff. At the end of this discussion, van Inwagen concludes: "there will be some premise or premises in any technically satisfactory argument for incompatibilism that the incompatibilist would have no reason to accept if he did not accept the validity of Beta" (98).

42 Thomas McKay and David Johnson (1996).

43 Alicia Finch and Ted Warfield (1998).

44 Joseph Campbell (unpublished), 23 in draft.

45 Joseph Campbell (2010), 71. A similar point is made in Ted Warfield (2000).

46 Alicia Finch (forthcoming). See also Daniel Speak (2011). Another objection to the modal conclusion of the Consequence Argument is given by Ted Warfield. Finch provides a response to this objection in her article.

Chapter Three

1 Robert Kane (2011), 27.

2 See Ted Honderich (2002a).

3 Ted Honderich (2002b), 5.

4 Ted Honderich (2002a), 464f.

5 Ted Honderich (2002b), 71.

6 Ted Honderich (2002a), 469. By "causal circumstance," Honderich means "a set of conditions or events that necessitates something later, an effect, and hence is in a kind of nomic connection with it; hence a causal circumstance makes it impossible that any event other than the effect would occur" (Honderich (2002b), 154).

7 Ted Honderich (2002b), 2. What is less clear in this quotation is whether Honderich understands Free Will primarily along the lines of a sourcehood condition or an alternative possibilities condition; both seem to be involved.

8 See, for instance, Ted Honderich (2002b), 3.

9 Ted Honderich, (2002b), 6.

10 Ted Honderich (2002b), 155.

11 Ted Honderich (2002b), 157.

12 Ted Honderich (2002a) 473f.

13 Ted Honderich (2011), 452.

14 Ted Honderich (2002b), 101.

15 Ted Honderich (2002b), 102.

16 Ted Honderich (2002b), 102.

17 Ted Honderich (2002b), 104.

18 Ted Honderich (2002b), 110. For a similar discussion, see also Honderich (2011), 448ff where he also suggests that there is empirical data supporting the view that we have two conceptions of free will.

19 Ted Honderich (2002b), 112.

20 Ted Honderich (2011), 451.

21 Ted Honderich (2011), 451.

22 Ted Honderich (2002b), 125.

23 Manuel Vargas (2004), 218f. For discussions of the recent historical development of revisionist accounts, see Vargas (2010a) and Vargas (2011).

24 Manuel Vargas (2005), 402. See also Vargas (2004), 227f and Vargas (2007a), 152.

25 Manuel Vargas (2007a), 132.

26 Manuel Vargas (2009), 48. For a further discussion about the apparently conflicting strands of folk thinking about free will, see also Vargas (2007a), 137f and Vargas (2011), 466f.

27 Manuel Vargas (2007a), 139.

28 Manuel Vargas (2009), 47.

29 Manuel Vargas (2005), 403.

30 Manuel Vargas (2005), 403. Vargas also refers to paradigmatic revisionism as a form of systematic revisionism, rather than "revisionism on the cheap"; see Vargas (2007a), 152.

31 See, for instance, Manuel Vargas (2005), 399ff.

32 Manuel Vargas (2005), 407.

33 Manuel Vargas (2005), 407.

34 See Derk Pereboom (2001) and (2005), as well as Galen Strawson (1994).

35 Manuel Vargas (2009), 52.

36 Manuel Vargas (2005), 409.

37 Manuel Vargas (2005), 401. Vargas describes Ira Singer and Susan Hurley as engaged in similar revisionist projects; see Vargas (2011), 468f.

38 See Manuel Vargas (2011).

39 Manuel Vargas (2011), 460. This is one reason that I think it apt to describe Honderich's view as a revisionist view.

40 Manuel Vargas (2011), 460. Once again, Honderich's view satisfies this way of differentiating revisionist views from conventional ones.

41 Manuel Vargas (2011), 463.

42 Manuel Vargas (2011), 463.

43 Manuel Vargas (2004), 235.

44 Manuel Vargas (2004), 232.

45 Manuel Vargas (2007a), 142.

46　Manuel Vargas (2009), 51.

47　Manuel Vargas (2004), 230.

48　See Manuel Vargas (2011), 470.

49　Furthermore, since, as noted earlier, both compatibilism and incompatibilism are typically taken to be necessarily true if true at all; thus, it is either the case that compatibilism is necessarily true and incompatibilism is necessarily false or that incompatibilism is necessarily true and compatibilism is necessary false. However, this further point need not concern us here.

50　Manuel Vargas (2004), 227f.

51　Manuel Vargas (2007a), 160. See also Vargas (2005), 418.

52　See John Martin Fischer (2007a), 44–7.

53　Manuel Vargas (2005), 423.

54　Manuel Vargas (2007b), 217.

55　This position is inspired by the title of R. E. Hobart (1934). For a different dialectical use of such a view, see Derk Pereboom (2008).

56　Manuel Vargas (2007b), 216.

57　Robert Kane appears to agree insofar as he calls Vargas' view "revisionist compatibilism ... [which] would also differ from ordinary compatibilist views" (Kane (2011), 27).

58　In personal correspondence, Jason Miller suggested the following related objection to the Logical Argument: "One might think that what 'free will' is somehow gets settled by what we *think* it is. So a revisionist who thinks the folk concept is (say) libertarian might hold that (a) free will is *not* compatible with determinism, given what we *now* mean by 'free will', and (b) we should revise our concept of 'free will' so that it means something that makes (a) false. But given that they think (a) is currently *true*, it's at least not clear to me whether it's fair to characterize their view as compatibilist according to the definition you offer." In response, I'm inclined to deny that the metaphysics of something as central to our self-understanding as free will is settled by what we think it is.

59　Ted Honderich (2002b), 110f.

60　Ted Honderich (2002b), 113.

61　In personal correspondence, Zac Bachman has suggested that "determining whether Honderich is a compatibilist or incompatibilist turns on what the 'kind of responsibility' that is compatible with determinism amounts to. We can distinguish, for example, the kind of responsibility that is required for punishment, blame, etc. on the one hand, and the kind of responsibility that is required for being the owner of artistic endeavors, finding meaning in life, love, interpersonal relationships, etc. I believe that it's [the former] notions of responsibility that are at the heart of the compatibility/incompatibility debate, and if this is the case, then he ought to be understood as an incompatibilist." As indicated above, Honderich does think there is a sense of freedom and responsibility that the truth of determinism means we cannot have. But there are other senses which we've seen he thinks remain. It is this latter claim which distinguishes him from Derk Pereboom who, as discussed in the next chapter, is an incompatibilist who thinks we are not free and responsible agents.

62 Manuel Vargas (2005), 420.

63 Compare Ned Markosian (1999), Timothy O'Connor (2000) and Harry Frankfurt (1971).

64 Manuel Vargas (2005), 417. See also Vargas (2004), 219.

65 See Chapter 8 for a further discussion of Fischer's view.

66 Manuel Vargas (2007a), 153. Consider also the following: "In this, the semi of semicompatibilism is like the semi of a semi-truck: it marks a particularly prominent instance of the kind, but an instance of the general kind nevertheless. All of which is to say that we also should not lose track of what the mainstream of the debate is about, and indeed, what compatibilism is usually taken to be about: the kind of power or agency required for being rightly blamed and praised in those characteristically moralized ways" (Vargas (2009), 58).

67 Manuel Vargas (2007b), 216. Elsewhere, Vargas also writes that if he's wrong about the descriptive aspect of folk thinking about free will, he has "a very natural fallback position for my account: conditional revisionism" (Vargas (2009), 55). I think that conditional revisionism is even more clearly a compatibilist account than is moderate revisionism for reasons that should now be obvious.

68 I'd have no problem calling it, for instance, "revisionist compatibilism" which would help to differentiate it from other forms of compatibilism that are not moderately revisionist. Rather, it is presenting moderate revisionism as an alternative to compatibilism that I take issue with.

Chapter Four

1 The same study indicates that 85 per cent of participants believe that dolphins have free will, and 75 per cent of participants think dogs do.

2 Here is the prompt and breakdown of responses in their survey:
   At least some of the choices you make while awake are free.

1	2	3	4	5	6	7	8	9
Definitely Disagree								Definitely Agree

Descriptive Statistics					
	N	Minimum	Maximum	Mean	Std. Deviation
Some_awake_ choices_are_free	50	1.00	9.00	7.8400	1.86657
Valid N (listwise)	50				

Some_awake_choices_are_free				
	Frequency	Per cent	Valid Per cent	Cumulative Per cent
Valid 1.00	2	4.0	4.0	4.0
4.00	1	2.0	2.0	6.0
5.00	1	2.0	2.0	8.0
6.00	4	8.0	8.0	16.0
7.00	6	12.0	12.0	28.0
8.00	9	18.0	18.0	46.0
9.00	27	54.0	54.0	100.0
Total	50	100.0	100.0	

3 http://philpapers.org/raw/survey.pdf (accessed 5 February 2012).

4 Interpreting the data is less than completely straightforward given the survey's possible responses. However, insofar as only 12.9 per cent of respondents in the present category indicated that they accepted or lean toward free will skepticism, I take it that the above description of the data is not inappropriate. It is interesting to note that in the same survey, free will skepticism increased to 18.4 per cent among current philosophy graduate students, and to 23.5 per cent among philosophy undergraduates.

5 Peter van Inwagen (1983), 206. Van Inwagen doesn't think that the existence of free will is as equally obvious, but that's because he thinks, as indicated in Chapter 1, that free will is just the ability to do otherwise.

6 Peter van Inwagen (1983), 223. Saul Smilansky (1990) raises a criticism of van Inwagen's view on just this point, which I explore below.

7 M. J. Scanlon (2005), 160.

8 See, for example, Joseph Campbell (2011), 1.

9 Ben Hart has pointed out that indirect proofs, as I discuss them here, parallel G. E. Moore's response to epistemic skepticism regarding the external world. There is a huge literature regarding epistemological skepticism that parallels much of the discussion of free will skepticism. A number of individuals have begun exploring the relationship between these two literatures; see, for example, Ben Hart (forthcoming) and Joseph Campbell (2011).

10 Peter van Inwagen (2008), 328. Later in the same essay, van Inwagen says the following about moral responsibility: "Since 'moral responsibility' figures prominently in my statement of the free will problem, one might expect that at this point I should define this term, or at least define some sentence or sentences in which it occurs—'x is morally responsible for y', perhaps. I won't do this. If I *did* offer a definition in this general area, it would be something like this:
  x is morally responsible for the fact that $p =_{df}$ it is x's fault that p.
But so much confusion attends the phrase 'moral responsibility' ... that I despair of straightening it all out in a paper that is not devoted to that topic alone" (ibid., 330f).

11 See, among others, Robert Kane (1996); Laura Ekstrom (1998); John Martin Fischer (2006), 21ff and Chapter 5; and Daniel Dennett (1984), Chapter 7.

12 Peter van Inwagen (1983), 155. Van Inwagen's argument takes as its starting point Richard Taylor (1963), Chapter 5, but differs from Taylor's in a number of important ways. For related discussions, see Dana Nelkin (2004a) and (2004b); E. J. Coffman and Ted Warfield (2005); and Derk Pereboom (2008a).

13 Peter van Inwagen (1983), 157.

14 Peter van Inwagen (1983), 156. Van Inwagen goes on in the same passage to say that the conclusion that deliberation requires free will is "as near to being uncontroversial as any philosophically interesting proposition can be." As we'll see in a minute, this conclusion is the subject of considerable controversy; whether this tells against van Inwagen's account or against the state of philosophically interesting propositions, I'll leave for the reader to decide. But even if van Inwagen is correct that Holbach believes he has free will, that obviously doesn't entail that he really *does* have free will.

15 An example here would be Peter Strawson's influential 1962 article "Freedom and Resentment." John Martin Fischer often talks as if he supports an indirect argument for the existence of free will; see Fischer (2006d), particularly Chapters 2, 3, and 5. However, as we'll see below, Fischer also advances a direct argument in response to the Existence Question.

16 Saul Smilansky (1990), 30 and 32.

17 See Derk Pereboom (2008a).

18 In personal correspondence, Manuel Vargas suggests that there is another way direct arguments for the existence of free will could go, which he calls "arguments from paradigm cases." On such an approach, one says that a particular case is obviously an instance of moral responsibility (and thus, on the definition of free will adopted above, a case of free will), and then works out an error theory about why others would ever doubt the existence of moral responsibility and free will. Peter Strawson's work would be one example of such an approach.

19 A number of the works in which Fischer develops and defends his compatibilist view of free will are co-authored with Mark Ravizza. Given that this view is further refined by Fischer in more recent single-authored work, in what follows I will refer to the view primarily as Fischer's account.

20 John Martin Fischer (2007a), 56. In particular, Fischer is inclined to accept the soundness of the Consequence Argument, discussed in Chapter 2, which argues that if determinism is true, then no one ever has the freedom to choose otherwise.

21 In the introduction to the volume containing Fischer (2007a) and (2007b), there is a chart attributing belief in the existence of free will to Fischer; see p. 4. Fischer has indicated in personal correspondence that he does affirm the existence of free will (as understood here) and moral responsibility to be a Moorean fact.

22 See Kane (2007a), 8–9.

23 See Robert Kane (2007a), 10–13.

24 Robert Kane (1996), 184.

25 Robert Kane (2005), 121–2. For an extended elaboration and defense of this argument, see Kane (1996), Chapter 7.

26 Robert Kane (2002b), 412. For a related discussion of the connection between free will and moral character, see Timothy Pawl and Kevin Timpe (2009). This is an issue which I discuss at greater length in Timpe (forthcoming).

27 Robert Kane (2002b), 411. This is why ultimate responsibility entails alternative possibilities, at least at some point in the causal history of an agent's actions. I return to this issue in Chapter 9 below.

28 The name "Anne" is given to the businesswoman by Derk Pereboom (2007), 102.

29 Robert Kane (2002b), 417. For a criticism of this example, see Pereboom (2007a), 101–5.

30 Robert Kane (2007a), 28.

31 Robert Kane (1996), 39 and 130.

32 Robert Kane (1996), 197.

33 Manuel Vargas suggests, in personal correspondence, that Nietzsche may offer an indirect proof for the non-existence of free will. Vargas suggests that Nietzsche "thinks that free will might be sufficient for moralized blaming, but he's independently skeptical about moralized blaming (e.g. on an interpretation where he's an error-theorist about morality in general), so there is good reason to be dubious that free will in the 'superlative metaphysical sense' can be had. Of course, he goes on to attack that notion on independent reason, but I wonder if he isn't at least implicitly committed … to an argument of the [indirect] sort." For a related discussion, see Brian Leiter (2010). It strikes me as a very strange claim to hold that free will is sufficient for moral responsibility, though I'm not sufficiently well versed in Nietzsche scholarship to comment more on Vargas' suggestion.

34 See, for example, Kadri Vihvelin (2008), 303.

35 Derk Pereboom (2007a), 93.

36 A third view holds that the required indeterminism is of neither of these sorts of causation, instead holding that free will requires no positive causal contribution at all. On some such views, exercising the kind of control at issue in free will need not be understood causally at all. Two prominent non-causalists are Hugh McCann and Carl Ginet. For a recent defense of such a non-causal view, see Stewart Goetz (2009). A very worthwhile discussion of these species of libertarian views is found in Randolph Clarke (2003).

37 Derk Pereboom (1997), 253.

38 Derk Pereboom (2008b), 1.

39 Derk Pereboom (2001), 79.

40 For the most recent defense of hard incompatibilism, see Derk Pereboom (2011).

41 Saul Smilansky (2002), 504 note 3.

42 Saul Smilansky (2002), 490f. Smilansky's view is more complex than is indicated here, in part due to his denial that there is just one kind of free will: "compatibilism and incompatibilism are indeed logically inconsistent, but it is possible to hold a mixed, intermediate position that is not fully consistent with

either" (Smilansky (2002), 491). For a full development and defense of his view, see Smilansky (2000).

43 Galen Strawson (1994), 5.

44 Galen Strawson (1994), 7.

45 For more on Strawson's argument against the existence of free will, see Joseph Campbell (2011), 56. More specifically, Strawson has in mind in this argument what he calls "true ultimate responsibility": "responsibility and desert of such a kind that it can exist if and only if punishment and reward can be fair or just without having any pragmatic justification, or indeed any justification that appeals to the notion of distributive justice" (Strawson (2002), 452). Strawson also defines true moral responsibility as "responsibility of such a kind that, if we have it, then it makes sense, at least, to suppose that it could be just to punish some of us with (eternal) torment in hell and reward others with (eternal) bliss in heaven" (Strawson (1994), 9). Strawson appears to think these two definitions are equivalent; however, see Randolph Clarke (2005), 20 for an argument that they are not.

46 Bruce Waller (2006), 85f.

47 Carlos Moya (2006), particularly chapter 5.

48 John Martin Fischer (2006a), 112.

49 John Martin Fischer (2006a), 113f.

50 John Martin Fischer (2006a), 116.

51 John Martin Fischer (2006a), 116.

52 Joseph Campbell (2011), 56.

53 Galen Strawson (1994), 12f.

54 Randolph Clarke (2005), 19. See also Al Mele (1995), 222.

55 Randolph Clarke (2005), 20. Ben Hart suggests a similar response to Strawson, one reminiscent of Reidian responses to epistemic skepticism. At the heart of this Reidian response is the claim that the belief in the existence of freedom and responsibility are more plausible than the unreasonable demands required by the skeptic. If that is the case, then the skeptic will have failed to provide sufficient reasons for believing in the principles, such as (P), which lead to skepticism. See Ben Hart (forthcoming). For a defense of the reasonableness of the Basic Argument, see Michael Anthony Istvan Jr. (2010).

56 Kadri Vihvelin (2008), 303 and 305.

57 Michael McKenna (2010), 432.

58 Remember, to say that *A* is incompatible with *B* is to say that there is no possible world containing both *A* and *B*. See also Joseph Campbell (2011), 54.

Chapter Five

1 For influential presentations of this argument, see Roderick Chisholm (1966) and Carl Ginet (1995).

2 In the earlier edition of this book, I referred to this as the Basic Argument. However, given the discussion of Galen Strawson's Basic Argument in Chapter 4, it is worthwhile to use a different name for the present argument. I select the Core Argument because this argument has been at the center for incompatibilism in recent decades.

3 Gerald Harrison (2006), 399.

4 Harry Frankfurt (1969), 829. Actually, Frankfurt's original name for this principle is "the Principle of Alternate Possibilities." Regarding the original title, Frankfurt says this:

> Many philosophers, including both supporters and opponents of my critique of the Principle of Alternate Possibilities, share the view that my name for the principle involves incorrect usage. They consider it obvious that the principle has to do with alternatives and not with alternates. Now I agree that "the Principle of Alternative Possibilities" would be more or less okay; but the extra beat clutters up the rhythm in a way that I don't like. So is it really clear that using the term "alternate" is egregiously unacceptable? In a selection process, the alternates are candidates to which or to whom we could have turned in case one of our preferred candidates had been unavailable. We don't refer to the alternates in these cases as "alternatives". That would mask the fact that they are second choices. When we speak of the possibility that a person could have done otherwise, we are speaking of actions that the person could have performed if he had not been able to do what he clearly preferred to do. Why aren't those rejected actions alternate possibilities, and properly referred to as such? (Frankfurt (1999), 372)

Peter van Inwagen has referred to Frankfurt's defense of his original title as "ill-advised" (van Inwagen (2004), 219).

5 *AP* is thus equivalent to premise (1) of the Core Argument. *AP* also needs to be understood so as to include a tracing clause, according to which a person can have free will at time *t* despite lacking alternative possibilities at *t* so long as her lacking alternative possibilities at *t* is the result of an earlier free choice of hers. Because (a) nearly everyone agrees that *AP* should be understood as involving a tracing clause and (b) explicit mention of the tracing clause would needlessly complicate much of what follows, in this chapter and throughout the rest of the book I will largely ignore this qualification. Nevertheless, the reader will do well to keep this qualification in mind. For a discussion of a number of the issues involved in tracing, see Timpe (2011).

6 Robert Kane (2002a), 17.

7 Harry Frankfurt (1969), 829. Similarly, David Hunt writes "While different analyses of the relevant sense of 'could' have led to very different ways of interpreting *PAP*, the principle itself (however interpreted) has inspired near unanimity across the philosophical spectrum" (David Hunt (2005), 126). Though they both date from after Frankfurt's article, the following two quotations illustrate the tendency that Frankfurt and Hunt here draw our attention to: "Responsibility presupposes freedom. If anyone is responsible for what he has done, then he must have been free to do otherwise" (Richard Taylor (1976), 293) and "Fundamental to our common-sense conception of human agency is the assumption that sometimes a person could have

performed some action that he did not perform" (Terence Horgan (1979), 345).

8 Michael McKenna (2010), 436.

9 Joseph K. Campbell (1997), 319. Campbell differentiates strong compatibilism from weak compatibilism, discussed below.

10 Peter Forrest (1985), 212f.

11 Torbjörn Tännsjö (1989), 191.

12 Torbjörn Tännsjö (1989), 190.

13 Tännsjö is himself aware that many will take the conclusion of his argument as a *reductio ad absurdum* of his preferred version of strong compatibilism; here I think he is likely correct.

14 David Lewis (1987).

15 David Lewis (1987), 291. The reader here will do well to keep in mind that Lewis intends soft determinism to be contrasted with hard determinism—the thesis that (a) determinism is true and (b) that the truth of determinism is incompatible with free will.

16 David Lewis (1987), 292. For a similar treatment, see Jonathan Westphal (2003).

17 David Lewis (1987), 292. Helen Beebee describes this distinction as follows: "one can perform an action that requires a miracle without thereby performing a miracle" (Beebee (2003), 260).

18 David Lewis (1987), 294. See also Lewis's discussion in David Lewis (1979).

19 Helen Beebee has argued that Lewis's view does commit him to the claim that free agents could cause laws of nature to be broken, despite the distinction between the two claims above. See Helen Beebee (2003). For a reply on behalf of Lewis's view, see Shane Oakley (2006).

20 Jim Stone (1998), 258.

21 Jim Stone (1998), 259.

22 Jim Stone (1998), 259.

23 Jim Stone (1998), 260f. Stone's article contains further qualifications on this idea, though these complexities need not concern us here.

24 Peter van Inwagen (1983), 114ff.

25 Other possibilities for the condition in question include "... if you had willed ...," "... if you had tried...," and "... if you had set out ... ." See the discussion in Roderick Chisholm (1967), which also contains criticism of these sorts of conditional approaches.

26 G. E. Moore (1912), 131. See also the discussions in J. L. Austin (1990), P. H. Nowell-Smith (1960), and Peter van Inwagen (1975), particularly 196f.

27 A. Y. Ayer (1997), 110.

28 For criticisms of conditionalism, see J. L. Austin (1990); Keith Lehrer (1966), (1976); Roderick Chisholm (1966); and Peter van Inwagen (1983), 114–26. For a defense of conditionalism in the face of some of the above criticisms, see Bruce Aune (1967).

29 Michael McKenna (2005a), 163.

30 Richard Taylor (1983), 44.

31 Hugh McCann (1998), 177.

32 Peter van Inwagen (2004), 222.

33 See, for example, C. A. Campbell (1957), Richard Taylor (1983), Peter van Inwagen (1983), Robert Kane (1985).

34 John Martin Fischer (2007a), 50.

35 In recent years, a number of compatibilists have developed classical accounts which are not committed to conditionalism. Space constraints, however, do not permit a discussion of these views at present. See, however, Kadri Vihvelin (2008a), (2008b); and Joseph K. Campbell (1997), (2005).

36 Harry Frankfurt (1969), 835f. I have omitted the subscript from "Jones$_4$" throughout this paragraph.

37 For a noteworthy introduction to this voluminous literature, see Michael McKenna and David Widerker (2003). See also John Martin Fischer (2002b) and (2010).

38 Michael McKenna (2005a), 162f.

39 Joseph K. Campbell (1997), 319. "Weak compatibilism" is also sometimes called Frankfurt-compatibilism for obvious reasons.

40 Harry Frankfurt (2002b), 28. Elsewhere, Frankfurt admits that "I have not always been clear myself about what the point [concerning *PAP*] is" ((2003), 344 note 2). John Fischer, another staunch defender of *FSC*s, writes that the "success of the Frankfurt-type strategy should not be judged on the basis of whether the Frankfurt-type cases in themselves decisively establish that moral responsibility is compatible with determinism. That they do not do all the work does not show that they do not do some important work" (John Martin Fischer (2002a), 8f).

41 John Martin Fischer (2010), 316 and 318.

42 John Martin Fischer (2002b), 291f. See also John Martin Fischer (2002a), particularly pages 4–12.

43 Kadri Vihvelin (2000), 1f.

44 Stewart Goetz (2009), 75.

45 There are other incompatibilist responses to *FSC*s than those considered here, though space does not permit a detailed discussion of them. For instance, in Vivienne Brown (2006), Brown argues that Frankfurt's argument against the ability to do otherwise essentially relies on a notion of choice, "but this exercise of choice isn't possible in a causally determined world, thus undermining the relevance of Frankfurt's example of the counterfactual intervener if causal determinism is true" (286). Another insightful and challenging incompatibilist criticism of *FSC*s can be found in Daniel Speak (2007). I return to Speak's discussion below in Chapter 7.

Chapter Six

1 Stewart Goetz (2009), 76.

2 Elsewhere, I have referred to the Dilemma Defense as the Kane–Widerker Objection, or the Kane–Widerker–Ginet Objection, named after its primary proponents. See Kevin Timpe (2003) and (2006b).

3 Harry Frankfurt (1969), 835f. As in Chapter 5, I have removed the subscript from "Jones$_4$" throughout this paragraph.

4 See John Martin Fischer (1994), 135f (1999b), 279; and John Martin Fischer and Mark Ravizza (1998), 110ff. For an early paper regarding the need for a prior sign, see David Blumenfeld (1971).

5 In an early paper, Robert Heinaman (1986) suggests that whether determinism or indeterminism is assumed in an *FSC* is vitally important, but he doesn't develop this idea to the degree that it is in subsequent discussions of the sort that I discuss below. Michael McKenna (2005a, 177) suggests that the Dilemma Defense line of response traces back to Peter van Inwagen (1983), 161–82.

6 For a different charge that *FSCs* beg the question, see P. A. Woodward (2002). For a reply, see Neil Levy (2004).

7 Robert Kane (1985), 51 footnote 25.

8 Robert Kane (1996), 142. See also pages 191f of the same volume, as well as Robert Kane (2000b) and (2003). For an application of the Dilemma Defense to Pereboom's Tax Evasion case, see David Palmer (2011).

9 David Widerker (1995), 248. The name *IRR* situation refers to the fact that the circumstances which make it impossible for the agent to perform the action in question are irrelevant to what the agent actually does since, as the situation actually unfolds, those circumstances are causally inert.

10 David Widerker (1995), 248f.

11 David Widerker (1995), 249f. I have slightly modified Widerker's exact phrasing to make the agent (Jones) a female, as having a gender difference between the agent and the intervener allows for clearer pronoun reference.

12 David Widerker (2003), 59.

13 David Widerker (1995), 249f. Widerker extends this line of argument to other sorts of *FSCs* in David Widerker (2000). The further complexities that Widerker considers here need not concern us at present. More recently, however, Widerker suggests that the Dilemma Defense fails; see Widerker (2006). For a helpful discussion of Widerker's change on this point, see Stewart Goetz (2009), Chapter 5.

14 Widerker is willing to grant that perhaps *PAP* is false for complex acts such as actually killing Smith: "a Frankfurt-type counterfactual intervener can deprive an agent of his freedom to carryout a given want or intention, but he cannot deprive him of his freedom to form it" (David Widerker (1995), 255). For similar lines of argumentation, see also Carl Ginet (1996), David Hunt (1996), and Laura Ekstrom (1998).

15 See, for instance, David Hunt (2003).

16 However, for a discussion of why I think that foreknowledge differs from causal determinism, see Kevin Timpe (2007b).

17 Alfred Mele and David Robb (1998), 98.

18 Alfred Mele and David Robb (1998), 102 footnote 12.

19 Alfred Mele and David Robb (1998), 101f.

20 Alfred Mele and David Robb (1998), 103.

21 As will be made clear in the discussion below, the "before" here can either be temporally prior, as in cutting preemption, or logically prior, as in trumping preemption.

22 This view of *FSCs* assumes the falsity of certain accounts of event (and action) individuation, such as those defended by Donald Davidson and Peter van Inwagen. See, for example, Donald Davidson (2001), particularly essay 8, and Peter van Inwagen (1983), particularly Chapter 5. For a criticism of such views, see Christopher Hughes (1994) and Jonathan Bennett (1988), 58ff. For a discussion of these issues as they related to free will, see Gordon Pettit (2005) and Kevin Timpe (2009).

23 John Martin Fischer and Mark Ravizza (1998), 159.

24 Cf. Linda Zagzebski (2000): "It is also true that in most descriptions of F cases [i.e. *FSCs*] the machine's operation depends upon what the agent does. ... An exception is causal over-determination scenarios in which the machine is set to cause a certain choice but the agent causes the same choice by her own power at the same time" (239 and 248, note 24). Like the exceptions Zagzebski mentions, the machine in the Trumping Case developed below does not depend on the agent's action for its own operation; however, unlike the exceptions she mentions, the Trumping Case is a case of trumping preemption rather than overdetermination.

25 Douglas Ehring (1997), 20f.

26 In Mele and Robb's terminology, "by t_2 P has neutralized all of the nodes in Bob for decisions that are contrary to a decision at t_2 to steal Ann's car (e.g. a decision at t_2 not to steal anyone's car and a decision at t_2 never to steal anything). In convenient shorthand, by t_2 P has neutralized N2 and all its 'cognate decision nodes'" (Mele and Robb (1998), 105).

27 For a further discussion of their example, see Alfred Mele and David Robb (2003). In this later article, Mele and Robb grant that the possibility that the primary issue underlying the difference between their evaluation of blockage cases and Kane's criticism of such cases, discussed below, is the metaphysics of causality.

28 David Hunt (2003), 170. See also the discussion in Hunt (2000), where he first introduces such cases.

29 Kane differentiates "pure blockage cases," in which the agent has no remaining alternative possibilities, from "modified blockage cases," in which only all of the agent's robust alternative possibilities are blocked (Robert Kane (2003), 95). The issue of robustness will be discussed at length in Chapter 7, and so I do not consider modified or partial blockage cases at length here.

30 David Hunt (2003), 171.

31 Derk Pereboom (2001), 18. Pereboom continues: "My own view is not that actual causal histories in blockage cases are clearly deterministic, but only that these considerations show that they might be. This type of problem should make one less confident when evaluating these difficult kinds of Frankfurt-style cases." For a similar conclusion, see Helen Steward (2009). For a stronger argument for the conclusion that "the blockage strategy ... is a dead end," see Carlos Moya Epsi (2003), 119.

32 Robert Kane raises a similar criticism of blockage cases in Robert Kane (2000c), as do Laura Ekstrom (2002), and Stewart Goetz in his (2002) and (2005).

33 Robert Kane (2003), 97 and the discussion on the following pages.

34 David Hunt (2003), 172.

35 David Hunt (2005), 131f.

36 John Martin Fischer (2000c), 146.

37 John Martin Fischer appears to agree in his (2002), 296.

38 Eleonore Stump (1996), 77f. By "correlates," Stump must mean that neural sequence 1 is necessary and sufficient for Jones voting for a Republican (and likewise for neural sequence 2 and Jones voting for a Democrat) in order for the intervener to be able to guarantee the desired outcome. For other discussions of Stump's example that focus on other issues than those below, see Stewart Goetz (2002) and David Widerker (1995), (2000), (2003).

39 If one wanted to allow for such further options, one could merely modify RCE. However, such further complications are not necessary for my purposes here and will hereafter be ignored.

40 If it detects x–y–z firing, it also cuts the causal chain arising from these neurons as mentioned earlier.

41 Jonathan Schaffer (2000), 165. A version of this example is given by Michael McDermott (1995), 530. Schaffer does not cite this earlier occurrence of the example, but the two are sufficiently similar to warrant the conclusion that Schaffer has McDermott's case in mind.

42 David Lewis (2000), 183. Lewis credits the discovery of trumping to Schaffer and the example used here to Bas van Frassen.

43 That is, the brain-stimulator's neural sequence preempting a different neural sequence elsewhere in the brain versus one dendrite trumping another dendrite in the same neural sequence. I thank Alicia Finch for pointing out the need for the further clarifications present in this paragraph.

44 In personal correspondence, Zachary Bachman worries that the Trumping Case as developed above is really a case involving overdetermination rather than trumping preemption. If this is so, then the case as here developed wouldn't serve my present purposes. But as I argue below in this paragraph, if trumping preemption is coherent, then we can construct an FSC based on it in some other fashion and the more general point holds.

45 Another way to avoid the Dilemma Defense is via middle knowledge. For FSCs developed along this line, see Eleonore Stump (2003) and Michael

Bergmann (2002). The Trumping Case presented here is preferable to these Molinist-inspired *FSCs* in that the former does not depend on something as philosophically contentious as middle knowledge.

46 This description of Erosion* is a compilation of Fischer and Ravizza's descriptions of Avalanche, Erosion, and Erosion* from John Martin Fischer and Mark Ravizza (1998), 155–60.

47 John Martin Fischer and Mark Ravizza (1998), 160.

48 David Lewis (2000), 182.

49 See John Martin Fischer and Mark Ravizza (1998), 162.

50 See Michael McDermott (1995), 524.

51 Eric Funkhouser (2009) is skeptical of the Trumping Case, but his skepticism is rooted in his skepticism of trumping preemption in general.

52 These two understandings, which they call the Broad Dialectical Situation and the Narrow Dialectical Situation, are also related to the two understandings of the Flicker Strategy, which I address in the subsequent chapter.

53 Ishtiyaque Haji and Michael McKenna (2006), 266. See also Haji and McKenna (2004).

54 Ishtiyaque Haji and Michael McKenna (2004), 303.

55 Ishtiyaque Haji and Michael McKenna (2006), 367.

56 Ishtiyaque Haji and Michael McKenna (2006), 367.

57 David Palmer (2005) argues, unsuccessfully in my view, that even the more limited way of understanding the role of *FSCs* at hand begs the question. Haji and McKenna respond in their (2006).

58 In fact, in a footnote Haji and McKenna write that their arguments were "offered as a limited defense of Fischer's contribution" to these issues (Haji and McKenna (2006), 367 footnote 8).

59 John Martin Fischer (1982).

60 John Martin Fischer (2000c), 144.

61 John Martin Fischer (2002b), 292.

62 John Martin Fischer (2010), 318.

63 John Martin Fischer (2010), 292. See also John Martin Fischer (1999a), 113 and (2002a) for similar arguments.

64 Stewart Goetz (2005), 87.

65 Fischer admits that there are problems with his current reply to Goetz in John Martin Fischer (2006e), 236.

66 Stewart Goetz (2005), 85.

67 Stewart Goetz (2009), 87f.

68 John Martin Fischer (2010), 325. He in fact describes his article as a "'coroner's report' on the status of the Dilemma Defense" (336).

69 It also assumes the success of buffer cases; see John Martin Fischer (2010), 327.

70 Interestingly enough, Fischer himself is inclined to accept that the truth of determinism would eliminate alternative possibilities, even though it's not an

official part of his semi-compatibilism. See also the discussion of the Weak Strategy in the next chapter.

71 For further debate of this issue not considered here, see Derk Pereboom (2006).

Chapter Seven

1 Peter van Inwagen (1983) contains an early presentation of the Flicker Strategy, though he does not call it such.

2 John Martin Fischer (1994), 134 and 140.

3 John Martin Fischer (1994), 136ff.

4 For those that favor a different version of the Flicker Strategy, I leave it to the reader to do the appropriate translation in what follows.

5 David Widerker and Michael McKenna (2003), 7.

6 Similar comments are made by Alfred Mele, another opponent of AP, when discussing the Flicker Strategy. See Alfred Mele (2003), 253.

7 John Martin Fischer (1994), 135.

8 John Martin Fischer (2002a), 6.

9 In fact, AP_f might be stronger than needed by the Weak Strategy, insofar as all the Weak Strategy needs is for some alternative possibilities to be necessary, whether those alternative possibilities are related to the action in question or not. What is central to AP_f is that A is not causally necessitated by anything prior to t.

10 Of course, the claim that the alternative possibilities that remain in $FSCs$ are morally relevant is contested by Fischer and kin, who claim that the remaining alternative possibilities are not "robust" enough to ground moral responsibility. I return to this issue below.

11 Alfred Mele (1998), 154. See also Mele (2003), 256.

12 Mike Murray suggested this way of putting the point in conversation.

13 Though a compatibilist herself, Kadri Vihvelin says the following about Frankfurt's attack on PAP and AP: "Frankfurt never pulled off his metaphysical conjuring trick. He left us with a promissory note, which his supporters have been trying to cash ever since" (2008b, 344).

14 Ted Warfield (2007), 288.

15 It should also be noted that arguments against incompatibilism from divine foreknowledge will not suffice to undermine AP_f in the sense at issue here. To see why, consider the following. Assume that God is essentially omniscient and has foreknowledge of free actions (the assumption that God is temporal and that His knowledge is, properly speaking, *fore*knowledge is not essential to the story. A similar case which allows for an atemporal deity could also be described). At t_1, God knows that Allison will freely do A at t_2. It does not follow that Allison cannot do other than A at t_2 in the sense at issue

here. Even if God knows what Allison will do, the conjunction of the laws of nature and the state of the entire physical universe at any time prior to t_2 are not sufficient for Allison's doing A at t_2. For an argument why free will and foreknowledge are not incompatible, see Timpe (2007b).

16 Michael Della Rocca (1998), 101 and 100.

17 Warfield (2007). See also Sam Black and Jon Tweedale (2002), 300f.

18 Alfred Mele (2003); see also R. Jay Wallace (1994), 263.

19 John Martin Fischer (1998), 164, emphasis added.

20 John Martin Fischer (1994), 145f. Fischer specifically acknowledges that the falsity of causal determinism might be taken to be one such factor. Furthermore, the Weak Strategy meets Fischer's desideratum that ascriptions of moral responsibility be based only on what happens in the actual sequence, not the alternate sequence. What the remaining flickers, no matter how "weak and thin," show is that the action in the actual sequence is not the result of causal determinism in the actual sequence, since that would completely eliminate all alternative possibilities of any sort. This also begins to point in the direction of sourcehood, to be explored in subsequent chapters.

21 John Martin Fischer (1999a), 119. Fischer credits this phrase to the illustrious Dan Speak.

22 John Martin Fischer (1994), 146. Fischer grants elsewhere as well that the arguments he offers against the flicker strategy are "not decisive" (Fischer (1999b), 286; (2002a), 2).

23 John Martin Fischer (1994), 159. See also Fischer (2006), 28 where he writes that the remaining alternatives are so "exiguous as to be irrelevant."

24 John Martin Fischer (1994), 140.

25 John Martin Fischer (2002a), 6.

26 The Robustness Requirement is what Dan Speak refers to as the indirect challenge of FSCs: "Fischer has countenanced the possibility that there will always be room in Frankfurt-style examples for some alternative possibilities. The indirect challenge to the relevance of the flickers of freedom does not require, after all, that the flickers be extinguished. Instead, Fischer argues that it is implausible to think that such thin alternatives could be the ground for our intuitions regarding moral responsibility" (Speak (2002), 93).

27 John Martin Fischer (1999b), 284f.

28 Helen Steward (2009) makes a similar point. According to Steward, an AP condition need not involve robust alternatives in order to form part of a sound argument for the truth of incompatibilism. She thus appears to embrace a version of the Weak Strategy discussed in the previous section.

29 John Martin Fischer (2002b), 288 and 301.

30 R. Jay Wallace raises a different objection to Fischer's understanding of robustness: "[Fischer's] response seems suspiciously ad hoc, however. After all, there is surely some sense in which the agents in Frankfurt's scenarios cannot do otherwise; it almost looks as if Fischer has singled out that sense and simply declared it to be the sense that matters to the debate. At the least, we need a convincing and principled reason [to adopt Fischer's definition of

robustness]" (Wallace (1994), 262). For a response to this charge, see John Martin Fischer (2006c), 321ff.

31 Derk Pereboom (2003), 188. Robert Allen considers a similar understanding of the Robustness Requirement in Allen (2004).

32 Michael McKenna (2003), 213. Elsewhere, McKenna says that "a robust alternative is one that a theorist could point to and say that the presence of it helps to account for the sort of control bearing upon responsible agency" (McKenna (2006), 216). I take it that he sees this way of describing the Robustness Requirement as equivalent with that given in the text above.

33 I previously phrased the Robustness Requirement in this way in my (2006b), 345. In personal correspondence (May 7, 2005), Pereboom suggests a similar understanding of robustness, one that is significantly weaker than his proposal considered in the text above: "the robustness of an alternative possibility specifies that it be *per se* relevant to explaining moral responsibility."

34 John Martin Fischer (1994), 140.

35 The attempt to provide a Strong Strategy can also be understood as an attempt to undermine what David Widerker calls "the Argument from Insufficiently Robust Alternatives" (Widerker (2005)).

36 John Martin Fischer (1994), especially 149–54.

37 John Martin Fischer (2002a), 10.

38 The discussion in Chapter 9 will return to this issue, but here let me simply indicate the direction that I will develop the argument there. If the factor of the actual sequence that grounds moral responsibility is a sourcehood condition, and that condition cannot be met if causal determinism is true, then moral responsibility will require there to be alternative possibilities insofar as they are sufficient to show that determinism is false. However, it may not be necessary that those alternative possibilities include voluntary action, since these further requirements aren't required to satisfy the sourcehood condition.

39 Another version of the Strong Strategy can be found in Garry Young (2007).

40 Daniel Speak (2002), 96.

41 In a footnote, Speak admits that "it might turn out that NO compatibilist will be persuaded" by his argument for this conclusion, but he thinks that this is "irrelevant" (Speak (2002), 103 footnote 10). Speak thinks that his response is superior to the Weak Strategy in that the former, unlike the latter, "can be offered to compatibilists on grounds they can be expected to accept," whether or not they actually do accept it.

42 Daniel Speak (2002), 97.

43 Daniel Speak (2002), 94.

44 Daniel Speak (2002), 97. In a footnote to this passage, Speak acknowledges that the Flicker Strategy should, in fact, do more than merely establish the possible relevance of the remaining alternative possibilities: "A complete defense of the flicker strategy would involve arguments not just in favor of the possibility of the relevance of these alternatives. Fanning these flickers should also involve an attempt to defend the plausibility of their relevance. I will not, however, attempt this here, although I hope my examples can at least begin

to build a case for the sort of plausibility I imagine incompatibilists ultimately want" (103, footnote 13).

45 Daniel Speak (2002), 97.

46 Daniel Speak (2002), 98. Speak subsequently develops more complicated versions of this scenario, paralleling the development of *FSC*s with ever-increasing complexity. However, the initial presentation of the case is sufficient for us to evaluate Speak's argument.

47 Daniel Speak (2002), 98. In the footnote to this passage, Speak further stipulates that the case is not one in which the agent performs his duty in some responsibility-undermining way.

48 Daniel Speak (2002), 100.

49 Michael McKenna (1997), 75.

50 For example, in David Hunt (2003), 182, footnote 29. See also John Martin Fischer (2003), 247: "If one coherent sort of scenario can be constructed in which we are confident that the agent is morally responsible yet lacks alternative possibilities, that would be sufficient for the purpose." For a dissenting view that a single counterexample to *AP* is insufficient to establish its falsity, see Bernard Berofsky (2003), 110.

51 Daniel Speak (2002), 100.

52 Daniel Speak (2002), 100.

53 For a different criticism of Speak's article, one that denies that moral obligation is independent from moral responsibility in important ways, see Ishtiyaque Haji (2003).

54 Daniel Speak (2002), 101.

55 Commenting on this paragraph, Speak writes: "What I hoped I was showing was that I could construct an obligation out of the very same causal powers available to an agent under Frankfurtian circumstances. If I could construct an obligation, then it seemed to me that the powers were enough for responsibility—even in the absence of the additional conditions that constituted the obligation. So, to my mind, the obligation that serves to bring out that *PRA* is satisfied. It isn't necessary for the satisfaction of *PRA*. It isn't in virtue of the obligation. ... The agential power that can be exerted in the face of a Frankfurt intervener is enough to ground an obligation. There's no reason, then, to think that it can't ground responsibility." The insistence on the importance of the agential powers here suggests to me that Speak would also think that what is crucial here is the action having its source in a relevant feature of the agent, thereby involving a sourcehood condition of the sort explored in subsequent chapters. For a similar view about the relationship between causal powers and obligations, see Michael Smith (2004) and Kadri Vihvelin (2000).

56 Daniel Speak (2002), 101.

57 Daniel Speak (2002), 101.

58 For similar discussions of how the addition of knowledge alters the nature of an *FSC*, see Neil Levy (2002) and Robert Allen (2004), 24ff.

59 It seems plausible to me that Garvin is not only morally responsible for his desire that Johansen be killed but also for Johansen's death. Garvin wants

Johansen killed; knows that refraining from pulling the trigger on his own will still result in Johansen's death; thinks that by waiting he will alleviate his moral responsibility for Johansen's death; does not even attempt to prevent the death; and waits for the sole purpose of bringing about Johansen's death through the means he knows are in place. Contrary to what Garvin may have been thinking, I think it plausible that he is morally responsible for Johansen's death despite the intervention. Finally, I say that Garvin may be only partly morally responsible for Johansen's death, because it seems as if the leader of the rebel force is also morally responsible for the role he plays in Johansen's death.

60 Brendan Larvor (2010), 507.

61 Brendan Larvor (2010), 507 (emphasis added).

62 Brendan Larvor (2010), 507. See also David Widerker (1995) and (2000) for a similar argument.

63 Ezio Di Nucci (2011) is a reply to Larvor on behalf of Frankfurt examples. However, even Di Nucci admits that "the counterfactual scenario is such that Jones does not act, and therefore does not kill Smith" (103). This however seems to concede the Strong Strategy to Larvor. Another promising version of the Strong Strategy is developed by Carolina Sartorio in a pair of recent papers, (forthcoming) and (2012a).

64 Michael Robinson (2010), 191.

65 John Martin Fischer (2002a), 8.

66 John Martin Fischer (1994), 83.

67 Michael McKenna (2005c), 233.

68 John Martin Fischer (1999b), 294. More recently, Fischer also writes that "rational people can disagree about whether the doctrines in question are indeed incompatible with the relevant sort of alternative possibilities. ... We seem to have arrived at a certain kind of stalemate" (Fischer (2002a), 2). See also David Hunt (2005), 130.

69 John Martin Fischer (2002a), 20. Frankfurt notes his agreement with Fischer regarding this point in Harry Frankfurt (2002b), 27.

70 Vivienne Brown (2006), 276.

71 Vivienne Brown (2006), 276.

Chapter Eight

1 Source incompatibilism is also sometimes called "causal history incompatibilism," "actual-sequence incompatibilism," and "hyper-incompatibilism." See, for example, John Martin Fischer (2006d), 7 and *passim*. Elsewhere, I have used the term "Frankfurt Libertarianism" to refer to the form of incompatibilism which rejects an alternative-possibilities condition for moral responsibility; see Timpe (2006a) and (2006b), particularly footnote 7. William Hasker uses the term "Frankfurt Incompatibilism" in Hasker

(2001), 107f. I first became familiar with the term in conversation with Ken Perszyk, who also kindly gave me the reference to Hasker's use of the term. This is the view I refer to as "Narrow Source Incompatibilism" in Chapter 9.

2 For a similar view, see Robert Kane (2007a).

3 John Martin Fischer (2002b), 288. The scenario above is also inspired by similar cases presented by Michael McKenna (2003), 206ff.

4 As discussed in Chapter 5, there are a number of compatibilists who think that the truth of causal determinism would not preclude alternative possibilities and defend compatibilist interpretations of *AP*.

5 Timothy O'Connor (2005), 216. Elsewhere, O'Connor makes this point as follows: "It is not enough that any or a range of possible actions are *open* to me to perform; I must have the right sort of *control* over the way the decision goes in a certain way" (O'Connor (2002), 197).

6 Also related at this point is what Robert Kane calls "the Libertarian Dilemma" (Kane (2005), 33f). More on the Luck Objection in Chapter 10.

7 John Martin Fischer (1982), 31. See also John Martin Fischer (2002b), 302.

8 Derk Pereboom (forthcoming), 1f in manuscript.

9 For similar criticism of the near "exclusive preoccupation with the alternative possibilities condition," see Timothy O'Connor (2005).

10 The language of "actual-sequence accounts" comes from Fischer. See, for example, John Martin Fischer (1999a), 125ff and Fischer (2006d), 68–78, 198–201. More on this in Chapter 9.

11 See Harry Frankfurt (1988), particularly Chapter 2.

12 Harry Frankfurt (1988), 15.

13 John Martin Fischer (2000c), 143.

14 I thank Neal Tognazzini for helping express these intuitions behind *SC*.

15 Harry Frankfurt (1988), 22.

16 Susan Wolf (2003), 377f.

17 Robert Kane (2005), 96f.

18 Harry Frankfurt (1988), 172. Elsewhere, Frankfurt also suggests a "satisfaction condition" as a way of avoiding the problems facing mere mesh; see Harry Frankfurt (1992).

19 Robert Kane (1996), 65.

20 Harry Frankfurt (1998), 32ff.

21 Harry Frankfurt (1988), 46.

22 Harry Frankfurt (2002b), 28.

23 Alfred Mele (2008), 270. See also Michael McKenna (2011) for a worthwhile discussion of Frankfurt's view on this point.

24 Other critical discussions of Frankfurt's account of freedom of the will and its relation to wholeheartedness can be found in Michael Bratman (2002), David Zimmerman (1981), Gary Watson (1975), and John Martin Fischer and Mark Ravizza (1998), particularly Chapter 7.

25 In recent works, Fischer (2007a, 2007b) explicitly describes his view as based on the notion of sourcehood.

26 Many of the works in which semi-compatibilism is developed are co-authored by Fischer and Ravizza; the view is also defended by Fischer alone in a number of other works. In what follows, I will tend to speak of Fischer and Ravizza as a pair given that the initial work articulating and defending the view was done by the two together.

27 John Martin Fischer (2000a), 326.

28 John Martin Fischer (2002b), 307.

29 John Martin Fischer and Mark Ravizza (1998), 82.

30 John Martin Fischer and Mark Ravizza (1998), 71.

31 John Martin Fischer and Mark Ravizza (1998), 75.

32 John Martin Fischer (2000b), 390.

33 Neil Levy describes the ownership requirement here as "an ultimacy condition for compatibilists. Just as source incompatibilists insist on an ultimacy condition, to bring it about that agents are not merely creatures of the conditions into which they were born plus their genetic dispositions, so ownership conditions are incorporated into historical accounts of moral responsibility to bring it about that agents are not merely creatures of their endowment" (Neil Levy (2011), 88).

34 John Martin Fischer and Mark Ravizza (1998), 196.

35 John Martin Fischer (2006d), 224.

36 See, for instance, John Martin Fischer (2006d), particularly Chapters 3 and 12.

37 William Rowe (2006), 298. Similarly, Michael McKenna (a compatibilist) writes "I believe that theirs is the best case for compatibilism to date" (McKenna (2005b), 132).

38 For other criticisms of Fischer and Ravizza's view, see Eleonore Stump (2002), Harry Frankfurt (2002a), and Michael McKenna (2005b). Seth Shabo (2005) and Michael McKenna (2000) raise a number of problems for the third element of Fischer and Ravizza's account of ownership. One particularly pressing problem for their view is that an agent can avoid moral responsibility simply by not seeing himself as the appropriate target of the reactive attitudes: "Ultimately, if one does not see oneself as responsible, then one is not responsible" (Fischer (2000d), 406). For a penetrating criticism of their view at this point, see Neal Judisch (2005), 123ff.

39 See, for example, Eleonore Stump (2002), Tomis Kapitan (2000), and Derk Pereboom (2001). Perhaps the most thorough development of this line of criticism is found in Todd Long (2004).

40 Harry Frankfurt (2002a), 61.

41 John Martin Fischer and Mark Ravizza (1998), 235.

42 John Martin Fischer and Mark Ravizza (1998), 235f. So far as I can tell, no work is being done here by the "electronic" nature of implantation; hypnosis would seem to be relevantly similar to an implanted Frankfurt-type device in

terms of undermining freedom. For this reason, I ignore this qualification in what follows.

43 John Martin Fischer and Mark Ravizza (1998), 236.

44 Neal Judisch (2005), 118.

45 Seth Shabo (2005), 107. Similarly, Judisch writes that "the introduction of the ownership condition is in large part motivated by their conviction that agents suffering from manipulation of just this sort are not morally responsible, at least in the typical cases" (Neal Judisch (2005), 122).

46 For a similar view, see Neil Levy (2011), 103ff, for—as Levy puts it—"the question of the origin of a desire is entirely irrelevant to our possession of the ability to endorse or reject it" (105).

47 Derk Pereboom (2001), 112f.

48 Derk Pereboom (2001), 113.

49 Derk Pereboom (2001), 122. From the context of this quotation, it is clear that Pereboom means a sufficient "freedom-relevant condition" for moral responsibility and not an overall sufficient condition for moral responsibility.

50 John Martin Fischer (2006d), 233.

51 For further arguments against Fischer and Ravizza's account of sourcehood with similar focus on their response to Pereboom's first case, see Derk Pereboom (2005), 239f; Pereboom (2007a), 99; and Neal Judisch (2005), 119ff. For a discussion of other problems facing Fischer and Ravizza's account, see also McKenna (2011).

52 Derk Pereboom (2001), 112. Note that Pereboom's argument is not only intended to cut just against Frankfurt and Fischer/Ravizza's view but also against other compatibilist accounts as well. See his discussion on pages 89–117.

53 Derk Pereboom (2001), 112f.

54 Derk Pereboom (2001), 113f.

55 Derk Pereboom (2001), 114. Pereboom's Case 3 bears a significant similarity to Susan Wolf's JoJo example, which she raises as an objection to source-based compatibilist views; see Wolf (1987), 53ff.

56 Derk Pereboom (2001), 115.

57 Derk Pereboom (2001), 112. See also Derk Pereboom (2008b).

58 Derk Pereboom (2001), 116; for similar thoughts, see Robert Kane (2000a). For a related discussion, see Alfred Mele (2008), 276ff.

59 For a similar discussion, see Michael McKenna (2004).

60 This second step of Pereboom's two-step is not uncontroversial. Berofsky, for example, calls into question the analogy on which the similarity claim is made. See Bernard Berofsky (2006), 434. Note also that what Mele calls the "no-difference premise" of manipulation arguments is stronger than the similarity claim above; see Alfred Mele (2008), 265f.

61 See Alfred Mele (1995) for an elaboration and defense of this position.

62 Alfred Mele (2008), 279. Mele himself says that this is not a manipulation argument, but an original-design argument (284f). For a discussion that it

may be appropriate to see the Zygote argument as a kind of manipulation argument, and why the exact classification doesn't matter, see Stephen Kearns (forthcoming), footnote 2. The central thrust of Kearns' argument is an interesting critique of Mele's Zygote Argument. For what I take to be a persuasive rebuttal of Kearns' argument, see Patrick Todd (forthcoming).

63 For the record, Mele is officially agnostic about this argument since he's agnostic about the truth of the first premise; see Alfred Mele (2006), 194. For a rebuttal to the claim that Ernie does not freely A given Diana's actions, see John Martin Fischer (2011), specifically 269ff. Fischer here also explicitly endorses the second premise of the Zygote Argument, which makes his response to Pereboom's manipulation argument discussed all the more perplexing.

64 Alfred Mele (2008), 279. See also Mele (2005) for related points about Pereboom's 4-case argument.

65 For a number of criticisms of these arguments that I do not have the space to discuss here, see Alfred Mele (2005), Ishtiyaque Haji and Stefaan Cuypers (2006), and Kristen Demetrious (2010).

66 As Mele notes, even if existing compatibilism accounts fall prey to manipulation arguments, "perhaps the story [at work in the manipulation argument] is not a counterexample to some superior candidate for being a set of conceptually sufficient conditions for free action and moral responsibility that is consistent with the truth of determinism and has not yet been proposed by compatibilists" (Alfred Mele (2008), 264).

67 Derk Pereboom (2001), 116.

68 I hesitate to say that Hal can bring about Allison's volition to kill her father (or any other volition for that matter) via manipulation since I'm inclined to think that manipulation would bypass Allison's volitional faculties thereby resulting in the volition being Hal's, not Allison's. For an elaboration of this point with which I have much sympathy, see Eleonore Stump (1988), 403f; and (1996), 80. Nevertheless, I set aside this worry for the present.

69 Michael McKenna (2008).

70 A similar idea can be found in Robert Kane's discussion of nonconstraining control in Kane (1996), 64–70.

Chapter Nine

1 Michael McKenna (2001). For an endorsement of source incompatibilism from the first part of the twentieth century, see Bradley (1927).

2 Eleonore Stump (2001).

3 See, for instance, Asselt, Bac, and te Velde (2010).

4 John Martin Fischer (1982), 32.

5 John Martin Fischer (1982), 33.

6 John Martin Fischer (1982), 33f.

7 Michael McKenna (2003), 201f.

8 Michael McKenna (2010), 437. McKenna, of course, rejects this line of thought.

9 I mean "grounds" here in the same way it is used in the following quotation from John Fischer: "Something grounds moral responsibility, in the sense in question, insofar as it explains (or helps to explain) why the agent is morally responsible, apart from simply being an indicator of something else that in fact explains the agent's moral responsibility" (2006d, 197). See also the discussion of the Robustness Requirement in Chapter 7.

10 John Martin Fischer (2007a), 44 and 46.

11 Ibid., 47.

12 John Martin Fischer (2000a), 323. See also John Martin Fischer (1999a), 129; (2006d), 183. For another presentation of this worry, see Manuel Vargas (2007a), 141f.

13 R. E. Hobart (1934).

14 R. E. Hobart (1934), 2 and 13.

15 P. H. Nowell-Smith (1948), 46. A recent interdisciplinary collection on free will also contains an essay defending this literal Hobartian position: "So we do have free will in a deterministic universe. Indeterminism, on the other hand, makes free will impossible. ... To the extent that determinism is true, we humans do indeed have something that we all innately feel and believe that we have: free will. In this most important sense, determinism makes free will possible" (John Baer (2008), 309).

16 Daniel Speak (2008), 124. For an incompatibilist defense of the resiliency intuition, see Helen Steward (2008).

17 Daniel Speak (2008), 124.

18 For a further development of these issues, see Kevin Timpe (2010).

19 See, for instance, Robert Kane (2007b), 179ff.

20 John Martin Fischer (2007a), 45.

21 I thank Zac Bachman for pushing me on this point.

22 For tentative and preliminary thoughts about this issue by influential compatibilists, see John Martin Fischer and Mark Ravizza (1998), 62–91.

23 I say "most" because compatibilist views like Hobart's are just as dependent upon the truth or falsity of determinism as is libertarianism.

24 William Hasker (1999), 87.

25 Robert Kane (1996) and Derk Pereboom (2001).

26 See, for instance, Eleonore Stump (1999), (2003).

27 Linda Zagzebski (2000).

28 David Hunt (2003). Michael Zimmerman also appears to embrace a version of Narrow Source Incompatibilism in Michael Zimmerman (1988), particularly Chapter 4. Randolph Clarke's view may also be interpreted in this way; see John Martin Fischer (1999a), 129f, footnote 66.

29 I thank Bob Kane for suggesting these terms. For a different use of similar terminology, see Randolph Clarke (2003), 9ff.

30 Another reason for making the distinction between the Narrow and the Wide forms of Source Incompatibilism is that while Kane's work was among the first to insist on the importance of ultimacy for incompatibilist accounts of moral responsibility, the term Source Incompatibilism is often used to denote simply that sub-group of Source Incompatibilists that I am calling Narrow Source Incompatibilists. Thus, according to current terminology, it is unclear whether or not Kane's position should be considered a form of Source Incompatibilism. At one point, Kane distances himself from Source Incompatibilism, despite his insistence on ultimacy (see Kane 2005, 124). By distinguishing between Narrow and Wide forms of Source Incompatibilism, I believe this confusion can be alleviated.

31 Not all Wide Source Incompatibilists require alternative possibilities at the very time of a free action, due to issues of tracing. An example here is Robert Kane (2005), 80ff. See also Kevin Timpe (2011).

32 Eleonore Stump (2001), 125–8.

33 Eleonore Stump (2001), 125. See also Eleonore Stump (1997), 106ff.

34 Eleonore Stump (1990), 277.

35 Eleonore Stump (1996), 88.

36 Eleonore Stump (1999), 312.

37 Eleonore Stump (1999), 301f.

38 Eleonore Stump (1999), 314. The reader should note that I am endorsing neither Stump's claim that the Flicker Strategist needs to assume 1 and 2 nor her claim that they lead to counter-intuitive results discussed below. Rather, I want to argue that *even if one rejects these assumptions*, Stump's account still leads to a version of the Flicker Strategy.

39 Eleonore Stump (1999), 314.

40 Eleonore Stump (1999), 315.

41 Eleonore Stump (1999), 315.

42 Eleonore Stump (1999), 317.

43 Stump says as much in a recent article, where she defines the principle of alternative possibilities as "the principle that alternative possibilities for action are required for moral responsibility" (2002, 139). Compare also Michael McKenna (1997), 76: "What it means to say that an agent is morally responsible for the action she does perform only if she could have avoided that action, is that she is morally responsible for performing that very token action which she did perform only if she could have avoided the performance of that very action."

44 Eleonore Stump (1988), 403f. See also p. 407: "On this view, the will is free with respect to a volition V just in case V is accepted by the agent because his intellect approves of V (at that time, under some description) as the good to be pursued, and there is no higher-order desire of the agent's with which V is discordant." Compare Michael McKenna (1997), 83 footnote 9: "I believe that the libertarian can reasonably argue that when an agent's actions, or the deliberative machinery of her actions, are brought about by reasons independent of the agent's own rational machinery, then the actions or the

deliberative mechanisms are *not* hers. This is not to say that it is *a priori* impossible for an intervener to cause an agent to act, or even to cause her to have such and such deliberations. It is only to say that the actions or the deliberations are not *hers*."

45 Eleonore Stump (1996), 80. For Stump, the need for the origination of an act to be in the agent's own intellect and will is what makes Aquinas' account an incompatibilist account: "What is necessary for libertarian free will is, as Aquinas says, that the ultimate source of the action be the agent's own will and cognitive faculties, whether or not the agent has alternative possibilities open to him in the circumstances" (88).

46 Other incompatibilists do think the causal origin of an action is an essential feature of that action. See, for example, Peter van Inwagen (1983), David Widerker (1995), and Gordon Pettit (2005). If these causal-genesis accounts are true, then *FSCs* would quite clearly fail to undermine *AP*, since the actual and alternate sequences contain actions with different causal origins. I argue against causal-genesis accounts of events and explore ramifications for debates about *FSCs* in Kevin Timpe (2009).

47 Eleonore Stump (1999), 322.

48 Eleonore Stump (2003), 151.

49 Eleonore Stump (1999), 313f, footnote 34.

50 Eleonore Stump (1999), 313f, footnote 34.

51 Eleonore Stump (2003), 151.

52 Even Shabo who, as discussed below, rejects the argument given above against Stump's view seems to agree that if I am correct then she is committed to an alternative-possibilities condition, "there is some reason to believe that other source incompatibilists will face the same worry" (Shabo 2007, 64).

53 John Martin Fischer (2007a), 61.

54 Seth Shabo (2007).

55 Seth Shabo (2007), 64.

56 Seth Shabo (2007), 69.

57 Seth Shabo (2007), 72.

58 Seth Shabo (2007), 72.

59 Seth Shabo (2007), 72.

60 Seth Shabo (2007), 73.

61 John Martin Fischer (2006f), 196.

62 John Martin Fischer (2006f), 196.

63 Alfred Mele (2006), 4. More specifically, Mele describes his view as "agnostic autonomism, the conjunction of the agnosticism just identified with the assertion that ... there are free and morally responsible human beings" (4).

64 Alfred Mele (1998), 151.

65 Alfred Mele (1998), 152f. A similar view is defended in William Rowe (2006). However, unlike the present view, Rowe's view builds upon Thomas Reid's work on agency, in particular his account of agent-causation. While I do not

think that my own view is wedded to agent-causation in the same way that Rowe's is, I think that his discussion of the TRAIN III example on pages 306ff makes a strong case in favor of the importance of alternatives due to sourcehood (whether or not sourcehood requires agent-causation).

66 See, for instance, John Martin Fischer (1998), 141; (1999a), 110f; (1999b), 280; (2002b), 288; and (2006c), 322.

67 John Martin Fischer (1999a), 110 (emphasis added).

68 John Martin Fischer (2006c), 323 and 325. For a similar view about the importance of alternative possibilities in this dialectic context, see David Widerker (2005).

69 John Martin Fischer (2010), 331. Relatedly, Kadri Vihvelin writes: "There may be a link between the two arguments [one that free will requires sourcehood and the other that it requires alternative possibilities], insofar as someone might argue that we have ultimate control over our actions and thereby our selves only if we can do otherwise, and this entails indeterminism. But we don't need to assume this link" (Vihvelin 2008, 311). As this chapter shows, I think this connection holds. But I don't assume it; I argue for it.

70 Stewart Goetz (2009), 89 and 97.

71 For similar views on this point, see David Hunt (2005); David Widerker (2005); Robert Kane (2007a). For a dissenting view, see John Martin Fischer (2007b), 185.

72 John Martin Fischer (2006d), 67.

73 For a similar claim, see Michael McKenna (1997), 74f.

74 See John Martin Fischer (2006d), 250 footnote 59; (1999a), 125 footnote 56.

75 John Martin Fischer (2005b), 148. For further discussion of this issue, see Gary Watson (2001); John Martin Fischer (2006d), 242ff.

Chapter Ten

1 Robert Kane (2002b), 407.

2 Robert Kane (2005), 37. Much of Robert Kane's (1996) work can be seen as providing an incompatibilist response to this kind of objection.

3 Alfred Mele (2002), 535.

4 Randolph Clarke (2003), 77f. Note that Clarke does not ultimately embrace the Luck Objection against incompatibilist views. See Randolph Clarke (1995), as well as Clarke (2003).

5 Daniel Speak (2011), 33. See also Christopher Franklin (2011a).

6 For helpful discussions about the metaphysical nature of luck, see Jennifer Lackey (2008), and E. J. Coffman (2007), and Neil Levy (2011).

7 A. J. Ayer (1954), 275.

8 Daniel Speak (2011), 33.

9 Daniel Speak (2011), 33.

10 Robert Kane (2007a), 31f. See also Neil Levy (2011), 41: "Chance, moreover, is not the same thing as luck: it might be *because* the chance at issue in libertarian accounts of free will should not be understood as luck that chance does not undermine free will."

11 Robert Kane (2007a), 27. See also page 36, as well as Kane's discussions of the indeterministic assassins on pages 17f and 38f.

12 Robert Kane (2007a), 27.

13 Robert Kane (2007a), 29.

14 See Stewart Goetz (2008), 61–6. See also Christopher Franklin (2011a) for a similar argument.

15 Thomas Nagel (1979), 26. As Dana Nelkin makes clear in her discussion of Nagel on this point, the quotation above should be understood as the claim that "moral luck occurs when an agent can be *correctly* treated as an object of moral judgment, despite the fact that a significant aspect of what he is assessed for depends on factors beyond his control" (Nelkin 2008).

16 Thomas Nagel (1979), 28.

17 Thomas Nagel (1979), 31.

18 As mentioned in Chapter 1, I think that agents can be morally responsible for their actions and the outcomes of their actions, and not just their volitions. For instance, the degree of an agent's moral responsibility may depend on whether she is successful in doing what she wills to do or not. However, I take it that responsibility for actions and consequences requires responsibility for the volition behind those actions, which is why I focus on the latter here. For a good treatment of some of the issues involved with resultant luck, see Carolina Sartorio (2012b).

19 Here, I am assuming a roughly Aristotelian account of the relationship between moral character and free choices. For a fuller treatment of this issue, see my Timpe (forthcoming), particularly Chapter 2.

20 Thomas Nagel (1979), 35.

21 Michael McKenna (2004), 171. Nevertheless, McKenna thinks that ahistorical versions of compatibilism have the resources to respond to global manipulation cases, even if there may be other reasons for preferring historical accounts. See McKenna (2004), 184ff.

22 Space prevents a complete exploration of the Luck Objection in all its forms; those interested in further pursuing these ideas are strongly encouraged to read Randolph Clarke (2003), Alfred Mele (2006), E. J. Coffman (2010), and Neil Levy (2011). For an excellent discussion of the problem of trans-worlds luck, see Manuel Vargas (forthcoming a), particularly section 5 and Daniel Speak (2011). Almeida and Bernstein (2011) is an especially good response to the "Rollback" version of the luck argument.

23 Neil Levy (2011), 12.

24 Neil Levy (2011), 13.

25 More specifically, he writes that he's "inclined to think that the degree of chanciness necessary for an event to count as lucky is sensitive to the significance of that event" (Neil Levy 2011, 17). Here, I'm inclined to agree.

For a related discussion, see my treatment of the context sensitivity of "might" in Kevin Timpe (2011), particularly § 6.

26 Neil Levy (2011), 41f. Keep in mind from Levy's definition of luck above that he's not claiming, as Hobart did, that it is mere indeterminism (what Levy calls "chance") which is at issue here. For him, luck is a technical term amounting to what I above called control-undermining luck

27 See Timothy Pawl and Kevin Timpe (2009), as well as Timpe (forthcoming).

28 John Kronen and Eric Reitan (2010), 201.

29 R. Jay Wallace (2006), 44.

30 The temporal qualifier is necessary because a person's agential structure—and what reasons she recognizes for acting—can change over time.

31 Neil Levy (2011), 84.

32 Neil Levy (2011), 108.

33 The issues here are related to Galen Strawson's Basic Argument, discussed earlier in Chapter 4. However, like Randolph Clarke (2005), I think that Strawson's argument overstates its case. Nevertheless, the general developmental worry is one with which I can sympathize. Robert Kane's account in *The Significance of Free Will* is related to this developmental worry. And Manuel Vargas raises the issue: "Consider the question of how we go from being unfree agents to free agents. This is a puzzle faced by all accounts of responsibility, but there is something pressing about it in the case of libertarianism. As children we either had the indeterministic structures favored by your favorite version of libertarianism or we lacked them. If we lacked them as children, we might wonder how we came to get those structures. We might also wonder what the evidence is for thinking that we do develop said structures" (Vargas 2007a, 148).

34 A second is that neither of the two main issues in the book—namely the debate between incompatibilism and compatibilism and the difference between source-based and leeway-based views—depends on the existence of free will.

35 Thomas Nagel (1979), 25.

36 Thomas Nagel (1979), 35.

37 Alfred Mele (2006), 76.

38 Manuel Vargas (forthcoming a), 4 in draft.

39 Manuel Vargas (forthcoming a), 4f in draft.

40 Vargas calls libertarians who employ this strategy "piggy-backers": "If one is a piggy-backer, then whatever compatibilist resources are sufficient for blocking the Luck Problem objection can be deployed by the piggy-backer libertarian" (Manuel Vargas forthcoming a, 10 in draft). Above, I'm suggesting that supercompatibilists could also be piggy-backers on libertarians.

BIBLIOGRAPHY

Albritton, Rogers (2003). "Freedom of will and freedom of action," in Gary
    Watson (eds), *Free Will*, 2nd edition. Oxford: Oxford University Press, 408–23.
Allen, Robert (2004). "Robust alternatives and responsibility." *Journal of Moral
    Philosophy*, 1, 21–9.
Almeida, Michael and Mark Bernstein (2011). "Rollbacks, endorsements, and
    indeterminism," in Robert Kane (eds), *Oxford Handbook of Free Will*, 2nd
    edition. Oxford: Oxford University Press, 484–95.
Audi, Robert (1974). "Moral responsibility, freedom, and compulsion." *American
    Philosophical Quarterly*, 11, 1–14.
Augustine (1993). *On Free Choice of the Will* (trans. Thomas Williams).
    Indianapolis: Hackett.
Aune, Bruce (1967). "Hypotheticals and 'can': another look." *Analysis*, 27, 191–5.
Austin, J. L. (1990). "Ifs and cans," in J. O. Urmson and G. J. Warnock (eds),
    Philosophical Papers (3rd edn). Oxford, Oxford University Press, 205–32.
Ayer, A. J. (1954). *Philosophical Essays*. London: Macmillan.
—(1997). "Freedom and Necessity," in Derk Pereboom (ed.), Free Will.
    Indianapolis: Hackett, 110–18.
Baer, John (2008). "Free Will requires determinism," in John Baer, James C.
    Kaufman and Roy F. Baumeister (eds), *Are We Free? Psychology and Free Will*.
    New York: Oxford University Press, 304–10.
Beebee, Helen (2003). "Local miracle compatibilism." *Nous*, 37, 258–77.
Beebee, Helen, Christopher Hitchcock, and Peter Menzies, (eds) (2010). *The
    Oxford Handbook of Causation*. Oxford: Oxford University Press.
Bennett, Jonathan (1984). *A Study of Spinoza's Ethics*. Indianapolis: Hackett.
—(1988). *Events and Their Names*. Indianapolis: Hackett.
Bergmann, Michael (2002). "Molinist Frankfurt-style counterexamples and the
    free will defense." *Faith and Philosophy*, 19, 462–78.
Bernstein, Mark (2005). "Can we ever be really, truly, ultimately free?" *Midwest
    Studies in Philosophy*, 29, 1–12.
Berofsky, Bernard (2000). "Ultimate responsibility in a deterministic world."
    Philosophy and Phenomenological Research, LX, 135–40.
—(2003). "Classical compatibilism: not yet dead," in David Widerker and Michael
    McKenna (eds), *Moral Responsibility and Alternative Possibilities: Essays on
    the Importance of Alternative Possibilities*. Burlington, VT: Ashgate, 107–26.
—(2006). "Global control and freedom." *Philosophical Studies*, 131, 419–45.
Black, Sam and Jon Tweedale (2002). "Responsibility and alternative possibilities:
    the use and abuse of examples." *The Journal of Ethics*, 6, 281–303.
Blumenfeld, David (1971). "The principle of alternative possibilities." *The Journal
    of Philosophy*, 67, 339–44.

Bradley, F. H. (1961). "The vulgar notion of responsibility in connection with the theories of free will and necessity," in Herbert Morris (eds), *Freedom and Responsibility: Readings in Philosophy and Law*. Stanford: Stanford University Press, 43–6.

Bratman, Michael (2002). "Hierarchy, circularity, and double reduction," in Sarah Buss and Lee Overton (eds), *Contours of Agency: Essays on Themes from Harry Frankfurt*. Cambridge, MA: The MIT Press, 65–85.

Brown, Vivienne (2006). "Choice, moral responsibility and alternative possibilities." *Ethical Theory and Moral Practice*, 9, 265–88.

Campbell, C. A. (1957). *On Selfhood and Godhood*. London: George Allen & Unwin.

Campbell, Joseph (1997). "A compatibilist theory of alternative possibilities." *Philosophical Studies*, 88, 319–30.

—(2005). "Compatibilist alternatives." *Canadian Journal of Philosophy*, 35, 387–406.

—(2010). "Incompatibilism and fatalism: a reply to Loss." Analysis, 70, 71–6.

—(2011). *Free Will*. Malden, MA: Polity Press.

—(unpublished). "The consequence argument."

Chalmers, David (1996). *The Conscious Mind: In Search of a Fundamental Theory*. New York: Oxford University Press.

Chisholm, Roderick (1966). "Freedom of action," in Keith Lehrer (eds), *Freedom and Determinism*. New York: Random House, 11–44.

—(1967). "He could have done otherwise." *The Journal of Philosophy*, 64, 409–17.

Clarke, Randolph (2002). "Libertarian views: critical survey of noncausal and event-causal accounts of free agency," in Robert Kane (eds), *The Oxford Handbook of Free Will*. New York: Oxford University Press, 356–85.

—(2003). *Libertarian Accounts of Free Will*. New York: Oxford University Press.

—(2005). "On an argument for the impossibility of moral responsibility." *Midwest Studies in Philosophy*, 29, 13–24.

Coffman, E. J. (2007). "Thinking about luck." *Synthese*, 3, 385–98.

—(2009). "Does luck exclude control?" *Australasian Journal of Philosophy*, 87, 499–504.

—(2010). "How (not) to attack the luck argument." *Philosophical Explorations*, 13, 157–66.

—(2011). "Alternatives for libertarians," in Robert Kane (eds), *The Oxford Handbook of Free Will* (2nd edition). New York: Oxford University Press, 329–48.

Coffman, E. J. and Ted Warfield (2005). "Deliberation and metaphysical freedom." *Midwest Studies in Philosophy*, 29, 25–44.

Davidson, Donald (2001). *Essays on Actions and Events*. Oxford: Clarendon Press.

Davison, Scott (1999). "Moral luck and the flicker of freedom." *American Philosophical Quarterly*, 36, 241–51.

Della Rocca, Michael (1998). "Frankfurt, Fischer and flickers." *Nous*, 32, 99–105.

Demetriou, Kristin (2010). "The soft-line solution to Pereboom's four-case argument." *Australasian Journal of Philosophy*, 88, 595–617.

Di Nucci, Ezio (2011). "Frankfurt counterexample defended." *Analysis*, 71, 102–4.

Ehring, Douglas (1997). *Causation and Persistence: A Theory of Causation*. New York: Oxford University Press.

Ekstrom, Laura (1998). "Protecting incompatibilist freedom." *American Philosophical Quarterly*, 35, 281–91.

—(2000). *Free Will: A Philosophical Study*. Boulder, CO: Westview Press.

—(2002). "Libertarianism and Frankfurt-style cases," in Robert Kane (eds), *The Oxford Handbook of Free Will*. New York: Oxford University Press, 309–22.

Finch, Alicia (forthcoming). "On behalf of the consequence argument: time, modality, and the nature of free action." *Philosophical Studies*.

Finch, Alicia and Ted Warfield (1998). "The *Mind* argument and libertarianism." *Mind*, 107, 515–28.

Fischer, John Martin (1982). "Responsibility and control." *The Journal of Philosophy*, 79, 24–40.

—(1994). *The Metaphysics of Free Will*. Cambridge: Blackwell.

—(1998). "*The Metaphysics of Free Will*: a reply to my critics." *Journal of Social Philosophy*, 29, 157–67.

—(1999a). "Recent work on moral responsibility." *Ethics*, 110, 93–139.

—(1999b). "Responsibility and self-expression." *The Journal of Ethics*, 3, 277–97.

—(2000a). "Problems with actual-sequence incompatibilism." *The Journal of Ethics*, 4, 323–8.

—(2000b). "Responsibility, history and manipulation." *The Journal of Ethics*, 4, 385–91.

—(2000c). "*The Significance of Free Will* by Robert Kane." *Philosophy and Phenomenological Research*, LX, 141–8.

—(2000d). "Chicken soup for the semi-compatibilist soul: replies to Haji and Kane." *The Journal of Ethics*, 4, 404–7.

—(2002a). "Frankfurt-style compatibilism," in Sarah Buss and Lee Overton (eds), *Contours of Agency: Essays on Themes from Harry Frankfurt*. Cambridge, MA: The MIT Press, 1–26.

—(2002b). "Frankfurt-type examples and semi-compatibilism," in Robert Kane (eds), *The Oxford Handbook of Free Will*. New York: Oxford University Press, 281–308.

—(2003). "Responsibility and agent-causation," in David Widerker and Michael McKenna (eds), *Moral Responsibility and Alternative Possibilities: Essays on the Importance of Alternative Possibilities*. Burlington, VT: Ashgate, 235–50.

—(2005a). "Free will, death, and immortality: the role of narrative." *Philosophical Perspectives*, 34, 379–403.

—(2005b). "Reply: the free will revolution." *Philosophical Explorations*, 8, 145–56.

—(2006a). "The cards that are dealt you." *The Journal of Ethics*, 10, 107–29.

—(2006b). "Free will and moral responsibility," in David Copp (ed.), *The Oxford Handbook of Ethical Theory*. New York: Oxford University Press, 321–254.

—(2006c). "The free will revolution (continued)." *The Journal of Ethics*, 10, 315–45.

—(2006d). *My Way: Essays on Moral Responsibility*. New York: Oxford University Press.

—(2006e). "A reply to Pereboom, Zimmerman and Smith." *Philosophical Books*, 47, 235–44.

—(2006f). "Summary of *My Way: Essays on Moral Responsibility*." *Philosophical Books*, 47, 195–7.

—(2007a). "Compatibilism," in John Martin Fischer, Robert Kane, Derk Pereboom, and Manuel Vargas, *Four Views on Free Will*. Malden, MA: Blackwell, 44–84.

—(2007b). "Response to Kane, Pereboom, and Vargas," in John Martin Fischer, Robert Kane, Derk Pereboom, and Manuel Vargas, *Four Views on Free Will*. Malden, MA: Blackwell, 184–90.

—(2010). "The Frankfurt cases: the moral of the stories." *Philosophical Review*, 119, 315–36.

—(2011). "The zygote argument remixed." *Analysis*, 71, 267–72.

Fischer, John Martin and Mark Ravizza (1998). *Responsibility and Control: A Theory of Moral Responsibility*. Cambridge: Cambridge University Press.

Foot, Philippa (2002). "Free will as involving determinism," in *Virtues and Vices*. Oxford: Oxford University Press.

Forrest, Peter (1985). "Backward causation in defence of free will." *Mind*, 94, 210–17.

Frankfurt, Harry (1969). "Alternate possibilities and moral responsibility." *The Journal of Philosophy*, 66, 829–39.

—(1988). *The Importance of What We Care About*. New York: Cambridge University Press.

—(1992). "The faintest passion." *Proceedings and Addresses of the American Philosophical Association*, 66, 5–16.

—(1998). "Discussion with Harry Frankfurt." *Ethical Perspectives*, 5, 15–43.

—(1999). "Responses." *The Journal of Ethics*, 3, 369–74.

—(2002a). "Reply to Eleonore Stump," in Sarah Buss and Lee Overton (eds), *Contours of Agency: Essays on Themes from Harry Frankfurt*. Cambridge, MA: The MIT Press, 61-63.

—(2002b). "Reply to John Martin Fischer," in Sarah Buss and Lee Overton (eds), *Contours of Agency: Essays on Themes from Harry Frankfurt*. Cambridge, MA: The MIT Press, 27–32.

—(2003). "Some thoughts concerning PAP," in David Widerker and Michael McKenna (eds), *Moral Responsibility and Alternative Possibilities: Essays on the Importance of Alternative Possibilities*. Burlington, VT: Ashgate, 339–46.

Franklin, Christopher (2011a). "Farewell to the luck (and *Mind*) argument." *Philosophical Studies*, 156, 199–230.

—(2011b). "The problem of enhanced control." *Australasian Journal of Philosophy*, 89, 687–706.

Frede, Michael (2011). *A Free Will: Origins of the Notion in Ancient Thought*. Berkeley: University of California Press.

Funkhouser, Eric (2009). "Frankfurt cases and overdetermination." *Canadian Journal of Philosophy*, 39, 341–70.

Ginet, Carl (1990). *On Action*. Cambridge: Cambridge University Press.

—(1995). "Freedom, responsibility, and agency." *The Journal of Ethics*, 1, 85–98.

—(1996). "In defense of the principle of alternative possibilities: why I don't find Frankfurt's argument convincing." *Philosophical Perspectives*, 10, 403–17.

Goetz, Stewart (2002). "Alterative Frankfurt-style counterexamples to the principle of alternative possibilities." *Pacific Philosophical Quarterly*, 83, 131–47.

—(2005). "Frankfurt-style counterexamples and begging the question." *Midwest Studies in Philosophy*, 39, 83–105.

—(2009). *Freedom, Teleology, and Evil*. London: Continuum.

Haji, Ishtiyaque (2002). *Deontic Morality and Control*. New York: Cambridge University Press.

—(2003). "Flickers of freedom, obligation, and responsibility." *American Philosophical Quarterly*, 40, 287–302.

Haji, Ishtiyaque and Stefaan Cuypers (2006). "Hard- and soft-line responses to Pereboom's four-case manipulation argument." *Acta Analytica*, 21, 19–35.

Haji, Ishtiyaque and Michael McKenna (2004). "Dialectical delicacies in the debate about freedom and alternative possibilities." *The Journal of Philosophy*, 101, 299–314.

—(2006). "Defending Frankfurt's argument in deterministic contexts: a reply to Palmer." *The Journal of Philosophy*, 103, 363–72.

Harrison, Gerald (2006). "Frankfurt-style cases and improbable alternative possibilities." *Philosophical Studies*, 130, 399–406.

Hart, Ben (forthcoming). "Skepticisms, sourcehood, and luck compatibilism."

Hasker, William (1999). *The Emergent Self*. Ithaca, NY: Cornell University Press.

—(2001). "The foreknowledge conundrum." *International Journal for Philosophy of Religion*, 50, 97–114.

Heinamen, Robert (1986). "Incompatibilism without the principle of alternative possibilities." *Australasian Journal of Philosophy*, 64, 266–76.

Hobart, R. E. (1934). "Free will as involving determination and inconceivable without it." *Mind*, 43, 1–27.

Hobbes, Thomas (1994). *Leviathan*. Indianapolis: Hackett Publishing Company.

Honderich, Ted (2002a). "Determinism as true, both compatibilism and incompatibilism as false, and the real problem," in Robert Kane (eds), *The Oxford Handbook of Free Will*. New York: Oxford University Press, 461–76.

—(2002b). *How Free Are You?: The Determinism Problem* (2nd edition). New York: Oxford University Press.

—(2011). "Effects, determinism, neither compatibilism nor incompatibilism, consciousness," in Robert Kane (eds), *The Oxford Handbook of Free Will* (2nd edition). New York: Oxford University Press, 442–56.

Horgan, Terence (1979). "'Could,' possible worlds, and moral responsibility." *Southern Journal of Philosophy*, 17, 345–58.

Hughes, Christopher (1994). "The essentiality of origin and the individuation of events." *Philosophical Quarterly*, 44, 26–44.

Hume, David (1975). *Enquiry Concerning Human Understanding*. Oxford: Clarendon Press.

Hunt, David (1996). "Frankfurt counterexamples: some comments on the Widerker-Fischer debate." *Faith and Philosophy*, 13, 395–401.

—(2000). "Moral responsibility and unavoidable action." *Philosophical Studies*, 97, 195–227.

—(2003). "Freedom, foreknowledge and Frankfurt," in David Widerker and Michael McKenna (eds), *Moral Responsibility and Alternative Possibilities: Essays on the Importance of Alternative Possibilities*. Burlington, VT: Ashgate, 159–83.

—(2005). "Moral responsibility and buffered alternatives." *Midwest Studies in Philosophy*, 39, 126–45.

Istvan, Michael Anthony, Jr (2010). "Concerning the resilience of Galen Strawson's Basic Argument." *Philosophical Studies*, 155, 399–420.

Judisch, Neal (2005). "Responsibility, manipulation, and ownership: reflections on the Fischer/Ravizza program." *Philosophical Explorations*, 8, 115–30.

Kahn, Leonard (2011). "Moral Blameworthiness and the reactive attitudes."
    Ethical Theory and Moral Practice, 14, 131–42.
Kane, Robert (1985). *Free Will and Values*. Albany: State University of New York
    Press.
—(1989). "Two kinds of incompatibilism." *Philosophy and Phenomenological
    Research*, 50, 219–54.
—(1996). *The Significance of Free Will*. Oxford: Oxford University Press.
—(1999). "Responsibility, luck and chance: reflections on free will and
    indeterminism." *The Journal of Philosophy*, 96, 217–40.
—(2000a). "Non-constraining control and the threat of social conditioning."
    Journal of Ethics, 4, 401–3.
—(2000b). "Replies to Fischer and Haji." *Journal of Ethics*, 4, 338–42.
—(2000c). "Responses to Bernard Berofsky, John Martin Fischer and Galen
    Strawson." *Philosophy and Phenomenological Research*, LX, 157–67.
—(2002a). "Introduction: the contours of contemporary free will debates," in
    Robert Kane (eds), *The Oxford Handbook of Free Will*. New York: Oxford
    University Press, 3–41.
—(2002b). "Some neglected pathways in the free will labyrinth," in Robert Kane
    (ed.), *The Oxford Handbook of Free Will*. New York: Oxford University Press,
    406–37.
—(2002c). *The Oxford Handbook of Free Will*. New York: Oxford University
    Press.
—(2003). "Responsibility, indeterminism and Frankfurt-style cases: a reply to
    Mele and Robb," in David Widerker and Michael McKenna (eds), *Moral
    Responsibility and Alternative Possibilities: Essays on the Importance of
    Alternative Possibilities*. Burlington, VT: Ashgate, 91–105.
—(2004). "Agency, responsibility, and indeterminism," in Joseph Campbell,
    Michael O'Rourke and David Shier (eds), *Freedom and Determinism*.
    Cambridge, MA: The MIT Press, 70–88.
—(2005). *A Contemporary Introduction to Free Will*. New York: Oxford
    University Press.
—(2007a). "Libertarianism," in John Martin Fischer, Robert Kane, Derk
    Pereboom, and Manuel Vargas, *Four Views on Free Will*. Malden, MA:
    Blackwell, 5–43.
—(2007b). "Response to Fischer, Pereboom, and Vargas," in John Martin Fischer,
    Robert Kane, Derk Pereboom, and Manuel Vargas, *Four Views on Free Will*.
    Malden, MA: Blackwell, 166–83.
—(2011). "Introduction: the contours of contemporary free will debates (part 2),"
    in Robert Kane (ed.), *The Oxford Handbook of Free Will*. New York: Oxford
    University Press, 3–35.
Kapitan, Tomis (1986). "Deliberation and the presumption of open alternatives."
    Philosophical Quarterly, 36, 230–51.
—(2000). "Autonomy and manipulated freedom." *Philosophical Perspectives*, 14,
    81–103.
—(2011). "A compatibilist reply to the consequence argument," in Robert Kane
    (eds), *The Oxford Handbook of Free Will* (2nd edition). New York: Oxford
    University Press, 131–50.
Kearns, Stephen (2011). "Responsibility for necessities." *Philosophical Studies*,
    155, 307–24.

— (forthcoming). "Aborting the zygote argument." *Philosophical Studies*.

Knobe, Joshua (2004). "What is experimental philosophy?" *The Philosophers'
Magazine, 28*.

—(2007). "Experimental philosophy." *Philosophy Compass*, 2, 81–92.

Kronen, John and Eric Reitan (2010). "Species of hell," in Joel Buenting (eds),
The Problem of Hell: A Philosophical Anthology. Burlington, VT: Ashgate,
2010, 199–218.

Labooy, Guus (2002). *Freedom and Dispositions*. Frankfurt am Main: Peter Lang.

Lackey, Jennifer (2008). "What luck is not." *Australasian Journal of Philosophy*,
86, 255–67.

Larvor, Brendan (2010). "Frankfurt counter-example defused." *Analysis*, 70,
506–8.

Lehrer, Keith (1966). "An empirical disproof of determinism," in Keith Lehrer
(eds), *Freedom and Determinism*. New York: Random House, 175–202.

—(1976). "'Can' in theory and practice: a possible worlds analysis," in Myles
Brand and Douglas Walton (eds), *Action Theory: Proceedings of the Winnipeg
Conference on Human Action*. Boston: D. Reidel Publishing Company,
241–70.

Leiter, Brian (2010). "Nietzsche" in Timothey O'Connor and Constantine Sandis
(eds), *A Companion to Philosophy of Action*. Malden, MA: Blackwell, 528–36.

Levy, Neil (2002). "Excusing responsibility for the inevitable." *Philosophical
Studies*, 111, 43–52.

—(2004). "Why Frankfurt examples don't beg the question: a reply to
Woodward." *Journal of Social Philosophy*, 35, 211–15.

—(2009). "Luck and history-sensitive compatibilism." *Philosophical Quarterly*,
59, 237–51.

—(2011). *Hard Luck: How Luck Undermines Free Will and Moral Responsibility*.
Oxford: Oxford University Press.

Lewis, David (1973). "Causation." *The Journal of Philosophy*, 70, 556–67.

—(1979). "Counterfactual dependence and time's arrow." *Nous*, 13, 455–76.

—(1987). "Are we free to break the laws?" in *Philosophical Papers, Volume II*.
New York: Oxford University Press.

—(2000). "Causation as influence." *The Journal of Philosophy*, 97, 182–97.

Long, Todd (2004). "Moderate reasons-responsiveness, moral responsibility, and
manipulation," in Joseph Campbell, Michael O'Rourke and David Shier (eds),
Freedom and Determinism. Cambridge, MA: The MIT Press, 151–72.

Lycan, William (2003). "Free will and the burden of proof," in Anthony O'Hear
(eds), *Minds and Persons*. Cambridge, UK: Cambridge University Press, 107–22.

Markosian, Ned (1999). "A compatibilist version of the theory of agent
causation." *Pacific Philosophical Quarterly*, 80, 257–77.

—(2012). "Agent causation as the solution to all the compatibilist's problems."
Philosophical Studies, 157, 383–98.

McCann, Hugh (1998). *The Works of Agency: On Human Action, Will, and
Freedom*. Ithaca: Cornell University Press.

McDermott, Michael (1995). "Redundant causation." *British Journal for the
Philosophy of Science*, 46, 523–44.

McKay, Thomas and David Johnson (1996). "A reconsideration of an argument
against compatibilism." *Philosophical Topics*, 24, 113–22.

McKenna, Michael (1997). "Alternative possibilities and the failure of the counterexample strategy." *Journal of Social Philosophy*, 28, 71–85.

—(2000). "Assessing reasons-responsive compatibilism." *International Journal of Philosophical Studies*, 8, 89–114.

—(2001). "Source incompatibilism, ultimacy, and the transfer of non-responsibility." *American Philosophical Quarterly*, 38, 37–52.

—(2003). "Robustness, control, and the demand for morally significant alternatives: Frankfurt examples with oodles and oodles of alternatives," in David Widerker and Michael McKenna (eds), *Moral Responsibility and Alternative Possibilities: Essays on the Importance of Alternative Possibilities*. Burlington, VT: Ashgate, 201–17.

—(2004). "Responsibility and globally manipulated agents." *Philosophical Topics*, 32, 169–92.

—(2005a). "Where Frankfurt and Strawson meet." *Midwest Studies in Philosophy*, 29, 163–80.

—(2005b). "Reasons reactivity and incompatibilist intuitions." *Philosophical Explorations*, 8, 131–43.

—(2005c). "Neo's freedom … whoa!", in Christopher Grau (eds), *Philosophers Explore the Matrix*. New York: Oxford University Press, 218–38.

—(2006). "Guest editor's introduction." *The Journal of Ethics*, 10, 211–27.

—(2010). "Whose argumentative burden, which incompatibilist arguments?—getting the dialectic right." *Australasian Journal of Philosophy*, 83, 429–43.

—(2011). "Contemporary compatibilism: mesh theories and reasons-responsive theories," in Robert Kane (eds), *The Oxford Handbook of Free Will*. New York: Oxford University Press, 175–98.

Mele, Alfred (1995). *Autonomous Agents: From Self-Control to Autonomy*. New York: Oxford University Press.

—(1998). "Flickers of freedom." *Journal of Social Philosophy*, 29, 144–56.

—(2002). "Autonomy, self-control, and weakness of will," in Robert Kane (eds), *The Oxford Handbook of Free Will*. New York: Oxford University Press, 529–48.

—(2003). "Soft libertarianism and flickers of freedom," in David Widerker and Michael McKenna (eds), *Moral Responsibility and Alternative Possibilities: Essays on the Importance of Alternative Possibilities*. Burlington, VT: Ashgate, 251–64.

—(2005). "A critique of Pereboom's 'four-case argument' for incompatibilism." *Analysis*, 65:1, 75–80.

—(2006). *Free Will and Luck*. Oxford: Oxford University Press.

—(2008). "Manipulation, compatibilism, and moral responsibility." *Journal of Ethics*, 12, 263–86.

Mele, Alfred and David Robb (1998). "Rescuing Frankfurt style cases." *Philosophical Review*, 107, 97–112.

—(2003). "BBs, magnets and seesaw: the metaphysics of Frankfurt-style cases," in David Widerker and Michael McKenna (eds), *Moral Responsibility and Alternative Possibilities: Essays on the Importance of Alternative Possibilities*. Burlington, VT: Ashgate, 127–38.

Moore, G. E. (1912). *Ethics*. London: Williams & Norgate.

Moreland, J. P. (2009). *Th Recalcitrant Imago Dei*. London: SCM Press.

Moya, Carlos (2003). "Blockage cases: no case against PAP." *Critica: Revista Hispanoamericana de Filosofia*, 35, 109–20.

—(2006). *Moral Responsibility: the Ways of Skepticism*. New York: Routledge.

Nagel, Thomas (1979). *Mortal Questions*. Cambridge: Cambridge University Press.

Nahmias, Eddy (2011). "Intuitions about free will, determinism, and bypassing", in Robert Kane (eds), *The Oxford Handbook of Free Will* (2ⁿᵈ edition) New York: Oxford University Press, 555–76.

Nahmias, Eddy, Stephen Morris, Thomas Nadelhoffer, and Jason Turner (2006). "Is incompatibilism intuitive?", *Philosophy and Phenomenological Research*, 73, 28–53.

Nelkin, Dana (2004a). "Deliberative alternatives." *Philosophical Topics*, 32, 215–40.

—(2004b). "The sense of freedom," in J. K. Campbell, M. O'Rourke, and D. Shier (eds), *Freedom and Determinism*. Cambridge, MA: The MIT Press, 105–34.

—(2008). "Moral luck", in Edward N. Zalta (eds), *The Stanford Encyclopedia of Philosophy*. Stanford, http://plato.stanford.edu/entries/moral-luck/ (accessed 18 January 2012).

Nelson, Michael (2011). "Default compatibilism and narrative: comments on John Martin Fischer's ways and stories." *Social Theory and Practice*, 37, 35–45.

Nichols, Shaun and Joshua Knobe (2007). "Moral responsibility and determinism: empirical investigations of folk intuitions." *Noûs*, 41, 663–85.

Nowell-Smith, P. H. (1948). "Freedom and moral responsibility." *Mind*, 57, 45–61.

—(1960). "Ifs and cans." *Theoria*, 26, 85–101.

Oakley, Shane (2006). "Defending Lewis's local miracle compatibilism." *Philosophical Studies*, 130, 337–49.

O'Connor, Timothy (2002a). *Persons as Causes: The Metaphysics of Free Will*. Oxford: Oxford University Press.

—(2002b). "The agent as cause," in Robert Kane (eds), *Free Will*. Malden, MA: Blackwell, 196–205.

—(2005). "Freedom with a human face." *Midwest Studies in Philosophy*, 29, 207–27.

—(2011). "Agent-causal theories of freedom," in Robert Kane (eds), *The Oxford Handbook of Free Will* (2ⁿᵈ edition). New York: Oxford University Press, 309–28.

Oshana, Marina (1997). "Ascriptions of responsibility." *American Philosophical Quarterly*, 34, 71–83.

Palmer, David (2005). "New distinctions, same troubles: a reply to Haji and McKenna." *The Journal of Philosophy*, 102, 474–82.

—(2011). "Pereboom on the Frankfurt cases." *Philosophical Studies*, 153, 261–72.

Pawl, Timothy and Kevin Timpe (2009). "Incompatibilism, sin, and free will in heaven." *Faith and Philosophy*, 26, 396–417.

Pereboom, Derk (1997). "Determinism al dente," in Derk Pereboom (eds), *Free Will*. Indianapolis: Hackett, 242–72.

—(2001). *Living Without Free Will*. Cambridge, UK: Cambridge University Press.

—(2003). "Source incompatibilism and alternative possibilities," in David Widerker and Michael McKenna (eds), *Moral Responsibility and Alternative Possibilities: Essays on the Importance of Alternative Possibilities*. Burlington, VT: Ashgate, 184–99.

—(2005). "Defending hard incompatibilism." *Midwest Studies in Philosophy*, 29, 228–47.

—(2006). "Reasons-responsiveness, alternative possibilities, and manipulation arguments against compatibilism: reflections on John Martin Fischer's *My Way*." *Philosophical Books*, 47, 198–212.

—(2007a). "Hard incompatibilism," in John Martin Fischer, Robert Kane, Derk Pereboom, and Manuel Vargas, *Four Views on Free Will*. Malden, MA: Blackwell, 85–125.

—(2007b). "Response to Kane, Fischer, and Vargas," in John Martin Fischer, Robert Kane, Derk Pereboom, and Manuel Vargas, *Four Views on Free Will*. Malden, MA: Blackwell, 191–203.

—(2008a). "A compatibilist account of the epistemic conditions on rational deliberation." *The Journal of Ethics*, 12, 287–307.

—(2008b). "Defending hard incompatibilism again," in Nick Trakakis and Daniel Cohen (eds), *Essays on Free Will and Moral Responsibility*. Cambridge: Cambridge Scholars Press, 1–33.

—(2011). "Free will skepticism and meaning in life," in Robert Kane (eds), *The Oxford Handbook of Free Will* (2nd edition). New York: Oxford University Press, 407–24.

—(forthcoming). "Optimistic skepticism about free will," in Paul Russell and Oisin Deery (eds), *The Philosophy of Free Will: Selected Contemporary Readings*. Oxford: Oxford University Press.

Pettit, Gordon (2005). "Moral responsibility and the ability to do otherwise." *Journal of Philosophical Research*, 30, 303–19.

Pink, Thomas (2011). "Freedom and action without causation: noncausal theories of freedom and purposive agency," in Robert Kane (eds), *The Oxford Handbook of Free Will* (2nd edition). New York: Oxford University Press, 349–65.

Plantinga, Alvin (1974). *The Nature of Necessity*. Oxford, Clarendon Press.

Robinson, Michael (2010). "Modified Frankfurt-type counterexamples and flickers of freedom." *Philosophical Studies*, 157, 177–94.

Rowe, William (2006). "Free will, moral responsibility, and the problem of 'oomph'." *The Journal of Ethics*, 10, 295–313.

Russell, Bertrand (1914). "On the notion of cause," in *Our Knowledge of the External World*. London, Routledge.

Russell, Paul (1995). *Freedom and Moral Sentiment: Hume's Way of Naturalizing Responsibility*. New York: Oxford University Press.

Sartorio, Carolina (2012a). "Actuality and responsibility." *Mind*, 120, 1071–97.

—(2012b). "Resultant luck." *Philosophy and Phenomenological Research*, 84, 63–86.

—(forthcoming). "Causation and Freedom." *The Journal of Philosophy*.

Scanlon, Michael J. (2005). "Arendt's Augustine," in J. D. Caputo and M. J. Scanlon (eds), *Augustine and Postmodernism: Confession and Circumfession*. Bloomington: Indiana University Press, 159–72.

Schaffer, Jonathan (2000). "Trumping preemption." *The Journal of Philosophy*, 97, 165–81.

Searle, John (2001). *Rationality in Action*. Cambridge, MA: The MIT Press.

Shabo, Seth (2005). "Fischer and Ravizza on history and ownership." *Philosophical Explorations*, 8, 103–14.

—(2007). "Flickers of freedom and modes of action: a reply to Timpe." *Philosophia*, 35, 63–74.

Smilansky, Saul (1990). "Van Inwagen on the 'obviousness' of libertarian moral responsibility." Analysis, 50, 29–33.
—(2000). Free Will and Illusion. Oxford: Clarendon Press.
—(2002). "Free will, fundamental dualism, and the centrality of illusion", in Robert Kane (eds), The Oxford Handbook of Free Will. Oxford: Oxford University Press, 489–505.
—(2005). "Compatibilism: the argument from shallowness." Philosophical Studies, 115.3, 257–82.
—(2006). "What choice did I have?" The Times Literary Supplement, 29.
Smith, Michael (2004). Ethics and the A Priori: Selected Essays on Moral Psychology and Meta-Ethics. Cambridge, UK: Cambridge University Press.
Sommers, Tamler (2010). "Experimental philosophy and free will." Philosophical Compass, 5.2, 199–212.
Sosa, Ernest (2007). "Experimental philosophy and philosophical intuition." Philosophical Studies, 132, 99–107.
Speak, Daniel (2002). "Fanning the flickers of freedom." American Philosophical Quarterly, 39, 91–105.
—(2007). "The impertinence of Frankfurt-style argument." Philosophical Quarterly, 57, 76–95.
—(2011). "Libertarianism contra contrast." The Modern Schoolman, 88.
Steward, Helen (2009). "Fairness, agency and the flicker of freedom." Nous, 43, 64–93.
Stone, Jim (1998). "Free will as a gift from God: a new compatibilism." Philosophical Studies, 92, 257–81.
Strawson, Galen (1994). "The impossibility of moral responsibility." Philosophical Studies, 75, 5–24.
—(1998). "Luck swallows everything." Times Literary Supplement, 8–10.
—(2000). "The unhelpfulness of indeterminism." Philosophy and Phenomenological Research, 60, 149–55.
—(2002). "The bounds of freedom," in Robert Kane (ed), The Oxford Handbook of Free Will. Oxford: Oxford University Press, 441–60.
Strawson, Peter (1962). "Freedom and resentment." Proceedings of the British Academy, 48, 187–211.
Stump, Eleonore (1988). "Sanctification, hardening of the heart, and Frankfurt's concept of free will." The Journal of Philosophy, 85, 395–420.
—(1990). "Intellect, will, and the principle of alternate possibilities," in Michael Beaty (eds), Christian Theism and the Problems of Philosophy. South Bend: University of Notre Dame Press, 254–85.
—(1996). "Libertarian freedom and the principle of alternative possibilities," in Daniel Howard-Snyder and Jeff Jordan (eds), Faith, Freedom and Rationality. Lanham, MD: Rowman and Littlefield, 73–88.
—(1997). "The principle of alternative possibilities," in Charles Manekin and Menachem Kellner (eds), Freedom and Moral Responsibility: General and Jewish Perspectives. College Park: University of Maryland Press.
—(1999). "Alternative possibilities and moral responsibility: the flicker of freedom." The Journal of Ethics, 3, 299–324.
—(2001). "Augustine and free will," in Eleonore Stump and Norman Kretzmann (eds), The Cambridge Companion to Augustine. Cambridge, UK: Cambridge University Press, 124–47.

—(2002). "Control and causal determinism," in Sarah Buss and Lee Overton (eds), *Contours of Agency: Essays on Themes from Harry Frankfurt*. Cambridge, MA: The MIT Press, 33–60.

—(2003). "Moral responsibility without alternative possibilities," in David Widerker and Michael McKenna (eds), *Moral Responsibility and Alternative Possibilities: Essays on the Importance of Alternative Possibilities*. Burlington, VT: Ashgate, 139–58.

Stump, Eleonore and John Martin Fischer (2000). "Transfer Principles and Moral Responsibility." *Philosophical Perspectives*, 14, 47–56.

Tännsjö, Torbjörn (1989). "Soft determinism and how we became responsible for the past." *Philosophical Papers*, 18, 189–201.

Taylor, Richard (1963). *Metaphysics*. Englewood Cliffs, NJ: Prentice Hall.

—(1976). "Action and responsibility," in Brand and Douglas Walton (eds), *Action Theory: Proceedings of the Winnipeg Conference on Human Action*. Boston: D. Reidel Publishing Company, 293–310.

Timpe, Kevin (2003). "Trumping Frankfurt: why the Kane-Widerker objection is irrelevant." *Philosophia Christi*, 5, 485–99.

—(2006a). "A critique of Frankfurt-libertarianism." *Philosophia*, 34, 189–202.

—(2006b). "The dialectic role of the flickers of freedom." *Philosophical Studies*, 131, 337–68.

—(2007a). "Source incompatibilism and its alternatives." *American Philosophical Quarterly*, 44, 143–55.

—(2007b). "Truthmaking and Divine Eternity." *Religious Studies*, 43, 299–315.

—(2009). "Causal history matters, but not for individuation." *Canadian Journal of Philosophy*, 39, 77–91.

—(2010). "Demotivating semicompatibilism." *Ideas y Valores: Revista colombiana de fiosofia*, 58, 109–24.

—(2011). "Tracing and the epistemic condition on moral responsibility." *The Modern Schoolman*, 88, 5–28.

—(forthcoming). *Free Will in Philosophical Theology*. London: Continuum.

Todd, Patrick (forthcoming). "Defending (a modified version of) the zygote argument." *Philosophical Studies*.

Van Asselt, Willem, J. Martin Bac, and Roelf te Velde, eds. (2010). *Reformed Thought on Freedom: The Concept of Free Choice in Early Modern Reformed Theology*. London: Baker Academic.

Van Inwagen, Peter (1975). "The incompatibility of free will and determinism." *Philosophical Studies*, 27, 185–99.

—(1977). "Ontological arguments." *Nous*, 11, 375–95.

—(1983). *An Essay on Free Will*. Oxford: Clarendon Press.

—(1989). "When is the will free?" *Philosophical Perspectives*, 3, 42–53.

—(1994). "When the will is not free" *Philosophical Studies*, 75, 95–113.

—(2004). "Van Inwagen on free will," in Joseph Campbell, Michael O'Rourke and David Shier (eds), *Freedom and Determinism*. Cambridge, MA: The MIT Press, 213–30.

—(2006). *The Problem of Evil*. New York: Oxford University Press.

—(2008). "How to think about the problem of free will." *Journal of Ethics*, 12, 327–41.

Vargas, Manuel (2004). "Responsibility and the aims of theory: Strawson and revisionism." *Pacific Philosophical Quarterly*, 85, 218–41.

—(2005). "The revisionist's guide to responsibility." *Philosophical Studies*, 125, 399–429.

—(2007a). "Revisionism," in John Martin Fischer, Robert Kane, Derk Pereboom, and Manuel Vargas, *Four Views on Free Will*. Malden, MA: Blackwell, 126–65.

—(2007b). "Response to Kane, Fischer, and Pereboom," in John Martin Fischer, Robert Kane, Derk Pereboom, and Manuel Vargas, *Four Views on Free Will*. Malden, MA: Blackwell, 204–19.

—(2009). "Revisionism about free will: a statement and defense." *Philosophical Studies*, 144, 45–62.

—(2010a). "The revisionist turn: reflection on the recent history of work on free will," in Jesus Aguilar, Andrei Buckareff, and Keith Frankish (eds), *New Waves in the Philosophy of Action*. Copenhagen, Denmark: Palgrave.

—(2010b). "Responsibility in a world of causes." *Philosophical Exchange*, 40, 56–78/

—(2011). "Revisionist accounts of free will: origins, varieties, and challenges," Robert Kane (eds), *The Oxford Handbook of Free Will* (2nd edition). New York: Oxford University Press: 457–74.

—(forthcoming). "Why the luck problem isn't," *Philosophical Issues*, 22.

—(forthcoming). "Situationism and moral responsibility: free will in fragments," in Till Vierkant, Julian Kiverstein, and Andy Clark (eds), *Decomposing the Will*. New York: Oxford University Press.

Vihvelin, Kadri (2000). "Freedom, foreknowledge, and the principle of alternative possibilities." *Canadian Journal of Philosophy*, 30, 1–24.

—(2008a). "Compatibilism, incompatibilism, and Impossibilism," in Theodore Sider, John Hawthorne, and Dean Zimmerman (eds), *Contemporary Debates in Metaphysics*. Malden, MA: Blackwell, 303–18.

—(2008b). "Freedom, foreknowledge, and the ability to do otherwise: a reply to Fischer." *The Journal of Philosophy*, 38, 343–72.

Wallace, R. J. (1994). *Responsibility and the Moral Sentiments*. Cambridge, MA: Harvard University Press.

—(2006). *Normativity and the Will*. Oxford: Oxford University Press.

Waller, Bruce (2006). "Denying responsibility without making excuses." *American Philosophical Quarterly*, 43, 81–9.

Warfield, Ted (2000). "Causal determinism and human freedom are incompatible: a new argument for incompatibilism." *Philosophical Perspectives*, 14, 167–80.

—(2007). "Metaphysical compatibilism's appropriation of Frankfurt," in · Dean Zimmerman, *Oxford Studies in Metaphysics*, vol. 3. Oxford: Oxford University Press, 283–95.

Watson, Gary (1975). "Free agency." *The Journal of Philosophy*, 83, 517–22.

—(1987). "Free action and free will." *Mind*, 96, 145–72.

—(2001). "Reasons and responsibility: review essay on John Martin Fischer and Mark Ravizza, *Responsibility and Control: A Theory of Moral Responsibility*." *Ethics*, 111.2, 374–94.

Westphal, Jonathan (2003). "A new way with the consequence argument, and the fixity of the laws." Analysis, 63, 208–12.

Widerker, David (1995). "Libertarianism and Frankfurt's attack on the principle of alternative possibilities." *Philosophical Review*, 104, 247–61.

—(2000). "Frankfurt's attack on the principle of alternative possibilities: a further look." *Philosophical Perspectives*, 14, 181–201.

—(2003). "Blameworthiness and Frankfurt's argument against the principle of alternative possibilities," in David Widerker and Michael McKenna (eds), *Moral Responsibility and Alternative Possibilities: Essays on the Importance of Alternative Possibilities*. Burlington, VT: Ashgate, 53–73.

—(2005). "Blameworthiness, non-robust alternatives, and the principle of alternative expectations." *Midwest Studies in Philosophy*, 29, 292–306.

—(2006). "Libertarianism and the philosophical significance of Frankfurt scenarios." *The Journal of Philosophy*, 102, 163–87.

Widerker, David and Michael McKenna, eds (2003). *Moral Responsibility and Alternative Possibilities: Essays on the Importance of Alternative Possibilities*. Burlington, VT: Ashgate.

Wierenga, Edward (1989). *The Nature of God: An Inquiry into Divine Attributes* Ithaca: Cornell University Press.

Wolf, Susan (1987). "Sanity and the metaphysics of responsibility," in Ferdinand Shoeman (eds), *Responsibility, Character, and the Emotions: New Essays in Moral Psychology*. Cambridge: Cambridge University Press, 46–62.

—(1990). *Freedom Within Reason* New York: Oxford University Press.

—(2003). "Sanity and responsibility," in Gary Watson (eds), *Free Will* (2nd edition). Oxford: Oxford University Press, 372–87.

Woodward, P. A. (2002). "Why Frankfurt examples beg the question." *Journal of Social Philosophy*, 33, 540–47.

Young, Garry (2007). "Igniting the flicker of freedom: revisiting the Frankfurt scenario." *Philosophia*, 35, 171–80.

Zagzebski, Linda (1997). "Foreknowledge and human freedom," in Philip Quinn and Charles Taliaferro (eds), *Companion to Philosophy of Religion*. Malden, MA: Blackwell, 291–8.

—(2000). "Does libertarian freedom require alternative possibilities?" *Philosophical Perspectives*, 14, 231–48.

Zimmerman, David (1981). "Hierarchical motivation and freedom of the will." *Pacific Philosophical Quarterly*, 62, 354–68.

Zimmerman, Michael (1988). *An Essay on Moral Responsibility*. Totowa, NJ: Rowman & Littlefield.

INDEX